How The Hippies Ruin't Hillbilly Music

To Tony Thanks for the guitar lesson in 1963

How The Hippies Ruin't Hillbilly Music

◆

A Historical Memoir 1960–2000

St. "Wish" Wishnevsky

iUniverse, Inc.
New York Lincoln Shanghai

How The Hippies Ruin't Hillbilly Music
A Historical Memoir 1960–2000

iUniverse books may be ordered through booksellers or by contacting:

iUniverse
2021 Pine Lake Road, Suite 100
Lincoln, NE 68512
www.iuniverse.com
1-800-Authors (1-800-288-4677)

Graphics by Teresa Wiginton

Pictures From the Collections of:
Nancy Sluys
Steve Wishnevsky
Tom Mylet
Chris Sekerak

ISBN-13: 978-0-595-42305-7 (pbk)
ISBN-13: 978-0-595-86644-1 (ebk)
ISBN-10: 0-595-42305-1 (pbk)
ISBN-10: 0-595-86644-1 (ebk)

Printed in the United States of America

To all those who were too busy to contribute to this work.

Now they have to write their own books.

Contents

Author's Note xi

The Moral xiii

Foreword xv

Chapter One: Prehistory 1

Classical Folk 2

Union Grove Festival 4

Galax Old Fiddler's Convention 5

Swarthmore, For Instance 7

Petrillo Music Strike 8

The Smith Anthology 8

Chapter Two: Mike Seeger Interview 10

Chapter Three: Greenwich Village 13

The Jewgrass "You Should Pardon the Expression" Experience 13

Roger Sprung Interview 15

Julian Winston Deposition 17

Mike Resnick Interview 18

Chapter Four: The Dawn of the Hippie 21

Peter Stampfel Interview 21

Memories of Alan Block Rory Block 25

Chapter Five: And Here's Where I Come In. 26

A Brief Folk Music Memoir by Stan Gilliam 37

Stompin' '76. 41

Sociology and other Delusions 43

Jeremiah Skarie Interview 44

Chapter Six: Hippies, Hippies, Hippies 51

Jim Stanko Letter 52

Henry the Fiddler 53

Henry "Hank" Sapoznik Interview Excerpt by Mark Rubin 53
Jacki Spector Interview 54
Johnny Sturgill Interview 57
Fiddling Nancy Banjo Interview 64
It's My Story and I'm Sticking With it. Joe Thrift 75
Nancy Corey Interview 76

Chapter Seven: Middle and West Coasts 80
Ken Bloom Interview 80
Letter From Chris Wig 89
John "Doc" Holliday Telephone Interview 90
Todd H. Cleave 91

Chapter Eight: Movin' South 93
Tom Mylet Deposition 93
Stalking the Wild Bojo 98
Jerry Correll 100
Donna Correll Interview 101

Chapter Eight and a Half: Henry Heckler Reminisces 105

Chapter Nine: Clogging the Electric Glide 106

Chapter Ten: Meanwhile, Back in the Eighties 113
SAMURAI 113
Mary Edna Thompson 118
Tom Bailey 119
Dave Grant Obituary By REED WILLIAMS—Daily Progress staff writer 121
Susan Sterngold 122
Drew Smith 122
Kielbasa Bill 123
Mark Rose Interview 124
Spiritual Journey 128
The Death of the Stalls 129
Mark Rose Interview, Continued 131
Tom Neuhauser 135
Michael Jones Letter 136
A genuine transmission from the day job computer of: Mark Rubin 137

Chapter Eleven: Real Southerners 139
A Letter From Lenora (Fox) Rose 139
Kirk Sutphin Interview 143
Bill Lowe Deposition 145
William G. "Jerry" Jordan "Jellywhitebread" 146
Bill and Janice Birchfield 147

Matt Kenman . . . 148
Gail Gillespie Deposition . . . 151
Mitchell Badgett Letter . . . 152
Lynn Worth An essay for your project. . . . 153
T. J. Worthington Interview . . . 154
Danny Casstevens Interview . . . 155

Chapter Twelve: Fur'ners and Worse . . . 157
"The Welshman" Robert Gabb . . . 157

Chapter Thirteen: The Beat Goes On. . . . 159
Richard Turner Interview . . . 159

Chapter Fourteen: Hippie Kids . . . 160
Matthew Ball Interview . . . 160

To Be Continued 163

Portfolio . . . 165

Appendix: Some Old Time Band Names . . . 173

Index To Photographs . . . 177

Endnotes . . . 179

Author's Note

All these are true names and stories, with the exception of the Bojo Tales, which are composites of the common stupidities we all committed. Other people's histories have been mildly sanitized to protect their reputations. Mine have not been. Either I had a wilder time than most, or else have no reputation to protect. It makes little difference

Contributors' words are in italics and mine are in regular type. I have not retained the transparency of an historian, because I was involved in the Revival from about 1970 or even earlier and this is as close to a memoir as I am ever liable to write. I also snuck in a couple of my poems that address the themes of this book far more succinctly than any prose could.

My first musical instrument was a Kay banjo my mother bought me with Green Stamps in 1963. I think she wanted to keep me away from those commie beatniks who played guitars. This was not the first or the least of her misapprehensions

The Moral

Riley Baugus who hails from Walkertown, North Carolina, tells of walking down Broadway past Ernest Tubb's record store and hearing John Cohen say, "Back in the early sixties nobody was playing this music but Alan Jabbour and us." And Riley says, "But we were!"

Foreword

The lure might have been a static-clouded signal from late night AM radio, a seductive gleam from a pearl inlaid banjo, or an odd record in a Salvation Army Store, but an unusual thing has happened to a lot of more or less sane people for the last fifty years.

You might call it "The Old Time Revival" or even the "Revenge of the Nerds", but an obscure musical form that once was the heart and soul of the American people refuses to die. There are as many definitions of Old Time Music as there are people involved, but what it *was* is easy to define. It was casual homegrown music, indigenous to the farming communities of the Thirteen Colonies. It was mostly from England, Scotland and Ireland, as were most of the people in the colonies, but traces of every culture in Europe could be found. It was a fiddle-based music for dancing, as rough and ready as the people who danced to it.

Americans being rebels and outcasts, the music soon mutated, picking up tunes and instruments from every port a sailing ship could reach. The banjo arrived from Africa, the guitar from Spain and the mandolin from Italy. Those who could afford one used the double bass, once the only instrument allowed by the Puritans. American ingenuity soon provided the Dobro, the harmonica, the Autoharp and the Sears Roebuck catalogue to buy them out of.

Other ancient instruments survived, long after polite society had forgotten what it had once ignored. Pan pipes, bag pipes, cane flutes and the dulcimer provided counterpoint to the ubiquitous fiddle. Desperate ingenuity produced the cake-can banjo, the diddley-bow, the washtub bass, spoons, bones, and limberjacks, and many more devices to "let the music out". This music, like the people who made it, was far beneath the notice of the Eurocentric musical establishment, but the lower class played their fiddle tunes and danced their rustic dances without the approbation of their betters for several hundred years.

And then an even odder thing happened. A few of the most privileged, best-educated American children became enthralled with the music of the forgotten and the neglected. Open-back banjoes shone brighter than the shiniest Stratocaster, rosin-caked fiddles became more attractive than sequined disco shoes. Something was afoot.

There were other straws in the wind. A micro-budget TV show featuring washed-up country musicians, "Hee Haw", lasted 585 episodes. A minor rock band "The Nitty Gritty Dirt Band" sold millions of copies of a three-record set of obsolete music. An anachronistic movie sound track "Oh Brother, Where Art Thou?" stayed on the charts for years.

Something was happening, and nobody knew what it was, did they, Farmer Jones?

Chapter One: Prehistory

The Nineteenth Century "Minstrel Craze" might have alerted ethnomusicologists, but they hadn't been invented yet. Perhaps the first of that line and the grandfather of the "Great Folk Craze" was Harvard's Francis J. Child. His five volume "The English and Scottish Popular Ballads" 1882-98 is the "canon", the basis of scholarly recognition that "mere folk" could produce art in the absence of guidance by their betters.[1]

Even before that, mostly unknown to folkies, Sir Walter Scott's first work was a collection of ballads from the Scots Border regions. This war-racked land was the original home of America's "Scots Irish" mountaineers, who are actually neither Scots nor Irish. Scott traveled through the Scots Borderlands collecting lost poems and ballads, publishing three volumes by 1803.[2]

Other famous writers investigated Folk Music, including Carl Sandburg (1878–1967). Sandburg was a poor boy, son of Swedish immigrants. He quit school in the eighth grade and hoboed cross-country in the 1890's. His experiences on the road and the rails exposed him to folk songs and instilled in him a distrust of capitalism. Sandburg published "The American Songbag" in 1927 and it is still in print, containing two hundred and ninety songs and blues.[3] This collection was never as popular with the folkies as the Lomax books, perhaps because Sandburg was too low class to be accepted as a Folk Expert.

But none of them, except Sandburg, was interested in Minstrel music. They collected ballads as romantic survivals of the minstrels of Chivalry. They were into the racial purity of Anglo-Saxon or Scots traditions. No Irish need apply. Sam Clements was less well bred, and he was interested in Darkies and crackers and their music. He also played piano and guitar. Here is his description of a mid-century genteel parlor on the Mississippi:

> *Piano—kettle in disguise—with music, bound and unbound, piled on it, and on a stand near by: Battle of Prague; Bird Waltz; Arkansas Traveler; Rosin the Bow; Marseilles Hymn; On a Lone Barren Isle (St. Helena); The Last Link is Broken;*
>
> *She wore a Wreath of Roses the Night When Last We Met; Go, Forget Me, Why should Sorrow o'er that Brow a Shadow Fling; Hours There Were to Memory Dearer; Long, Long Ago; Days of Absence; A Life on the Ocean Wave, a Home on the Rolling Deep; Bird at Sea. Spread open on the rack, where the plaintive singer has left it ... Tilted pensively against the piano, a guitar—guitar capable of playing the Spanish Fandango by itself, if you give it a start.*[4]

Note that the music includes "Rosin the Bow", "Arkansas Traveler" and "Spanish Fandango," all of which have graced the Old Time repertoire.

At roughly this time the first truly American music shambled to life, much to the distress of the genteel. Only Jazz, Rock, Punk, and Rap have been as disreputable. It was raucous, irreverent, exquisitely low class and outrageously popular. And you could dance to it. I give it an 84. Minstrel or "Blackface" music had a symbiotic relationship with Old Time, with songs and musicians moving back and forth in a manner seemingly designed to infuriate academics and racists of all colors, but it is sufficient to cite songs like "Old Zip Coon/Turkey in the Straw", "Dixie" and "Arkansas Traveler" to see the influence that Minstrel had on Hillbilly and vice versa.

Clarence "Tom" Ashley was one of the many musicians who had careers in both Old Time and Blackface. It might be easy to condemn such fluidity, using the morality of a later age, but the operative imperative was "Never Turn Down a Gig." The run of gigs might be a square dance at the school, a paid dance for whatever passed for "quality", some sort of benefit picnic, or just a front porch picking session with jug. There was music in church, in the nursery, and once a year there was music down in Winston-Salem at the tobacco auction. The farmers would wagon down their yearly cash crop and whores, moonshiners, and musicians would be there to make sure they had a good time with their money. Wives and families got what was left.

Similar patterns existed all over the country. Before the invention of the phonograph, musicians had to create their own gigs and few receipts were kept. In the early days of mail order, musical instruments were staples of home entertainment, and the country went through crazes, first player pianos and then Ukes, Hawaiian Steel Guitars, Mandolins, and banjos, banjos, banjos. And then that Tom Edison guy tried to invent a talking doll. The Victrola became first a toy for the rich, and soon a necessity for the poor, much as the player piano had become a generation before.

The first recording that is generally classified as Country Music, was Vernon Dalhart's "Wreck of the Old '97" in 1924. Jimmie Rodgers and The Carter Family were the first Country superstars and both were recorded on the same day—August 1, 1927—in Bristol, Tennessee. [5]

At this point, genres were imposed on the wash of American Music as record company marketing devices. The first genre to come out was perhaps "Race Records"; "Hillbilly" music came soon after, along with records of "Old Country" music. My Ukrainian grandparents had a dozen blue Columbia discs. The first item they bought to celebrate their success in America had been a Victrola.

Once the recording industry was well established, there was an immediate dichotomy between "Recording Artists" and just folks who picked a little. And a few people discovered there was money to be made in music that wasn't semi-classical or vaudeville. Records were originally sold from furniture stores, where the "Victrolas" were displayed, and assorted chiselers, fast buck artists and music lovers fanned out across the country recording songs for cash money and liquor.

Classical Folk

At the same time, a few classically trained musicians were following Child's footsteps and recording, archiving, and adapting traditional melodies to classical compositions. One of the first and oddest was John Jacob Niles. He was a native of Louisville, Kentucky, born in 1892. He collected folk songs from childhood and composed his first song at fifteen, later studying Composition in France. He published his first folk music collections in 1925, and adapted songs such as "I Wonder As I Wander", and "Black is the Color of My True Love's Hair". He died in 1980 and is memorialized in the John Jacob Niles Center for American Music at the University of Kentucky.[6]

Nile's "dulcimers" were like nothing else on heaven or earth, medieval in appearance, and he sang incredibly lovely songs in an unearthly falsetto. He may have had a better voice than Joan Baez in her prime.

More mainstream than John Jacob Niles was Aaron Copland, "America's Greatest Composer". He followed long-established precedent in being influenced by Folk Song. Copland was the son of immigrants, born in Brooklyn. He Anglicized his surname from Kaplan to Copland, as he became more involved in Composition.

Studies in Paris left him with the desire to create works that were "American in character", a common anti-elitist attitude during the Depression. Copland took his inspiration from folklore, revival hymns, and cowboy songs. His ballet "Appalachian Spring", which refers to flowing water, not the season, uses several fiddle tunes as themes. [7]

Another vein in this corpus was the father and son team of John and Alan Lomax. John A., the father, was born a few years after the Civil War, and attended Harvard as a grad student in 1907. His professors encouraged his interest in Cowboy Songs, leading to the book "Cowboy Songs and Other Frontier Ballads" in 1910.

He went on to collect more than ten thousand recordings for the Library of Congress. In 1931, his wife died, leaving four children, the youngest only ten. John Jr. encouraged his father to take to the road again, recording and giving lectures. Another son, Alan, later served as his father's assistant and successor.

A year later, Macmillan Publishing Company accepted Lomax' plan for an inclusive anthology of American Folk music. He made arrangements to collect more songs using a disc-recording machine that weighed three hundred pounds. In order to produce his monumental book, "American Ballads and Folk Songs" Lomax required the services of an arranger. He found two, Charles and Ruth Seeger, who were also incorporating traditional themes into their work. Charles Seeger played a leadership role in the 1930's Composers Collective in New York City and in the foundation of the American Musicological Society and the Society for Ethnomusicology.[8] He also seems to have been something of a genteel leftist. It is odd, or merely American, that the concept of Folk Music could have been taken up as a Holy Writ by both the Volkish Aryan types and the Struggling Masses pseudo-commies.

Charles had two sons and three daughters by two wives, and three of these children made notable impacts on American music. Pete Seeger was the prime mover of the Great Folk Scare, Peggy was responsible for bringing real Celtic music to the U.S., and Mike was instrumental, pun intended, in the Old Time String Band Revival.

These works led to the first Folk Festivals. One of the first was the White Top Festival, which was created by a lawyer, his musical wife, and John Powell, another composer who used traditional music. It was held on the highest mountain in Virginia, just above the North Carolina line.

The first of the White Top festivals was held August 15, 1931. They wanted the old-time "folk" music of white mountaineers, and they emphatically did not want "tawdry" hillbilly as heard on the radio. Thus the flier for that first festival specified that "Only old time music [will be] considered in the contests: no modern songs, tunes, or dances." Local musicians responded in considerable numbers. The tunes the musicians were to play were carefully screened. "Salty Dog" and "Don't Let Your Deal Go Down" were not acceptable, but "Jimmy Sutton" and "Cumberland Gap" were.

A hundred or so contestants registered from southwest Virginia and nearby counties in Tennessee and North Carolina. About three thousand people gathered to see the three dozen actual performers. Cash prizes were the draw; ten dollars each for the fiddle, banjo and string band winners, five dollars for the singers and cloggers, and two dollars and a half for the best harmonica player.

During the next several years, the festival grew beyond the trio's wildest imaginings. Eleanor Roosevelt attended the festival in 1932, and her picture is still proudly displayed in the Park Headquarters building. As the years passed, the festival became more elaborate, and it came to take itself quite seriously as a cultural event. By 1936 academics were thick enough on the ground to hold a ten-day White Top Folk Conference at Marion College before the festival.

After visiting the festival, musicologist Charles Seeger was skeptical of the "well-meaning, self-advertising city cultivators of the folk" who were running the festival. Seeger noted that the musicians' poor neighbors had to stand outside the roofed pavilion if they couldn't afford the forty cents admission.

Ultimately John Powell became the worst of the festival's problems. When Seeger said that the political-cultural ideas that underlay the event were "reactionary to the core," he was referencing Powell. For all his posturing as composer and champion of the "Folk", Powell had organized the Anglo-Saxon Club of America in Richmond, which was open only to white males. The Club gained passage of Virginia's Racial Integrity (Miscongeniation) Law of 1923. "Negro music," Powell said, was "meager and monotonous," but the "beauty of Anglo-Saxon folk music surpasses any other in the whole world … [and] promises a solution to our [national] problem." None of the three thousand blacks who lived nearby were allowed up to the top of the mountain as spectators or performers.[9]

By the time the United States entered World War II, the festival was dead. White Top was one of four elitist festivals founded in the southeast after 1928 (Bascom Lunsford's Mountain Dance and Folk Festival, Jean Thomas's American Folk Song Festival, and Sarah Gertrude Knott's National Folk Festival).

Meanwhile, the "locals", who could recognize a money making idea when they saw one, started their own festivals. Indeed, they may have been carrying on quietly for years. Albert Hash, fiddle maker from White Top, told me that in the old days they used to have gatherings in the alpine meadow that gives White Top its name. He said that the fiddlers would gather on one side, and the gospel revival people would set up tents on the other side, and the moon-shiners would park their wagons in the middle and sell impartially to all.

A famous tale was told of Art Wooten, legendary fiddler and imbiber, who fell backwards off the stage in the midst of a hot tune, and was held up and passed hand to hand to a place where he could be stood up onto the stage again; "And he never missed a note!" A scholarly citation for this would push the invention of "crowd surfing" back a half-century. Although the academics will state that the White Top Festival was one of the first, the tradition was a lot older. The first big one was Union Grove, North Carolina.

Union Grove Festival

The Union Grove Festival history cites the first fiddle festival in America as November 30, 1736, in Hanover County, Virginia. The first Union Grove festival—and the name refers to a *grove* of trees that was used as a church by a *union* of congregations—was held in 1924, promoted by county school teacher, H. P. VanHoy. By its fiftieth anniversary the festival was attracting "one fourth the current college enrollment of the south-east", Hells Angels, Hari Krishnas, and a hundred thousand wildly assorted party-fiends to a town whose everyday population was 125 souls.

H. P. was a fiddler himself, from a long line of fiddlers, and raised in a tradition of music. One custom was the "Fifth Sunday Singing". Methodist preachers had every fifth Sunday off, so the congregations got together and sang and had a communal dinner. There was secular music too. H. P. was mentioned as playing a festival in Statesville, in 1912, which had been holding festivals since at least 1908. The local school needed money and in 1924, H. P. suggested that a festival charging 25 cents a head would provide some cash. It was such a good idea, H. P. was put in charge. They drew a hundred and fifty people and six bands. The gate was divided 50/50, and the school netted fifty giant dollars.

By 1930, the festival got notice in the Statesville paper, and there seems to have been a Blackface Comedian category. By 1942, they had outgrown the auditorium and used the gym also. Six years later, they could afford a P. A. In 1957, they made allowances for Rock and Roll and Calypso music, (!) and drew 2,300 people and forty bands. The flyer advertised "Folk Lore, Old Time, Country, Western and Popular Music. The next year, 1959, Mike Seeger, Bob Yellin, and the "Greenbriar Boys" made their debut. In 1961, New York

Times "Folk Music Critic" Robert Shelton put Union Grove on the cultural map with an article, and the next year saw the first circus tent set up on the school grounds.

In 1964, Union Grove declared itself "The World's Champion Fiddlers' Convention." A newspaper quoted a finger-blistered contestant, "It don't matter a damn, le's play!" By 1967, "Sing Out!" had a feature article, and noted the arrival of "About a million and nine of the great unwashed from parts unknown." The hippies had arrived, and the folkies were professionally underwhelmed.

The 1968 convention made Newsweek, Time, and the "Today" show, where Clark Kessinger displayed his trophy to Hugh Downs. This success led to local agitation to move the festival off school grounds, and the next year the big yellow and green tent was moved to Pierce Van Hoy's 70 acre farm. That year, 1970, was my introduction to the festival and "Old Time music as she is played". Paid admission was 25,000, but that was a joke, as the fences were designed to keep cattle in, not hippies out.

This year also marked a family falling out between two of H. P. 's sons, Pierce and Harper. Harper was down on drunks and hippies, and wanted a more traditional, family-oriented event, and Piece wanted the good times to roll. Harper split off, and started his own festival, "Fiddlers' Grove", which still survives. At Pierce's, about the only rules were that horns, drums and electric instruments were not allowed on stage.

1972 was the year of the deluge, and 45,000 paid wallowed in a sea of gumbo. There were 199 bands and first prize was now $1,000.00 for best fiddler. As I remember it, the rain began in earnest Saturday night, during the final competition, and the crowd noise was so intense that nobody heard the downpour. I walked out to find a poor-toilet, and saw a solid sheet of water pouring off the tent. Next morning, the grounds looked like a battlefield, with drifts of camping equipment left wherever they had fallen. The local farmers made a pretty penny hauling hippie vans to the highway, you may be sure. The festival lasted eight more years, getting crazier every minute.[10]

Similarly, after the White Top Festival was well established, the nearby town of Galax established a festival of their own; their motivation was simpler and purer than that of the academics.

Galax Old Fiddler's Convention

The very first Galax Old Fiddler's Festival was Friday night, April 12, 1935 at the schoolhouse, the only building in town big enough to hold the crowd. Several hundred still had to be turned away. The Bogtrotters of Galax were the winning band. I am informed that there are, in fact, bogs near Galax. A special cup for best overall musician, no pun intended, went to Edgar Rodgers, who came all the way from Stuart, Virginia.

Such a success demanded an encore, and so the second festival was held that October for two days. 146 musicians entertained 1,300 paid admissions. The Bogtrotters won "Most Entertaining Band". They were Crockett Ward, fiddle; Dr. W. P. Davis, Autoharp; Uncle Alex Dunford, fiddle; Fields Ward, guitar and Wade Ward, banjo.

The pattern was set, and the winner's circle for the next few decades showed lots of Wards on various instruments and Meltons on dulcimers. "Mr. Lomax from the Library of Congress" recorded the 4th Convention in 1937, and it was noted with some pride that "due to the abundance of folk and traditional music, stayed three days more."

The 1938 Convention was the first one to be held in Felts Park, although hard data is sketchy as the relevant bound volume of the local newspaper was misplaced when the County Library was moved. Alan Lomax came down to record the Convention in 1941.

Art Wooten, "an immaculately dressed musician from Marion" won both trophies and "more first places in more events than probably anyone else had done in a long, long time. This surprised no one." He won Fiddler, Novelty Fiddler, First Place Band, and All Around Entertainer. He wowed the audience with his "One Man Band" contraption, a wooden frame full of threads and spools and cams that allowed him to play guitar and banjo with his feet, while fiddling. I have seen Art Wooten's band machine and it was no crude device. It used pencil erasers to chord the strings on guitar and banjo, played in the standard four keys, (A, C, D, and G) and had an eccentric mechanism to reproduce the "frailing" motion of an Old Time banjo player. Art Wooten was several kinds of Genius, and a Southern gentleman of the Old School. Had he not been taken drunk at an inopportune juncture, he would have been remembered as one of the Founding Fathers of Bluegrass music.

Another noteworthy performer was "Big Jim" Scott, of Wade Ward's band who, at 7 foot 6 inches, "overshadowed" the bass fiddle he played on a strap and danced the flatfoot in his size 18 shoes. I mention this to delineate the high point of "real" Old Time and to demonstrate the lack of academic rigor in the proceedings.

In 1958, the winds of change blew in. A certain "Michael Seegar" of Baltimore, Maryland, won Old Time Banjo, and Bob Yellin, of New York City, came in second in Novelty. The Idyll was over.

It looked like the tide was turned back next year, George Pegram started winning and usually split the banjo prize with George Stoneman. Even at this late date there was still no official notice of Bluegrass. There was only Banjo and Band. In 1962 Tom Ashley won Second Place Folk Song, backed up by Doc Watson. And Mike Seeger recorded the festivities for a Folkways record.

In 1963, "Winnie" Winston, the much beloved folkie from NYC, placed second in Bluegrass Banjo, and Roger Sprung got Second Place Clawhammer Banjo, in the first year of differentiation. It took until 1971 to have separate categories for Bluegrass and Old Time Bands. That year, Bob Flesher of Fairfield, Connecticut won Clawhammer Banjo. An editorial in the Carroll News noted dryly "... has drawn some welcome converts ... if that is the word ... from rock music. The new converts, who wear their hair long, have an earnest conviction about what is true folk music and what isn't, and when they believe, they believe ... And if the fiddler's conventions and similar get-togethers all over the nation are a link between the generations, we say let it be." Which was a hell of a lot more accurate commentary than many big city journalists were writing at the time. The dam had busted.

The next year Walt Koken of Highwoods got Third in fiddle, Roger Sprung won Bluegrass Banjo, and two hippies, Bob Flesher and Tony Marcus, (of R. Crumb's Cheap Suit Serenaders) were one and two in Clawhammer. "The Fat City String Band" came in Second in Old Time Band.

The '74 Convention, which was the first I attended, had bands from Sweden and Japan, and a "family of three was seen several times "touring the city" in a taxi with New York City tags" (sensation). The best hippie band was "Hot Mud", in eighth. [11]

This was about the time that young Peter Parrish fell under the influence of a stray Wade Ward record, and made his way from England in a one-man banjo invasion and moved to Piney Creek, North Carolina, married the junkman's daughter (the prettiest girl in the county), and eventually became a Methodist preacher. He preached Dave Sturgill's funeral.

Meanwhile, the Great Folk Scare was gathering steam. Here is a typical event, culled from a Swarthmore Alumnae web site:

Swarthmore, For Instance

Swarthmore's Folk Festival had its origins in February 1940, when Alice Gates of the Women's Physical Education Department organized a "barn dance" at the College. Then in the fall of 1943, Gates proposed that the group should create and run an intercollegiate folk festival. They got funding from the Cooper Foundation and went to New York, where they heard Richard Dyer-Bennett, a little-known performer. He was invited to be the feature at the folk festival.

The festival was held in May 1945 and a second festival was planned for 1946. Dyer-Bennett suggested Leadbelly as the featured performer, who gave two of the greatest musical performances ever heard at Swarthmore.

The 1948 festival starred Susan Reed and Margot Mayo's American Square Dance Group, and the 1949 festival featured John Jacob Niles and Woody Guthrie.

In 1953 the featured performer was Pete Seeger. The year 1955, when Josh White and Jean Ritchie performed, was Swarthmore's Woodstock. The official tabulation was 2,725 outside attendees, outnumbering the student body three to one. Dress styles of the outsiders aroused negative reactions. Many of the young visitors, both male and female, wore blue jeans (!).

The administration agreed to hold a festival in 1957 with the understanding that problems relating to outsiders would be addressed. John Jacob Niles, the ultimate non-hippie, was invited back as the feature.

Odetta performed at the 1958 festival, and crowds were again an issue. The 1959 concert was given by three Swarthmoreans: Robin Christensen, Ralph Rinzler, and Roger Abrahams. The 1960 concert featured the New Lost City Ramblers. In 1961 there was no festival; instead, the committee sponsored the appearance of several folk performers, including Jean Ritchie, in individual concerts. Once re-established, the festivals were held annually until 1967.[12]

Petrillo Music Strike

One of the oddest watersheds in American popular music came in 1942 with the Petrillo Music Strike. Many of the most popular Big Bands had disbanded as their musicians had been drafted. This left a vacancy in the music supply, especially for war brides and defense workers at home. They had lots of money and nothing to spend it on except the movies and records.

Although it is contrary to our experience, records were not then played on the radio. All radio music was live, and all the networks had their own orchestras and specialized in carrying live music "From the Stardust Room, high above the famous Apex Hotel". Records were sold from furniture stores, or in the mail. The American Federation of Musicians liked it that way, and although it is not to be inferred that the AFM was connected to Mob interests, it was based in Chicago and bootleggers had gained control of the nightclubs back in the speakeasy days.

When Petrillo was elected president of the AFM in 1940, he saw recordings as a threat to his union's viability. To counter this he led a strike, "Petrillo's War" in 1942, to get royalties on sales of records, seeing broadcasts of live music as limiting the number of live gigs. Recording companies refused Petrillo's demands so he instituted a national ban on all phonograph recordings. AFM members also refused to perform live on the radio. The ban lasted more than two years and was only lifted when the recording companies agreed to pay AFM fixed royalties. [13]

In the interim, radio stations and record companies turned to non-union musicians and others un-available for the draft. One consequence of this was the sudden craze for "Hillbilly" music, one ramification of which led to Woody Guthrie and his cousin Jack having their own successful radio show on KFVD in Southern California. In this period, new forms of music flourished and crept into view. Bluegrass, Bebop, and Rhythm and Blues all were born about this time.

When the war was over, and the strike settled, records were being played on the radio, and Petrillo had won one of the most Pyrric victories in musical history. Woody Guthrie and Leadbelly and Pete Seeger were about to launch "The Great Folk Scare".

The Smith Anthology

There is one more strong thread in the revival, a six record "Anthology of American Folk Music". Edited by Harry Smith, there are eighty-four cuts gleaned off of his collection of obscure 78 rpm records. These eighty-four cuts have jump-started more careers, from Peter Stampfel to Joan Baez to Bob Dylan to Jerry Garcia, than any other document in American music.

Smith, 1923-1991, was dead center of the American avant-garde. Although best known as a filmmaker and musicologist, he called himself a painter, and his projects called on his skills as an anthropologist, linguist, and translator. Harry's parents were Theosophists, and their pantheistic ideas persisted in his fascination with unorthodox spirituality and comparative religion. By the age of 15, Harry had recorded songs and rituals in several Puget Sound Indian dialects. Smith studied anthropology at the University of Washington, and during a weekend visit to Berkeley he attended a Woody Guthrie concert and experimented with marijuana for the first time.

In San Francisco Smith built a reputation as one of America's leading experimental filmmakers. He moved to New York in the early fifties. There, he offered to sell his collection of American vernacular music to Folkways Records. Instead, Moses Asch challenged Smith to cull his collection into an anthology. Smith's involvement with recording continued into the sixties and seventies as he produced and recorded the first album by "The Fugs" in 1965. Smith spent his last years as "shaman in residence" at Naropa Institute, the Beatnik University. In 1991 he received a Chairman's Merit Award at the Grammy Awards. He proclaimed, "I'm glad to say my dreams came true. I saw America changed by music." [14]

The important thing to realize is that nobody had heard these eighty-four songs before. Nobody could unless they were as nuts as Harry Smith was. Nobody else was.

I'm no expert on this collection or old records, but even I can count twenty-five of the eighty-four cuts are from the Appalachian area and perhaps twenty of them from within two hundred miles of Galax, Virginia. The Stoneman Family, the Carters and Charlie Poole were homies, for sure. This did prove to have some beneficial effects on one of the poorest parts of the country, but not for years yet.

So a very few urbans were studying and collecting these old records, and others were listening to late night radio, picking up exotic strains of bluegrass and raw country from clear channel radio stations like WSM in Nashville and WWVA in Wheeling, West Virginia.

Chapter Two: Mike Seeger Interview

I wouldn't know where to start ... it's my life ... It's true ... I don't think the (Conscientious Objector Status) had a lot to do with my music making, but it was a part of my life. Do you know about my upbringing? I should start at the beginning ... As they say in the South, "it would be a great blessing to you".

My father was a musicologist and composer of Modernist Music. And my mother was a composer as well. They both played piano. And in the early Thirties, partly due to politics, they discovered American Folk Music. They brought me and my three sisters up on traditional songs. And they got my older brother Pete interested in it too. This is in the mid-Thirties. I didn't play any music; I just sang these songs until I was almost eighteen years old. Then I started playing guitar and then very soon, banjo, then fiddle, mandolin and fiddle, and I've just been interested, involved in this music since I was two years old.

I was a Conscientious Objector during the Korean War, and worked in a State Hospital where I met Hazel Dickens, and I got very much involved in playing and listening to Bluegrass. And then I began heading back to older traditional music.

And then of course, the "New Lost City Ramblers" got started. Which, a combination of Old Time String Band and Old Time solo music, has been my focus ever since 1958. And combined with playing old time music and collecting from old time southern people has been the center of my life for the past forty-five plus years. It's been my full time living."

Pete Stampfel said you were the first multi-instrumentalist in the Great Folk Scare and you were such a huge influence.

Correct that to say Maryland ... I didn't have much to do with New York. Really, Tom Paley was the first multi-instrumentalist in the New York area, and he really had a lot to do with the New York people. But as far as the late fifties and early sixties, it was the "New Lost City Ramblers". And the new thing was my playing the fiddle. See, people played banjo country style then ... Tom especially, had a record out in the fifties, and he played mostly Old Time music on the banjo and guitar. And what set the "New Lost City Ramblers" apart was that we were a string band with a fiddle. And we made a real point of playing as close as we could to traditional style. We strived for that.

Tom and John had access to collectors of 78 rpm records. I didn't. I was reared on Library of Congress field recordings ... but what the Smith collection did was to provide us with a beautifully selected group of 78 rpm records and increased our curiosity about what else must be out there. The way I look at it is this: We're part of a revival. It goes back further than I can give you really good knowledge about. Into people who collected ballads for their literary content. And then some people in the early Twentieth Century started saying "There are some really good tunes there". And then my folks, their real thing was, "There's really good music there".

And then Pete and Woody, they actually played traditional music. By getting city and country people together, and then what we did was basically just extend that a bit further into really seriously making a point of just letting the music speak for itself. As much as we could. And we would obviously choose what we thought was important. And it was based on the knowledge we had of the previous folks."

Were your parents in contact with Aaron Copland and John Jacob Niles?

My Father met Niles at a yoga camp in the early Twenties, so he was aware of him then. In fact he had a dulcimer made along the line of Niles'. My dad knew Copland in the early thirties, and my mother and father both made orchestral arrangements of a couple of different folk songs and then they made all these piano arrangements (for Lomax), especially my mother.

Niles was just a character from Kentucky, and he did a bunch of unusual things. He was in a sense a revivalist, although he was from Kentucky. They are all part of the early revival, Niles from the Twenties, and Josh White from the Thirties, and Paul Robson from the early Twenties. That's the very early folk song tradition and they, except for Josh White, very much influenced by the classical, or parlor music. And so we, Pete to a certain extent, we of the string band revival, are a real revival.

The next wave, as far as I'm concerned, was the group from around Chapel Hill—Alan Jabbour—but I don't know how much they were influenced by us. They claimed that they weren't. I can't remember what years ... but Alan Jabbour was very important and the "Fuzzy Mountain"and the "Hollow Rock" were very important because of their emphasis on fiddle tune. And then, following them, the important ones were "Highwoods". The twin fiddle aspect came out of the "Fat City String Band". "Fat City" was Walt Koken and Mac Benford. And they had been together since late and middle Sixties. Peggy, my sister, was the first woman Old Time banjo player, from the early Fifties. First city woman probably. But she wasn't part of the revival over here because she was in England.

How did you see the tension between the newcomers and the mountain people work out?

Most of the people from the mountains love the music and just like to play it with other people. Just like we do. Some people say, "Oh, you Yankees, you do it your way," but it's mostly kidding ... Tommy Jarrell was just welcoming of everybody.

What do you think of modern, experimental old time?

I know the "Hix" and the "Horseflies" of course. I look at it this way: old time music in the old days had all kinds of approaches, from very, very traditional and wild and creaky, and they played old time music in the old time way, all the way to people like Charlie Poole who was very progressive. And then, of course, some who thought they were the latest jazz around, such as Clayton McMichen ... and I figure it's the same way now. And some people love to play those obscure fiddle tunes in scratchy old time style. I like that ... because some of them are really good and have the feeling ... some smooth it out more and then some do "Horseflies" or the "Hix".

What do you think the Japanese are getting out of Old Time Music?

(Laughs) I don't know ... I think to some extent they get what we get out of it, the fun of playing something ... you can play from day to day ... and have access to, and get pleasure out of playing for yourself ... Maybe playing to show off a little bit ... but mostly playing for yourself ... But I don't know, and you should probably ask them ... Because it would be fascinating to know...."

Classical musicians that come down ... like your parents ... What's the gut level on that?

They didn't play old time music ... they sang old time songs in a very citified way ... although my dad started playing parlor guitar shortly after the turn of the century, that is the previous century ... in the same style as a lot of country people played ... Alan Jabbour was classically trained, I believe, and it works with his style of fiddle playing. Sometimes it helps. A lot of people started playing Suzuki method ... which is a great way of coming into this, if you're going to come in through classic music, because it's ear training ...

Mike Seeger on the Revival:

There are probably a few thousand people playing this music now. Whereas old-time music used to be played by rural and small-town people, mostly involved in agriculture, and sometimes in the mines and mills, it is now played by people who have a common urban-based experience. Probably five and no more than ten musicians make their full-time living playing old-time music, depending on your definitions of "old-time" and "a living." [15]

Meanwhile, in the wilds of Greenwich Village, the natives were getting restless.

Chapter Three: Greenwich Village

The Jewgrass "You Should Pardon the Expression" Experience

Although the progression went from Old Time to Bluegrass among the originators of the music, in the north the process went the other way, with a small cadre of mostly Jewish Bluegrassers generating a larger movement of urban Old Timey people.[16]

In 1946 or so, the more or less communist "folk" musicians of New York City, began to make it a custom to meet at the fountain at Washington Square Park in Greenwich village, and hold "hootenannies". These were communal songfests, with printed lyric sheets, based on idealized memories of union rallies and led to the publication of "The People's Songbook". This thick volume was published in 1947 and was still in print last time I looked

This in turn became the nucleus of People's Songs, a leftist organization led by Irwin Silber and Pete Seeger, which served to print political song parodies and announce gatherings. And that became the decidedly non-glossy magazine, "Sing Out! The Folk Song Magazine", a quarterly established in 1950, featuring traditional and contemporary folk songs, feature articles and interviews, reviews, plus columns on the folk process. They are still a bunch of genteel commies, but you should have known that already. [17]

"Sing Out!" spawned its fellow traveler "Broadside Magazine". Broadside was the first publishing credit for Bob Dylan and Janis Ian and dozens more.[18]

They also probably were the people who organized the "Dylan Sold Out" campaign punctuated by the famous booing incident at Newport Folk Festival. I was there.

But in the beginning, people made it a habit to meet at the fountain in Washington Square Park to play. Eventually they got enough organization to get the required permit, although I suspect there was always a certain amount of anarchy involved.

The "Hoots" started in 1946, and were held every Sunday afternoon between 2:00 PM and 6:00 PM from April to October. The permit the musicians were required to obtain from the city specified "folksinging with instruments".

There was also a fair amount of folk and country programming to be heard on New York City radio stations after the war, most notably Oscar Brand's Folk Song Festival on WNYC Sunday evenings beginning in 1945. As I write this, Oscar Brand has just celebrated his sixtieth year on the air.

A certain George Margolin was credited with starting the tradition. Typical songs included; "Roll the Union On," "Jimmy Crack Corn" and "I've Been Working on the Railroad". The fountain, once the site of the City Sheriff's gallows, attracted musicians, some of who became famous indeed. Notables included Pete Seeger and his half-brother Mike, Woody Guthrie, Bob Dylan, and Harry Belafonte. And of course, any sunny day would attract any amount of buskers, jugglers, mimes, and people who just needed a spot to practice a few guitar chords. Izzy Young described walking around the fountain in the late 1950s like "turning the dial of a radio. You walked around and listened to the groups you liked".

As the Hoots evolved, younger players moved into the Square, playing traditional songs at blistering tempos, with fancy "breaks" in between verses. Prominent lights included Roger Sprung, who was known as the "King of Washington Square", his brother George Sprung, Matt Umanov of Matt Umanov Guitars, Bob Yellin, and Izzy Young, the proprietor of the Folklore Center and the "Mayor of Greenwich Village".

Izzy Young's Folklore Center was on MacDougal Street and, founded in 1957, it became the locus for the West Village folk scene. The first band to play bluegrass in the park (and probably in the entire northeast, as they recorded their first album in 1953) was the "Shanty Boys", featuring Roger Sprung, Lionel Kilberg and Mike Cohen. By 1957, "bluegrass players kind of took over Washington Square Park." It was, as Alan Lomax famously put it, "folk music in overdrive". Banjo player and klezmer pioneer Hank Sapoznik called the park's fountain "the Western Wall of Folk Music."

"The Greenbriar Boys", a group that formed in the park in the late Fifties and recorded in 1962, was composed of Ralph Rinzler, Bob Yellin, Paul Prestopino, Eric Weissberg, and John Herald. Only a handful of women ever participated in Sunday Washington Square jams, and there is little evidence of a single female bluegrass player between 1946 and 1961. Ellen and Irene Kossoy were the best-known women to play in Washington Square, though their frailing banjo style made them distinctly Old Time. Kossoy Sisters' most recent credit is their version of "I'll Fly Away" in the movie "Oh, Brother, Where Art Thou?"

This tendency has continued to the present day, with women banjoists tending to play Old Time, perhaps due to the influence of Peggy Seeger. It has only been the influence of Alison Krauss in the last decade that has brought more women into straight Bluegrass, while Old Time singers like Gillian Welsh seem more comfortable as solos or duos. The duo of Hazel Dickens and Alice Gerard was the only prominent female-led bluegrass band of the 1960s and was based in the D.C. area, although I find them more "Carter Family" than hard-core Bluegrass.

Once Bluegrass and Old Timey fans could support a recording cottage industry, tiny labels sprung up everywhere. The big names in the industry became Rounder, Rebel, County, Sugar Hill, and Flying Fish. Jews were at the helm of every one.

Participants' explanations of why Jews were so involved in bluegrass, related to Pertz through personal interviews and correspondence, have ranged from the flippant (Matt Umanov: "Who's run this town for the last hundred years?") To the defeatist (Roger Sprung: "there is absolutely no explanation for it whatsoever ... I don't think you're going to have too much to write about"). Almost everyone interviewed said, "We just loved the music".

There was a certain amount of culture clash, however. Pertz' thesis is focused on the Jewishness of the New York musicians, but the Southern originators were so ignorant of New York folkways that Pertz includes the following quote:

"Boys, stay away from them donuts. They ain't got no sugar in 'em", said Bill Monroe after tasting his first bagel.

On March 13, 1961, the New York City Commissioner of Parks denied the permit requested by "Izzy" Young, Alan Lomax and Greenwich Village attorney Ed Koch. They formed a committee to agitate for the permit's renewal. This outfit organized a demonstration on Sunday, April 9. The turnout exceeded their expectations. The police cracked down that day in a classic "Police Riot" which the papers reported as the

"Folk Song Riot". Although the Committee was successful and the right to sing was restored a few months later, it was the end of an era. Some see the Folk Song Riot as the start of the Hippie East Village and the Great Folk Scare.

Roger Sprung Interview

Roger Sprung is a very tall, imposing man with a noble beak of a nose and the face of a cigar store Indian. He frequently wears a dented derby hat of great antiquity. He can be seen at festivals in an elderly van that sprouts arcades of tarps sheltering tables of antique banjoes and accessories, as well as his tapes and records and CD's. The marquee over the top reads "Sprung Is Here", and he is supposedly here on business, but is easily distracted into a jam session or an errand to back up a chance-met young lady for Folk Song competition.

So you're Roger Sprung, the first man to learn Bluegrass banjo in New York City?

I would say so. One of the first on the East Coast.

So what made you think of that, how did that come to you?

There was a lot of Folk Music, I liked traditional Folk Music and my brother, who loves to sing, goes down to Washington Square in Greenwich Village. And years, four years, or so, he's been there. I was a Boogie-Woogie pianist, I liked Boogie-Woogie piano.

Is that where the bowler hat comes from?

No. One question at a time. So he says, "Why don't you come down?" So finally, one year, I say, "OK, I'll come down". I went down and I see everybody, all ages playing banjoes and guitars and things like that. I said, "This is great!" And the piano went out the window. I played two months on the guitar and then I heard the banjo, and I started playing the banjo. And that was it. Because New York has every kind of music there is.

What year was this?

That was 1947.

Scruggs had only invented that style a few years before that, right?

Bill Monroe says he started it in '45. And I just met a guy who said, "There's a guy name of Earl Scruggs, you ought to get his records". So I went up to Rosie Allen's Record Shop in New York and I got Earl Scruggs' 78's and I started to learn the banjo. And I started to copy the style and it all started. That was it.

Did you have a Gibson banjo?

No. At that time I bought a Kay. I got it from my grandfather's hockshop. And I had to pay my Mom back for that. And then I sold that and got two banjoes. And I sold that and got four banjoes. Before you know it, I'm in business.

So you're from an old New York family?

80th Street and Broadway in Manhattan, and I'm still there.

And your grandfather?

My grandfather was in Manhattan. He had a house out in Rockaway. And he had a hockshop. On about 17th Street and Ninth or Tenth Avenue.

Was he an immigrant?

I'm not sure. I think his father was.

Did he play music?

No, my grandmother on that side played piano, but I haven't heard much of it. My mother played one song on the ukulele, '"Sipping Cider Through a Straw". I played piano from five to seventeen years old.

So here you are, and I understand a big Hootenanny scene …

Yeah, around the fountain area. Different groups around the fountain.

The Greenbriar …

No, no, no, It wasn't an intentional split. People just ... "The Greenbriar Boys" came much later ... way after that. In fact, somebody wrote in the paper that I found John Herald. It was in the papers last week. Because he died. And I have to go up ... Well, I want to anyway, he was a nice guy ...

Was this only Sundays ...?

Every Sunday in the warmer weather. I went down there because I had to go on Oscar Brand's program, on WNYC, which wasn't too far from there.

I see that you won here at Galax, a long time ago.

A couple of times. I won vocal here, I won Clawhammer and I won Banjo here. I just read about it ... '64 I won Banjo ... I don't know, you have to look it up.

So who brought you down, how did you find out about Galax?

That's a good question.

Did Mike Seeger?

No. He didn't come down to the Square that much either.

So that was '64. I started playing in '63, Newport Folk Festival. I think I remember seeing you there ...

Yes, the old one. I've been to a few of them.

Were you on stage?

Yes, I did some songs with Oscar Brand. I was on his program, and we did some songs. He's wonderful. He doesn't even have to sing, he just has to talk. He's very entertaining.

The longest running radio show ...

It's still going. He was on Sundays. That's how I got to meet a lot of Folk Singers.

Did you play for a lot of people?

Yeah, banjo and fiddle. I have a brochure with a discography. From Glen Yarborough to ... a lot of people ... "'Sawbuck Singers" ... In fact, I did a re-recording from Sam and Kirk McGee ... They weren't there. They had the recording there and they wanted some banjo added. So they don't know about it, but I added banjo.

I see you here every year.

I almost didn't make it this year. But I came. But, they might have buried me, if I didn't go to the hospital. But I make it here every year. The forty-second year [since 1963]. When I was in the army, it was tricky. I was in Fort Dix and you don't get off every weekend ... get weeks off. But I got out.

Did you teach a lot of people?

Huge amounts. I teach, buy, sell and play. I teach in my brother's house, in New York City ... George, who dragged me down to Washington Square. And I teach at my house up in Newtown Connecticut, every day except Wednesdays. Wednesdays in New York.

How were your relations with Dave van Ronk?

Wonderful. Got the book.[19] *I'm mentioned in it. There is one experience I had with him I will never forget. There was a party, I think a farewell to a guy going into the Army, up in the Bronx. We were all seated around the room, and we were playing away and all of a sudden there is a rap at the door, it's the super. And he says, "You guys, I don't know if you know it or not, but the ceiling—part of the ceiling in the room downstairs—collapsed." But he says to me, "Don't worry about it. I knocked down the rest. So have a good time." Dave was there ... a big fuzzy bear. The song I do of his, which is great, is "Virgin Mary Had a Little Baby". Wonderful song. I feel he really worked on each song as a project. He really polishes up his songs, takes time for each song and polished them up beautifully.*

Tell me, what is Roger Sprung leaving to music?

That you're going to have to ask the people. I don't know. In the paper, they said I found John Herald. I don't find people! He played with us, down the Square, and he's a good player. I don't find them. I have a style that nobody has ... But then I went to see Don Reno, and I went to see a lot of people, and I started playing, and that's it. That's all. You have to ask the people. I'm amazed at some of the people. But there's a lot of people who don't tell what I've done for them. There's two girls, that don't give me any credit, and boy, I taught them a lot. They were up at my house learning songs and they did so with friends of ours. And they give me no credit.

I read about them, about Washington Square.

Everything seems to start there. I will give myself credit for that. I was one of the first there. But not the first, though. There was this guy George … It will come back to me.

Julian Winston Deposition

Julian "Winnie" Winston died in the summer of 2005 while this book was being written, and had been kind enough to fill out a questionnaire via email. He was eulogized by NPR's Terry Gross, and mentioned with affection by everyone who knew him. The adjective "well-beloved" is precisely applicable. [20]

I was born in NYC and headed south as soon as I had my driver's license. Spent time with Bascom Lunsford at his house, went to Asheville, Galax, and a number of other places before many other "Yankees" got there. I had a good bluegrass band in NYC. I was on the "Old Time Banjo Project" by Electra. I played a stint (short) with Bill Monroe.

When I was 10, my parents got a job at a "creative arts" camp. I went along. While there, I learned a few chords on the guitar. My parents bought me a low-end Martin guitar (O-17) when I returned home in September, and I kept up my interest. Although I was taking piano lessons, I continued to play the guitar. Eventually, I persuaded my parents to let me take guitar lessons. I studied for a year with Jerry Silverman, who was involved in the NYC folk scene and with "Sing Out!" magazine.

In 1955, back at the camp, I met Paul Prestopino who turned me on to the whole folk music scene. In one fell swoop I learned about the Carter Family and all the other players on the "Anthology of American Folk Music", the five stringed banjo, both Scruggs and OT styles, and Travis style guitar playing.

I came back to the city, bought a cheap banjo and a Martin D-18, and started to hang out at Washington Square Park where many musicians would congregate on Sunday afternoons. Among them; Tom Paley, Roy Berkeley, Luke Faust, and Dick Greenhaus, as well as bluegrass players like Eric Weissberg, Marshall Brickman, Bob Yellin, and Roger Sprung. The separation between OT and other styles was not as distinct then as it has since become, and much of the repertoire moved fluidly back and forth. A player like Dave Van Ronk, who would make a name for himself as a blues player, was often seen playing OT tunes on the banjo. I played both guitar and banjo. I was interested in all styles, and worked at becoming fluent in them. I spent a lot of time listening to the "Anthology" and learning the songs that were found there. After hearing the "Greenbriar Boys" (in their first incarnation) I put the guitar aside and took to the five string banjo in earnest.

Mostly, I was a solo performer. In 1959 I had an opportunity to play with Harry and Jeannie West, a couple of transplanted southerners who lived in NYC. Harry played mandolin, Jeannie played guitar, and I joined playing five string banjo. We were joined, on occasion, by Artie Rose who played Dobro. The music they played was bordering on OT and bluegrass, although their presentation was more laid back than the "driving" style of bluegrass.

I did continue to hone my bluegrass skills with another group of musicians from New Jersey and a number of musicians from the Connecticut bluegrass scene. By 1964 I was the "hot" banjo player in New York. I played in "The New York Ramblers" with David Grisman (mandolin), Gene Lowinger (fiddle) and a number of guitar players including Eric Thompson, Jim Field, and Jody Stecher. I can be heard with the Ramblers on "Bluegrass Breakdown" (Vanguard) and with Grisman on "Early Dawg" (Sugar Hill).

At the same time I began to drive to other venues. My first long trip was to the festival at Asheville, NC that was run by Bascom Lunsford. Harry and Jeannie were friends of Bascom and I got to spend some time with the old gentleman. I got to meet and play with George Pegram at that time. A year later I went to the Galax Festival where I met Wade Ward and Clarence Ashley. I was also regularly driving down to West Grove, PA to see the bluegrass shows at Sunset Park. I did play as a "Bluegrass Boy" in 1964 when Bill Monroe came to Pennsylvania. I didn't travel with his band. It was a great experience.

In addition to those already mentioned, I went to a number of the Indian Neck gatherings in New Haven, CT, most of the shows put on by the Folksinger's Guild in NYC, and, when it started up, the Philadelphia Folk Festival. In 1965 I went to the first "Bluegrass Festival" at Cantrell's Horse Farm in Roanoke, VA. I saw them all but was especially enamoured of Don Reno and Red Smiley, and Jim and Jesse—who had Alan Shelton playing banjo with them.

Were drugs or alcohol a factor?

Not until later. I began smoking dope in 1965—way after I fell into the scene. Marijuana did have an effect, in that I began to "hear" the music differently and began experimenting with alternate timings and tonalities. I grew up in a "lefty" NY family. They had always listened to folk music, although my choices were, eventually, somewhat puzzling to them as I started to hang out with some severe "red-necks!"

Did other musicians mentor you?

Only in that I learned from them by observing them. I guess the first was Paul Prestopino. After that I watched Luke Faust and Tom Paley for my "old-time" banjo stuff. Playing with Harry and Jeannie was certainly a "mentoring"—I learned about working in a band and a bunch of good old tunes in the process. Old Time gave me a social scene in which to operate, and many friends. I can't imagine what my life would have been without music.

The best part of Old Time?

The heartfelt soul of the music.

The worst?

People trying to play it without understanding it. It is NOT just notes.

Do you think non-Appalachian people can play OT?

Yup. I did! And I was well accepted by the folk I learned from. I was "the Yankee boy who picked the five."

Mike Resnick Interview

I grew up in Brooklyn, and got interested in acoustic music through Pete Seeger and the Hootenannies. This might have been around 1951. I met Roger Sprung in 1952. And then I got to hear Southern Old Time Music, which was being brought up north by a couple of people, John Cohen and Tom Paley, early on the scene. They would perform as a duo. This was before they formed the "New Lost City Ramblers". So you could go to an Off-Broadway theater in Greenwich Village, and for two dollars you could hear them do stuff they had learned off of old records. There was a man named Harry West, who grew up in North Carolina; he lived in New York and worked as a private detective. He was very influential, a seminal figure, playing and teaching and transmitting Southern music, and of course the banjo. He was married to Jeannie West.

They formed this duo, and were at parties and played this music and got a number of New York people interested. Also there was Jean Ritchie, who grew up in Kentucky. Guy Carawan[21] who did spend time in the South. He was a union organizer, and came up and performed. This was all in the early Fifties. He was with Guthrie and Pete Seeger, and Bess Hawes. At any rate, I got to like this Old Time Music and wanted to hear more of it, wanted to hear what was more authentic. I found out there was a festival in Asheville, North Carolina, run by Bascom Lunsford. So I arranged to go down in the summer of 1957 and that was my first experience in the South. I was very taken with the scenery and the music. I went with a man named Richard Hollenburg who is now a professor of History at Cornell University. And we met up at that time with Ed Kahn who became the President of the John Edwards Memorial Foundation, which was started by an Australian who was very interested in Old Time Music and had a huge collection of 78 records.[22]

Ed Kahn died prematurely. But there we were in 1957, in Asheville and we decided that we were going to try to travel around and meet up with the real practitioners of this music. And we did meet quite a number of interesting people in the area. We went to Harmony, North Carolina. We met Marcus Thornton, we met Samantha Bumgardner, a woman who was one of the early ... she recorded as early as 1944. She played banjo and fiddle. Very powerful woman, who Pete Seeger credits with inspiring him to play the banjo. We met Clarence Green and did some recordings and heard it first hand. It was very inspiring. And then came back to New York and resumed our lives. I was in medical school at the time.

By this time, there were re-issues of 78's coming out. The earliest was the Anthology of American Folk Music, which Harry Smith put together. But then there were many LP's of 78's ... "Blue Sky Boys", "Skillet Lickers", that's how we had access to this music, through 33 1/3 records. Folkways was putting it out. So that was my introduction. Then people from the south, like Bill Monroe, Doc Watson, started traveling up north, on the college circuit, and they also appeared in concert halls, Town Hall, I remember, in the early '60's.

I got a guitar, and that was about 1955 ... then I got a banjo, then a mandolin. Tried to play them all, in that Southern Style as closely as I could. And then my internship and residency interfered with my musical development. I stopped being an Orthopedic Surgeon a couple of years ago, otherwise I'm still working.

What does this music mean to you intellectually?

"I don't know about any intellectual reason, I think because it gave me goose bumps, I had an emotional reaction to it. Some of the songs of hard times ... I identified with "Down on Penny's Farm" and "Cotton-mill Colic" and those hard times songs. I grew up in a working class family, accustomed to going to union meetings and so forth with my father. I grew up in Brooklyn. My grandparents were immigrants.

"A lot of the songs we learned from this 92 year old Balalaika player reminded us in form and content of Old Time. The A and B parts, the repetition ... it was dance music, basically."

When I was about eight, I was playing Ukrainian records on my grandparents' wind up Victrola and my mother, who was from the South, said, "I can't stand that music, it's all the same thing, over and over."

And I pointed out that it was the same as square dance music. Which made her even madder. As a southerner with pretensions, she didn't like Country Music. She liked Mario Lanza. My dad, who didn't speak English until kindergarten, loved Red Foley.

"My grandparents came from what is now Belarus and their Yiddish Folk that my mother learned and sang, were totally welcome. We heard a number of stories especially down South, here, of middle-class people who really rejected the country music, so to speak, felt it was of no account, or trashy. Hillbilly was derogatory. Quite a few people were amazed when the practitioners like Wade Ward, who they held in no esteem whatsoever, or Tommy Jarrell, now had streams of people who visited them like icons, that would sit at their feet and learn this music. Local people had other connotations for it.

"The next time I came South was with Drew Smith in 1977 to Galax. We met quite a few people from town. We didn't start coming down to the field; we stayed in a motel, until we met Susan Sterngold. Any part of the Southern culture was very interesting to me. I think the music that we liked primarily was the so-called Mountain Music, whether it came from Georgia or Alabama or Virginia, it was certainly Appalachian culture. There wasn't anything below Washington ... Before Clifftop started, we were regular travelers to the Carter Fold. They had a festival, also. They were extremely welcoming.

"Drew and I have formed a band called 'Ben Borsch and the Beats'."

One door closes and another opens. About 1960 something unprecedented in the entire history of humanity insinuated itself into the consciousness of the avant garde. It was a complex molecule derived from a fungus that grew on rye flour. It was called LSD, and as the man said "If you don't think it's amazing, just go ahead and try it." [23]

Things got weird and a thousand flowers of strangeness bloomed in slums and wastelands all over America. One of the first bloomings was in Greenwich Village. They called it a youth rebellion, but that was the very least of it, and the musicians were some of the first to sense the sea change. The beats hated Folk, as being childishly cheerful, and the Rock and Rollers, such as they were in 1960, never saw the Folkies coming. How could you be on stage without matching uniforms?

But people like Peter Stampfel, Jim Kweskin, John Sebastian, Bob Dylan, Joni Mitchell, and thousands more were on their way. And all of these mentioned had some trace of Old Time Music in their musical gene pool. Stampfel became a fiddler, Kweskin helped reinvent Jug Band, Sebastian was in The Even Dozen Jug Band, and Dylan mined the whole history of Folk Music. Even Joni Mitchell played dulcimer

Chapter Four: The Dawn of the Hippie

Peter Stampfel Interview

Peter Stampfel is one of the most influential musicians of his generation. He kicked the Old Time Revival into hyper-space with his band "The Holy Modal Rounders" and was an early member of the world's first Punk/Art/Performance/Psychedelic band "The Fugs".

Who were you when you were fourteen?

Lower class Milwaukee. My dad was a factory worker. When I graduated from high school in 1956 and went to the University of Wisconsin at Milwaukee, I was the first kid in the family to go to college. I met a beautiful girl in my anthropology class; she was married and she and her husband, Rob Hunter, not to be confused with the Grateful Dead Rob Hunter, were very close friends. Rob Hunter played folk music since he was 12—five-string banjo, guitar, and was deeply into Pete Seeger and Bluegrass. So that was my first exposure to folk music.

I played violin in high school orchestra and I tried to play saxophone for about a year when I was in high school. I took saxophone lessons as well as violin. We got … in 7th grade you get a pep talk. Everyone takes chorus. The chorus teacher gives everyone a pep talk on how you should learn to play a musical instrument because it will instill your future life with great joy.

So I decided to go for the violin which I actually started playing in 10th grade. Rather, in 3rd grade, it was offered in Milwaukee to all students but the teacher was an evil man. I managed to escape his clutches after begging and pleading and crying for several months but I won't go into details. So I got the violin from some neighbors who had it up in their attic. People have always been giving me fiddles from their attic. Well, anyway, when I heard the five-string banjo for the first time … which I had on the song "Tzena, Tzena, Tzena" by the Weavers … only I didn't know that was a five-string banjo. I hated banjos; I thought banjos were awful and accordions were awful, you know. But when I heard the five-string banjo for the first time, I just knew I had to play it. It was just an instantaneous feeling, you know.

No thinking was involved, it just came. Anyway, I didn't start playing until '58, and I went to Nashville with Rob Hunter in 1957 to the "Grand Ole Opry" and I fetched coffee for Bill Monroe in Bean Blossom, Indiana, and spilled it all over my hand and burned myself. But I heard the "New York City Ramblers" when they came out with their album in 1958 and that was my first exposure to Old-Timey. So that's where I got to the Old-Timey. When I got to New York in 1959, I was exposed to the Smith Anthology and that is where I realized that Old-Timey was more mysterious and strange than I ever imagined.

One of the things that attracted me to your music was that you had a kind of hair-raising affinity to the surrealistic … "Hello leaf, hop back on the tree, turn the color green the way you used to be". What attracted me to Old Time, to use Pete Seeger's analogy, is that it's like a stone that has rolled down a stream until it's polished.

Well, I think there was a truth, a genuineness—I hate to use the word "authenticity" but it is one of those buzzwords. However, it just seems like it was a degree more real than most music. I was passive. I love old stuff—I look in the old magazines and pictures and maps—and the smell of old stuff. I really haven't read too much, like I'm not really into 19th century literature or anything like that. I mostly read new-age stuff but I've always liked some old, old stuff. Did you read "Cold Mountain"? When he is talking about the banjo and fiddle music? Like he is describing something that never really … I mean the idiot savant banjo guy and incorrigible, genius fiddle player … I don't know whether they could have happened. It sounds like a strange mysterious platonic ideal of old strings. But after reading that book, I determined to make up old fiddle tunes that were that strange. I mean I just read the book a couple of years ago and I figured the best way to do[it] was to play the fiddle tunes on the Smith Anthology.

Side Two has one of the best collections of fiddle tunes that I have ever heard in one place in my life. But it is not only they were from different … it's like each one was from a different planet; they're so distinct. Anyway, I've picked up on all these except for the "Brilliancy Medley" by Eck Dunford, which I can't handle … It's too hard for me, it goes by too fast.

Back then, you were mostly a banjo player?

I learned banjo in 1958. I started playing it in Southern California. I went out to San Francisco to see what the beat stuff was about, and ended up staying with my grandma in Compton, of all places … and I learned banjo, but when I got to New York in '59—I'm a slow learner, you know—everyone played better than me. There were like hundreds and hundreds of banjo players. But in carrying my fiddle with me, almost unconsciously … and there were only two fiddle players in New York, Alan Block and Danny Zee … and I started playing along with the fiddle along with the Smith Anthology, you know, and thought that it was twenty times better than playing violin ever was. So I started playing fiddle because there were tons of banjo players and they could all outplay me, but no one played fiddle except for these two guys. So there was a need for me.

My friend Rob Hunter introduced me to Folk Music, followed me to New York, and we met this guy named George Dawson and we formed a string band because there was this Jewish Girl's Home for Bad Girls—a Halfway house for bad Jewish Girls … they were having a parent's meeting, which was a very awkward situation … and the girls hustled the person into having us three guys play for everybody … which was a long funny story. And so, suddenly here was this chance to make twenty-five dollars so we formed a band. Because twenty-five dollars was a lot of money in 1960. We were actually the first Old Timey band on the Lower East Side, "The Strict Temperance String Band of Lower Delancy Street."

"The New Lost City Ramblers" were a couple of social levels above that?

Musical levels, about that … Actually George Dawson and Rob Hunter played damn well. But the musicianship of the "New Lost City Ramblers" … Tom Paley was the first guy to introduce good chops to the New York City Folk Scene. And he is actually a native New Yorker, which makes it even stranger. But before him no one really played that well on the scene. And he introduced serious chops in the late 1940's, at which point having serious chops became critical. And ten years later, there were hundreds of guys on the scene, who could play like crazy. Eric Weissberg, Dick Rosmini, Perry Letterman … And Mike Seeger was the first person to have mastered all the instruments … guitar, fiddle, banjo, mandolin, autoharp … He was the guy that made everyone say, "Oh, Ok, That's what you do, you play everything!" So, in so many ways the Ramblers made an indelible mark on the whole folk music scene. And the reason that they didn't cover any Harry Smith Anthology songs was because Harry gave the rest of his collection, the out-takes, to the New York Public Library where Ralph Rinzler catalogued them. And the Ramblers got all their tunes from the out-takes of Harry Smith's collection. John, Mike and Tom are absolutely the key to this whole Old Timey thing, absolutely.

In the "Strict Temperance Band" ... You played banjo?

No, I played fiddle and mandolin, Rod Hunter played guitar, and George Dawson played banjo.

So you guys were the one and only string band in 1960?

There were a number of Bluegrass bands, ad hoc Bluegrass bands, but besides the "New Lost City Ramblers" we were probably about the only ... The thing is, that there wasn't really any venue for us to play at. There was a folk dance bunch ... Margot Mayo[24] *ran a folk dancing weekly get-together and people would play music after the dancing. This had been going on since the Forties maybe. And that was about the only place people played traditional music. Gerde's Folk City didn't open until 1960. There weren't any Old Timey bands around really. Allan Block's Sandal Shop on 4th Street, between 6th and 7th Avenue ... People would play there every Saturday. Alan was a fiddle player from Oshkosh, Wisconsin.*

So that was sort of an ad hoc string band because it was banjoes, fiddles, guitars, mandolins, together. So there were a lot of us got together and played string band music but it was all, you know, loose.

When I listen to your early records, I find you sound so much like Tommy Jarrell, it's unbelievable ...

Like who?

But you didn't know who Tommy Jarrell was?

I still don't know ...

Tommy Jarrell ... He's deceased, but he was the local god of Old Time fiddle. Because he learned in an archaic style. In the '70's, he was in his eighties, and when he learned, he played in a very archaic style, what they called the "Round Peak" style.

Round Peak? What's that mean?

It's a locale. In North Carolina. But naturally every little group of Old Timey people thinks that they are the center of the universe.

You say that there are 30,000 people in Old Time music currently?

That's just a ballpark guess.

Do you have any idea—ballpark guess—of the number of people involved in from 1960 to 2000? Has it been going up or is it fairly stable? Was there a peak that it is down from?

There was a huge peak in the middle Seventies.

Oh, really?

When Union Grove Fiddle Festival was going on ... And now there are like two big festivals a year here. We see people from Japan and stuff ... The truest festival is this weekend at Elk Creek, Virginia. The two big ones are Mt. Airy, "Always the First Weekend in June" and that's the best one. And then there is the bigger, more commercial one, called the Galax Old Fiddler's Convention. That's the second week in August.

Yeah, I've heard about that one.

And then from '90 to now, it's been down, but recently a lot of the local, local kids have been picking up Old Time as a kind of punk music.

One thing about the phenomenon of punk rockers discovering traditional, and started playing that, because punk rock is kind of a very rebellious, teenage music ... And when you get a little older, you start being concerned about how long your ears are going to last, and melodies and things. The Folk Scene tended to be so chops oriented that it's really difficult for a lot of people to create circa '20's music like, in "O Brother, Where Art Thou"?

It's supposed to be 1936, but the guitar playing is technically advanced ... I mean, like God bless everyone involved with that ... I don't mean to be putting anything down, but it just didn't really sound really Old Timey. And I think the punkers who got country, because of having an aesthetic that involved simplicity and crudeness, are often more capable of rendering the old music in an accurate style. Because they don't have an attitude about like the need to have fantastic chops and display them constantly.

Yes. Exactly right. I got a letter from a guy in a band called "The Bad Livers"

Danny Barnes is the banjo player in "The Bad Livers" ... all the people with amazing chops . He is the one with the most soulful note choices of any banjo player that I have ever heard. He is just ... he is an exception to the rule. He is a phenomenal banjo player.

You don't go to festivals?

I actually never have gone to a fiddle festival. I went to the Philadelphia Folk Festival ... in 1965, I think it was. But that's about the only folk festival I have ever been too.

I would like to hear more about your lyrical approach.

When I started picking up songs off of old records, often there would be a line or two, or a verse or two, that were hard to figure out. And I would end up approximating what I heard.

The Folk Process.

Exactly. And what I found out was that ... invariably, when I found out what the real words were ... every time, I found that what I had made up was, I thought, better. And after this happened ... I mean, until about 1961 or 1962, my line was "Don't play any post 1939 notes. Don't sing any post 1939 stuff". I wanted to be a re-creator. And then I thought, "What if some one could magically bring the Smith Anthology guys, when they were still in their twenties, to the modern world" ... now we're talking 1963 ... and if they were exposed to Rock and Roll. What would they do then?"

This was when the first Holy Modal Rounders record was recorded?

Right. Before I ran into Steve Weber, I started thinking suddenly of the combination of Old Timey plus Rock and Roll. But not Country Rock ... I mean Old Timey Rock as opposed to contemporary Country Rock, you know. And anyway, at that point, I decided that making up new words gratuitously rather than simply trying to fabricate approximations was ... So I started doing that. Because I did have kind of an affinity towards words, but it took me a hell of a long time to ... My song-writing ability took decades to really come together, because I'm a really ...

Slow learner.

Right.

I'm beginning to not doubt your word, of course. That's what attracted me to your band ... It was just little bit skewed, a little bit off, but it made sense. Like, "Hanging out her wash, in the pouring rain, I thought New York had gone insane." That could happen. You could be walking down the street and that could happen.

I'm not sure if that was Robin Rumaili or Steve. But Robin Rumaili and Mike Hurley have been making up songs earlier than I was. And they also had a pretty good Old Time feel as well. So they were some of the first ... beside Bob Dylan ... you know, people that actually had a clue about the old stuff, who can make up credible songs as well.

But until Bob Dylan started doing it, and achieving some real amazing success, really quickly, it was sort of ... like flying ... But once you started doing it, I started "I want to do it too." But, it just took me an awful long time to get the hang of it. I just didn't have the instant affinity that Dylan had. What attracted me to Folk Music in general, was the really great songs, in capital letters, and the really strange songs and the really odd structures and ... Like the way "Man of Constant Sorrow" didn't start on the tonic chord ...

I guess van Ronk was earlier.

Van Ronk was earlier. His biography just came out. It lays out the Folk Scene in greater detail than anything I've ever seen. Because he was in his forties. If you want to know about the New York City Folk Scene, it's all there.

Do you play out now?

I play with this guy John Kruth and we do a lot of double banjo stuff. In fact we are going to get together with John Cohen later this week, hopefully, and do some triple banjo stuff. We are playing with a bass player, occasionally a tuba player, a drummer and a jazz clarinet guy. Going into jazz, actually.

Memories of Alan Block
Rory Block

My father settled into a tiny shop on MacDougal Street not much larger than a kitchen counter, and there began his custom leather business that later became famous. Having no room inside, he stretched his materials out across the sidewalk and made sandals in front of the pedestrians.

The Allan Block Sandal Shop relocated to its well known address on West 4th street, at the head of Jones street, where frequent sightings of Bob Dylan and John Lennon were all part of the incredible live atmosphere of the place.

One day when I was twelve my father walked in the door and exclaimed that he met an old farmer in the street selling corn. He told us he wouldn't be playing "violin" anymore, but a new style called "Old Timey" which he learned about from this farmer. He took the instrument from its case and announced that from now on this was a "fiddle." He demonstrated the style, which was scratchy and bouncy.

My father eventually became the reigning impresario of the incredibly vital folk revival scene in the West Village, hosting regular Saturday afternoon jam sessions in his sandal shop after music in the park was banned. The players and spectators literally spilled out onto the sidewalk while the center of the room steamed up from the intensity of the music as my father held court and directed. His thing was "holding down the beat", and from time to time an excited musician would receive a gruff reprimand as my father snapped, "Speeding up!"

My father has since moved into the remote reaches of the backwoods and quietly continues his leatherwork and music, and has also published several books of poetry. I think he is still searching for that old farmer with the corn.[25]

Chapter Five: And Here's Where I Come In.

Through no fault of my own, being young and innocent at the time, I was raised up in darkest Alabama, in Greensboro. The radio back then had no shame either, and played "Rag Mop", "Blues in the Night", and Hank Williams without prejudice. Then, in 1950, when I was five, we moved to Yankeeland, and I didn't hear anything I liked on the radio until "The Kingston Trio" tried to get Charlie off the MTA with a banjo. I was soooo tired of Italians, whether crooning or doo-wopping.

Then the radio played "Walk Right In" and "Don't Think Twice", and I found out I was a folkie. Gasp. Things went from bad to worse. I saw this guy, Nick Tesla, sing "The Man Who Shot Liberty Valence" at the school talent show. He played guitar. I thought "I could do that! I'm a nerd too ..." I was lost.

The wild woman of the school, Evie Nelson, sold me a Stella guitar for $10.00. She was way out there, she sang jazz, and drove barefoot. My mom bought me a Kay banjo for Green Stamps, and I bought this Red Book by somebody named Seeger and learned two chords. I went to this coffeehouse in the basement of a church to show off my expertise, and Evie hooked me into backing her up on "Take this Hammer." Three guys that wanted to screw Evie applauded, and it went to my head.

A friend of mine from down the street, Pete, had a Framus twelve string, and this other guy, Tony, could tune it. Tony went to private school and was privy to much esoteric knowledge. Dark clouds gathered. Pete was the kind of guy who had candy striped shirts on purpose, and we listened to "Dave Guard and the Whiskey Hill Singers", fell in love with Judy Henske, and tried to learn another chord. He was in college, and went to see odd groups from time to time. One time he came back with this really strange record. It had a black and white cover, with a picture of two obviously demented guys. They were armed with fiddle and guitar, and were from some other planet. Pete was shocked. One of them had scratched his butt right there in public!

The music on the record ... It was really simple, and really.... Off. It was the "Holy Modal Rounders". I have not yet recovered.

I used to listen to PP&M, Marty Roberts, Ray Charles, and my dad's Burl Ives and Josh White, and Tennessee Ernie Ford records. However, dad had a record by John Jacob Niles so "The Holy Modal Rounders" were not *quite* the strangest thing I had ever heard.

At this coffeehouse, "The Blue Door", there were a bunch of Dylan wanna-be's, a few Baez clones, some nondescripts, and three over-the-edge guys. One was me, the 150-pound dork who wanted to be Josh White; one was Tony Thomas, the black kid that wanted to be Hobart Smith, and one guy who was happy being himself. Don "Moose" Sineti had a Whyte Lady banjo, three more chords than me, and a dozen "New Lost

City Ramblers'" songs. He had a strong frailing lick, a huge voice, and the build of a linebacker. He tried to help me play banjo, but I never could get the lick. He is now the prime interpreter of whaling era Sea Chanties in New England. When I finally learned to frail, I sounded like Moose.

In 1963 I went to the Newport Folk Festival and saw Skip James, Son House, Lighnin' Hopkins and Gary Davis on the same day. The other influences that weekend were this guy on the beach telling me to tie the banjo strap to the hoop and not the neck. "Otherwise it will never stay in tune". His voice in the dark was familiar and eventually I figured out it was Pete Seeger. Thanks, Pete.

I had heard of Woody Guthrie at that point, but hadn't realized that he was as authentic an Old Time musician as there was. Hillbilly music. At one time I had a tape of Woody, Cisco Houston, Sonny Terry and Brownie McGee, playing Old Time music, roughly defined as "anything you could square dance to". Here is the table of contents from a typical pirated Woody album, which might stand in for a set list, circa 1939, for a working musician:

1. John Henry
2. Worried Man Blues
3. Pretty Boy Floyd
4. Lost John
5. Bury Me Beneath The Willow
6. Ezekiel Saw The Wheel

7. Lonesome Day

8. Buffalo Skinners

9. Gypsy Davy

10. Cumberland Gap

11. Poor Boy

12. Chain Gang Special

13. Columbus Stockade

14. Hard, Ain't It Hard

15. More Pretty Girls Than One

16. Long John

I can safely say, that by the time I had been beating on that banjo for a year, I could fake every song on that list, or one just as corny. Woody also gave some good advice in one of his autobiographies: "If you're playing behind a fiddler, remember, he doesn't want to hear you. He wants the audience to hear him, and you are to support him. So don't get fancy and don't show off. Don't go up the neck and don't play more than you have to. Just shut up and play 'G'."

After I assimilated the Newport experience, the Kay banjo got traded in on a Guild F-20, and I sold my soul to the blues. Six years later, my hippie friends and I finally achieved our dream and went to the Newport Folk Festival and the Jazz Festival in the same year. They were two weeks apart, and we spent every penny we had and were partied out.

While at the Jazz Festival, we had been parked next to some black junkies from Middletown, New York. They told us about a huge party coming near there, but we discounted their advice, considering the source. That party was Woodstock. By the time we got off our partied-out asses and decided to go, it was too late. Words were spoken; remorse was expressed, alas.

To cheer us up, a guitar-playing buddy of ours, Bob Mills, promised to take us to a huge party next spring in far-off North Carolina. We went, like, "sure, Bob". Bob said; "When you get there, you will not only forget all about Woodstock, you will walk around for four days saying 'I don't believe this shit." Like, sure, Bob.

Dammed if he didn't show up with a baby blue Dodge van and drag the whole smelly pile of us down to some place called Union Grove, North Carolina for Easter. He paid our tickets in, and told us to wander around until we felt at home. It took three steps. Succeeding steps became progressively more unsteady until one had to sit down for a rest. One of the places I sat down at was a campfire where an old man was simultaneously playing banjo with his cowboy hat, drinking something out of a Mason jar, smoking pot, hugging on the hippie girls, telling lies, singing, braying like a mule, and carrying on like two and one-half wild men.

It was George Peagram. And I knew I was in the presence of a presence. The old blues guys, like Son House, had such charisma and such joy which came from surviving all the trouble black men could endure. And this white guy had all that and more. And could dance. Made you think.

One of my fellow travelers was W. B. Reid, who is now a fixture in the West Coast Old Time Scene, but back then was a somewhat lost kid named Bruce. He had been living on our open back porch in Connecticut all winter on a rotting couch under a sleeping bag. The stage in Union Grove was in a huge smoky circus tent, and the seating was 2 x10 pine benches with no backs. All were taken. We found a piece of 2 x 4 on the ground, and made a seat out of that and one of the many wine bottles that littered the ground. One of us at a time was sort of comfortable sitting on the 2 x 4, until the owner came back from the john and demanded his board back.

Bruce was enthralled. The bands kept coming across the stage, each playing a single song as fast as possible, and the crowd would go wild every three minutes. We really had no conception of the difference between Old Time and Bluegrass, and could have cared less perhaps, if we had been on drugs or something. Bruce declared it "Sweat Music" and was hooked. I was there for the party.

We made it a ritual to go to Union Grove every Easter even after we moved to Vermont. We would dig down through the snow to find a car that might run, get a hot battery and a plate, and roar off. A day later we would be lying under blooming dogwood trees wondering why we ever had to go back to Vermont.

The drill was to wander the main roads until somebody invited you to play or take dope or some other diversion occurred. It was set up as a three-lobed figure eight, sort of a cloverleaf pattern, from the Big Top up the midway to the Crafts Barn, left back around the underground midway, up past the beer tent, up to the musicians' camp, which was on a small hill, around the main drag of the campground and back to the beer tent. It took a beer to do a lap, and the fire department was happy to sell you a "nurn". There was a hamburger stand there someplace, but they were pretty forgettable. Drink and walk and walk and drink, until you fell down or got invited to set and pick a while.

They had a midway on the main road from the Big Top to the Crafts Barn that held the paying vendors. Then as the road went back around the, shall we say, casual vendors set up their wares which included tables of pot and moonshine. I would make up a few dozen rosewood dope pipes and spread a blanket and sell them for money to get home on. The pipes were only a few dollars each, but it only took twenty bucks or so of gas to get back home. Call it ten pipes, a day's work. That left me with a few pipes to trade for dope, $15.00 a bag for homegrown and plenty left for beer and acid and stuff. I was a cheap date.

One time I had over $300.00 left at the end of the festival, and took the time to call up an airline to see how much a plane ride to Jamaica was. It was just at $300.00. I could have got there and back, but had no money to live on there. If I had had $400.00 I would have gone for it, and gotten into real trouble. Thank you, Lord of Poverty.

One of the real landmarks was the little blue "Sunshine Taco" bread truck. The first year they had a few people in there working like beavers to sell tacos a few hours a day. I was most impressed by the pint Tabasco bottle. Then the next year they had a compound and still were shoving tacos out the window of the little blue truck. If there was a tomato or onion left within a hundred miles of Union Grove it wasn't their fault. They must have been baling up the money.

Down the road was this tall emaciated guy, who always seemed to be clad only in ratty brown hunter pants, no shirt, always terminally messed up. The poor-toilets tended to be in a state of overflow, and this guy always seemed to be passed out in the slime. We undertook a mission at the risk of our health and sanity, and drug him out one time and propped him up with a beer uphill from the sump. But the next time around, he was back wallowing in the piss-mud again. Moral there someplace.

We were making dope pipes for a living, and one day, John Sturgill, son of Dave, saw a particularly nice one,[26] and said; "If you can do that, you could make guitars." And Dave said that if I wanted to work for him, I would at least have food to eat, and a place to stay, which was better than what I had at home. Me and Doug Reid the fiddler and Tom Puppetmaker reconnoitered to Piney Creek, home of the Sturgills on the way home. We pulled into a market in Sparta, the county seat, and two guys in a wore-out Ford took one look at us and handed us a bag of green and said, "Y'all, come down and live here. We need more cool people in this county." That kind of took the edge off of the "Deliverance Terror".

When I got back to Yankeeland, my wife was understandably pissed, and my boss at the hang glider factory was also put out. The fact that he hadn't paid my wages for a few weeks was, in his mind, irrelevant. So, when I told wife-person I had been fired, she invited me to leave. I outsmarted her. I did what she told me to do.

I moved to downtown Hartford, and found a crash in an apartment building filled with whores and dope dealers and hippies on Frederick Street. I had put a deposit on one of Dave Sturgill's guitars with ten silver dollars and that had not helped my marital relations either. So I fell back in with evil companions with a great sigh of relief. These particular freaks were Bob Mills, the culprit who had introduced us to Union Grove in the first place, Daniel Melvin Mudgett, a great guitar player, and Bud Russell, an engraver and mechanic. These were all musicians from our recently defunct coffeehouse, "The Forum". Bob and Mudgett and me were more or less working installing aboveground swimming pools as a "Division of Red Eye Supply." We made enough to pay the rent and buy dope, if it was bad enough dope.

Mudgett had, or was being had, by a mad nurse named Sue. Sue had many admirable points, most of which were offset by her habit of extracting the maximum drama out of her relationships. An efficient method of accomplishing her goal was to have the maximum number of relationships. So it came to pass that Sue and I hitch hiked down to Piney Creek to investigate the living conditions for refugees. It was dead summer and North Carolina was at its best. The mountains were green and cool and nowhere near as humid as that great fetid swamp the natives call Connecticut.

Dave Sturgill let us stay in a ragged popup camper and it was only a mile walk to the beer store, so all was well. We perforce hitch hiked through Sparta, the Allegheny county seat, and one afternoon we were waiting in front of a little stone realty office right where the Little River crosses Rt. 21. Sue got bored, which took about three minutes, and stepped into the realty office to inquire about houses. The nice man offered to show us a few places and told us to follow him in our car.

Sue informed him that we had no car, and he didn't blink an eye. We jumped in his Jeep wagon, and he showed us a little frame house in town for $12,000.00. He found out Sue was a nurse, and he offered to find her a job and accept a copy of her Nurse's License for the down payment. He called the hospital, and they said she could have a job, sight unseen, and all she had to do was to ship a Photostat of her license to him and the house was hers. They shook hands and we hitch hiked back to Hartford. Plan.

One odd thing happened when we got back into town. It was about five in the afternoon on a Friday, and we were ragged, sun and road-burned and every bit as smelly as hippies were supposed to be. We walked up from the interstate through the business district, and several businessmen dragged us into a bar and forced drinks upon us. When we finally escaped and made it to the hippie bar, "Mad Murphy's", people applauded us as we entered. The rest of the night is somewhat blurred.

And few weeks later, Mudgett, Bud, Sue and me were off for Sparta. Her domestic arrangements soon got to me, and I moved to the Sturgill shop. Had to walk all the way, carrying a steel National guitar in a hard shell case with no handle. Worth it.

II

Dave Sturgill lived in a place called Piney Creek, North Carolina. He had been a motorcycle gypsy, violin maker, electrical engineer, pilot, geologist, gun maker, and President of Grammer Guitars. Grammer had been bought out from under him and he had become un-enamored with the Nashville scene. He went back to the family land in Piney Creek and started to make musical instruments. He had always most wanted to be a musician and so decided to "get a straw hat and grow a beard and be a hillbilly". "Uncle Dave" was born. He had a certain resemblance to Pappy Yokum, minus the corncob pipe. It was real easy to underestimate Uncle Dave.

He wasn't a very good banjo or fiddle player, and his style of guitar playing was too old-fashioned and energetic for the modern taste. All his instruments were a little too modern for the old timers and a little too old-fashioned and eccentric for the purists. Doc Watson he wasn't. But on his own terms, and he had to be taken on his own terms, he was one of the smartest and most interesting people I have ever met. He still had his first banjo, all hand-made in the 1920's. The head had an odd mottled pattern very like the skin of a calico cat … his mother was still mad at him.

Dave had a wall of drawers in the basement of the shop, with perhaps fifty large drawers. He had me look through them for some tool, and it was like rummaging through his brain. Drawers full of: homemade Geiger counters, percussion cap pistols, aeronautical instruments, mapping gear, Harley parts, bullet molds, reloading presses, engravers, plating equipment, oscilloscopes, vacuum tubes, telescope mirrors, and so on. Each drawer would have been a lifetime avocation for a normal genius, but it was just a small part of Dave's interests.

I got to sleep on the floor of Dave's office as the only place not covered with sawdust, and reveille was Dave tapping out letters on his typewriter. He had ulcers and often couldn't sleep.

As well as I remember, Dave had two sons working for him, John and Danny, and an odd dozen odd apprentices, including Joe Arminger from Baltimore, Chris Sekerak from Upstate New York, Bruce Carveth from Canada, Rob and Bet Mangum from Alabama, Susan Cahill from Florida, Carol Seace from Abingdon, Virginia, Steve Gendron, who was in the "Plank Road Band", and Jill Byington from Ithaca or some place. Dave's moneymaker was dulcimer kits and folk instruments, dulcimers, mountain banjoes, and flat top mandos. For the most part the folk instruments were made out of the kits, or other scraps, and were sold at festivals for a hundred dollars. For every five you made for Dave, the apprentices got to keep and sell one. You could make one a day perhaps. Well, I could. I had to.

Dave had a crew of old timers who came over to play and swap wood and instruments, which included Kyle Creed, Albert Hash, Dick Finney, Wayne C. Henderson, Gerry Casstevens, Art Wooten and many more. Work would stop at the drop of a thumb, and twenty people would gather in the front room to pick and grin. Although Dave was more enthusiastic than adept, the old timers liked him well enough. He had paid his dues, and had been one of the first people to develop the claw-hammer banjo style.

The display room was an annex of Heaven. The walls were lined with scores of instruments, and any small sound would excite resonances from the hundreds of strings. Dave, no fool, always made it a point to keep those strings tuned to pitch, which made his instruments subliminally sound better. It became my job to do the tuning, and I can remember the exact moment I developed an "ear" while doing that chore.

Old Time was a social music, where the emphasis was on making music with your friends rather than aiming for some aesthetic perfection. The mountain people had made music after the work was done, weekly or monthly, for relaxation or social events, and the typical musician developed to the limits of his talent and then stayed at that level. There was no time or leisure to develop technique as an end to itself.

The Appalachian region was one place in America where being a musician gained any respect. Several times I was pulled over by a North Carolina cop and when he saw the guitars in the car, started a conversation about how he or his daddy or granddaddy had played music. It was a welcome change from Connecticut where a guitar case was seen only as a device to hide dope. Another reason to stay was that you could get a carton of cigarettes, a six pack of beer, and a Stewart Sandwich for a five-dollar bill. That made the $100.00 a week you might have gotten for a dulcimer go a long way.

Our work week in the summer was a festival every week, sometimes more, and so we would sleep Mondays, make instruments for three or four days, load up and travel to the festival Thursday, play and party and vend Friday and Saturday, drive back Sunday and crash. Rinse and repeat.

III

In order to save money, Dave encouraged all us apprentices to form a band, so we would get our money back at festivals. He paid our way in, and to his credit, he never asked for his money back, so we had a little beer money. The better musicians among the apprentices were in Dave's band, "The Skyland Strings", but the rest of us had to do what we could. No one seemed to care that we were horrible and we always got our money back. We started with four or five guitar players and a mando player. Jill was on mando, resplendent in a pair of (I am not making this up) Ralston Purina red and white checkerboard bib overalls.

As I remember, the first band was Joe Arminger, Chris, AKA Pruney, Jill, Rob and Bet Mangum, and me. I was the best guitar player, if a fingerpicker, but I had held a banjo before, so I was the banjo player. Rob was a solid guitarist, so he got that gig. Bet looked good, so she held a dulcimer. Pruney had aspirations to, and actually owned, a fiddle, so that was his niche. Joe lasted half the first practice, and then discovered that he had musical integrity, and quit. He wanted to preserve his reputation and apparently did so. We concentrated on finding three-chord songs that we already knew, that might be considered Old Timey by the charitable. "New River Train" was a big hit, as was "Going Down the Road Feeling Bad". We felt fine, just sounded bad. Actually, Jill was really good on the mando and helped hold us together.

This band was known, usually, as "Rueben's Train." And then this guy got out of the navy, and went back to nature, and came up to Dave's to learn to make guitars ... His name was Joe Thrift, and immediately became known as "Red Joe". Albert Hash had made a fiddle that was exceptionally loud and red and named it "The Screaming Red Witch". Joe gravitated to this Red Witch like it cast a spell on him, and he bought it, and learned to scratch away on it. So then we had two fiddlers, that made up nearly one fiddler between them, and off we went.

Red Joe decided that we had best change our names every festival as a matter of self-preservation. He came up with such classics as "The Dead Horse Floggers", "The Wild Goose Chasers" and "The (Crotch) Cricket Pickers". I had a few myself; the best was "The Hungry Holler Highsteppers."

But the actual membership of the band changed from week to week, even day to day. The registration back then was casual at best, all you had to do was to show a ticket, and when you did your stint on stage, they would punch the ticket and give you back your money. I had always wanted to play in front of a big audience, like Newport Folk Festival, and although this wasn't quite like being Peter, Paul and Mary, I was getting my wish.

The crowds at Union Grove were huge, and enthusiastic, even crazed. The stage was enclosed in chicken wire, just like "Bob's Country Bunker", in case somebody launched a bottle in a paroxysm of ecstasy. From the stage all you could see was smoke, hair, flesh and blue denim. But it didn't matter. You played, the crowd danced and cheered and waved their hands in the air, and that was that. Next!

One time we had picked up an odd duck, the son of a diplomat, who had been raised abroad and accumulated some upper-class ideas. I will use his name, which was Winston Pettis, because he is probably an Ambassador some place and I want to ruin his image. He was a wonderful fiddler, well trained, but able to assimilate the controlled frenzy of the best of the Old Timers.

We finally reached the stage after hours in line, and I went up and set up the mics as best as I could in the minute the announcer was talking. All was ready, and I looked around; no Winston. He was over to the side of the stage with his penis stuck through the chicken wire, urinating on the dancers five or six feet below. I grabbed him and we did our song and got our money and split. I was monstrously pissed at him, but the uproar in the tent was so intense that nobody had ever noticed. Nobody but me, and I had been looking right at him.

Oddly enough, with all the constant playing, we actually got better and started to win a little money. The band was never the same, as apprentices came and went. And one day Dave came in with a hitchhiker he had picked up. This was unusual behavior for Dave, and the beneficiary of the charity was a little odd, also. He said that he had a dream about a mandolin with 15 strings and a peghead like an oak leaf, and Dave invited him to apprentice until he could make it. The enthusiastic young man agreed and dove into the shop with elan. He was, he announced, "Dave—'Mrs. Grant didn't raise no fools'—Grant." He knew more about music than a cow perhaps, but he had great ears and unlimited enthusiasm. He was promoted to washtub bass player.

I remember one time at Stompin' 76 when he and Mudgett not only worked out "Rose of Spanish Harlem" as a bluegrass song, but also discovered that the three of us could Eff. This is a musical form of hyperventilation that was featured in a song called "Little Effing Annie" by whatever group had recorded "Surfin' Bird" in the 50's. Don't tell me; let it remain a mystery. So at practice we slid into a hot Effing break, and Joe Thrift about had a bird, bird, bird.

There were lots of great bands then, a few of which have survived. I remember "Plank Road", "The Swamp Cats", "Hot Mud Family", "Red Clay Ramblers", "Fast Flying Vestibule" in particular. And of course, the sun center of all that hippie ass craziness was "The Green Grass Cloggers".[27]

What a group! They seemed to exist in a stomping storm of sawdust flying up and perspiration falling down, lots of big smiles and exuberance, and a certain amount of healthy substance abuse. The focus of the group, at least visually, was Earl White, usually the only black guy for miles, dancing up a storm in heavy boots and a fireman's helmet.

I did see a similar, if not identical, group put twenty hits of acid in a half gallon of Jack Daniels and suck it down and dance it off and be sober again after a half-hour set. A certain old timer, Willard Watson, jealous at being left out of the bottle circle, managed to snag the jug when there was an inch of sludge at the bottom, and made away with it. I saw him a month later, and asked him where he had vanished to. He allowed that he had come over feeling a mite peculiar and had walked home. That was from Fiddler's Grove to Deep Gap, a distance of some 54 miles, more or less.

Another time, when the Sturgill apprentices had managed to become the Cloggers' backup band, we all decided to take a few hours off to go swimming. Somebody knew where a swimming hole was, and so we all stripped down and splashed about. It wasn't more than knee deep, but had a sandy bottom, and was wet. After a while, they decided to try to clog a few sets nude, in the water.

I decided to retain my dignity and my glasses, if not my pants, and sat on the bank as observer. Bruce Carveth and the band stood in the shallows while the eight couples dared the raging torrent. Let us specify that these were all fine looking people, trim and fit from constant dancing. I forget if Red Joe was in the band or in the set, but he was there. It was probably all his idea in the first place.

The band fired up and the cloggers started churning, producing more spume than two hovercrafts and a mud-bogger, and everything disappeared in sandy spray. Occasional glimpses of knees, boobs, and hair were all that was visible. Alas.

The decadent spectacle lasted only about eight bars before the deluge hit the skin head of Bruce's banjo and the fiddler's bow hair. No kidding, they kicked up a lot of water. I will be willing to bet that the real old timers never did anything so silly. They were more serious about their craziness back in their day.

One had to be careful around the old timers, in dopal matters. At Union Grove one year, Dave Sturgill had two bands—one of his homies, and one of the hippies. One of the hippies brought down a huge tray of pot brownies. The Old Guys got pissed at not getting any brownies, all unaware we were saving them from the evils of dope, and launched a commando raid to share the wealth. WWII vets, you know. I happened to be in good with the old farts and was sitting in their LTD helping them kill a quart of Jim Beam when the pot kicked in. They were talking some wild stuff, on a memory trip, about cutting soapstone from the ground with crosscut saws, and making the old fashioned type of haystacks that were built around a post: "Just as smooth as a damn egg." They had not the slightest idea they were high as cross-eyed mooses, and I didn't feel it was my place to tell them.

These old boys—the Woodie Brothers worked on bulldozers ("bulldoziers" in the dialect)—had taken a shine to me and used to come by and lead me into the paths of sin. They would "run the roads"; which involved four or five old farts in a big old Ford, with a half-gallon of Jim. They had the county scoped out and the drill was to take a pull on the jug and chase it with a tiny sip of Fanta Grape pop. They had it worked out that they could get to the next drink machine by the time the old can emptied. Then they would drop a quarter and run the roads some more, until the Jim Beam was all gone, and home we would go. It is a felony these days.

That year at Union Grove I must have ate something that agreed with me a bit too much, and played a homemade Beverly Bass[28] all night. Come first light, I looked at my hands, and discovered, that although I had taped the last joints, I had been ripping the strings so hare I had torn all the skin off the other two joints of all four fingers. So I peeled off the tape and staggered to the nurse's tent. She had no sympathy, "You're the third idiot this morning to pick up a hot frying pan without a pot holder!" If you want sympathy, try a dictionary, not a nurse.

Pretty much anything went at Union Grove. There was this legendary biker type, Big Al, who had a Winnabego, and a stew pot and a cowboy hat and two girl friends, which he managed to turn into a money-making franchise. First he would make a pot of stew and put up a sign that said, "Free Stew/Show Us Your Nipples." So that made his camp a landmark, as such things went. Then Saturday, he would run a "Show us your nipples" contest. The deal was that young ladies would exhibit their charms on top of the Winnie, and Al would pass the hat to collect a pot for the winner. Pot was just one of the things that soon filled the hat.

His two skanks could be counted on to show more than any others, so he would turn a profit. I was standing there, trapped in this huge crowd of sweat and lust, while the drama reached its awful crescendo. Next to me were a corn-fed couple, healthy, blonde and about seventeen. They were obviously locals and the girl, who was truly lovely, was clutching her boyfriend's arm and begging him, "Let me go up there, Jimmie! Look at all that money and dope! You know I could win all that money! We could buy a car!"

And he was saying, "Betty Lou, if you go up on that camper and show your butt to all these people, I will b'god cold cock you and drag you off home, b'god!" I think I learned more about women from that one conversation than from all of literature.

Mysteries abounded. Near my Connecticut friends' camp was a little glade, and at the center was a rope tied to a very tall tree and a common plastic milk jug tied to the end. Every year I wondered what that was about; there never seemed to be anybody there. Years later I learned that the campers there would form a circle around the jug, and each would drink from the "punch", refill it with whatever he had—wine, moonshine, MDA, acid, crystal meth—and swing it across the circle to the next victim. The reason I never saw anybody was that they were all in comas by Thursday afternoon.

I suppose I should describe the physical plant. The VanHoy farm is located three hundred yards off of Interstate 77 in Iredell County in North Carolina, about an hour north of Charlotte. The land was about thirty percent piney woods, moderately hilly, with a deep gully towards the back and a medium sized creek. The twin foci of the festival were a full-sized yellow and green striped circus tent and a slab-built shed where the local Fire Department sold beer. They always had lots and lots of off-brand beer for a dollar a kinger, and sometimes the beer actually sat in the ice for long enough to get cool. They always had a spare semi trailer full of beer to move up to the back of the beer stand. There was also a midway of vendors, an office and an old barn for crafts. And a hundred thousand crazed hippies pretending to be rednecks and about that many crazed rednecks trying to learn to be hippies.

And a few serious musicians.

A Brief Folk Music Memoir by Stan Gilliam

When I was a child, there were 78's in our house in Kannapolis, NC. A lot of them were eventually broken, but I remember "Bully of the Town" and "Pass Around the Bottle" ... maybe by the "Skillet Lickers". My grandfather had bought that one. At church on Wednesday nights we sang 19th-century revival hymns. My grandmother sang folk songs she learned in the 1890's. My mother liked to sing "Red Wing." We listened to "Flatt and Scruggs" and Arthur Smith and the "Cracker Jacks" on radio and television. We sat on the porch and sang camp songs and hymns on summer nights. My sisters sang "Little Sally Walker," which they had learned from a black girl.

In the fourth grade, about 1956, I became aware of the existence of "folk songs" through the songbooks we used at school: "Erie Canal," "Streets of Laredo," "Sourwood Mountain," "On Top of Old Smoky", and so on. I realize now that these came to us because of the pioneering work of John Lomax, Carl Sandburg and others.

About 1960 I met Jan P. Schinhan, retired musicologist, who was head of the Folk Music department of the NC Federation of Music Clubs. He was looking for recordings of "authentic" singers, and so I began recording the songs of my grandmother who was about 72 at the time. I gave a tape to him and made another, which I still have. (Years later I wrote a paper on her songs for a folksong class at UNC-Chapel Hill.)

About 1962 I put an ad in the paper saying I wanted to buy old records, and I was able to get several pounds of them from a couple of sellers in my hometown. These included tracks by Charlie Poole, Fiddlin' John Carson, "Blind Boy Fuller", the "Georgia Crackers", and others. I made tapes of them and still love these old recordings. I painstakingly transcribed the lyrics to a number of them. The records eventually went to the Archive of Folk Music at Wilson Library at UNC-Chapel Hill.

The first time I heard live old-time fiddle was in the fall of 1963 at the Statesville Fiddler's Convention which I attended at the invitation of Thom Case, later of "Chicken Hotrod." Alan Jabbour played "Old Christmas." In college I continued to be interested in folk music and attended performances by Joan Baez and Doc Watson. In Wilson Library I was able to listen to great LP's by Buell Kazee, Blind Willie Johnson, Dorsey Dixon, and a lot more.

Twice in 1967 I visited the home of (Black Old Time Musicians) Odell and Joe Thompson. They and their friends played regularly on Friday evenings, I believe. One night they played around a campfire and another time inside. I mainly remember Joe's wonderful guitar playing. My personal highlight was leading the singing of "A Picture from Life's Other Side" with the group. In 1967 I attended my first Galax Fiddlers' Convention, and heard some of the real old timers there. In 1969 I attended the infamous Union Grove convention.

In 1974 I went to the Augusta Heritage Workshop in West Virginia to study ceramics for two weeks. There I encountered an exciting musical scene and met Nowell and Suzy Creaddick and Paul Reisler and others and began jamming to fiddle tunes in the Creaddick's living room. We had big square dances with a bonfire in the middle of a parking lot and a band in the middle of the circle. Those were great times.

I started attending Irish music nights at Oxbow Music around l978 (Nowell Creaddick again!), and met other players who were also "into old-time," and that is when I started jamming a lot, especially at house parties. I played piano for contra-dances and regularly accompanied the "Cane Creek Cloggers" at their rehearsals and performances until I left the area in 1983.

From 1983 to 1987 I worked in Dalton, Georgia and played bass and guitar with bluegrass bands. I also became acquainted with Art and Margo Rosenbaum, who introduced me to Phil Tanner and Joe Miller of the "New Skillet Lickers". Art Rosenbaum recorded my singing of my grandmother's songs and took the tape with him to Germany to use in his classes while he was on a Fulbright. At the Lookout Mountain festival I performed some of these songs, while sharing the bill with the "Rising Fawn Ensemble" and Fiddlin Bob Douglas.

During the 90's I played fiddle and piano for contra dances in Winston-Salem with the "Vintage String Band" and the "Randy Boys". And I participated in various incarnations of Steve Wishnevsky's "Wish Band".

I still love all the traditional music I ever played and heard, and I admire the talent and energy of the great practitioners, young and old. And I am grateful to people like Mike Seeger and Moses Asch who did so much to excite people about the early recordings and performers.

But my views on the contemporary "old-time scene" are somewhat jaded. In fact, I hate it. I no longer attend festivals. The festival campgrounds are dominated by exclusive cliques. As a southerner with genuine traditional music in my blood, I sometimes resent the star system of carpetbagger musicians who have co-opted traditional music and become its arbiters. Unfortunately, a few "famous" musicians act as gatekeepers, determining what is appropriate for their slavish and less-talented followers (musical tourists) to play. The recordings of the latter group are almost uniformly unlistenable.

I see the "old-time scene" as a somewhat artificial subset of the grander "folk and traditional culture" which includes arts and crafts, language, beliefs, foodways, and so on. The festival scene has its myopia and even a meanness which is out of keeping with the generous spirit of the real old timers who seldom expected to be known outside their hometowns and who freely taught their skills to younger musicians. I am thinking of Tommy Jarrell, Dellie Norton, Dewey Balfa, Melvin Wine, and the Hammonds Family.

The funny thing about the old-time music scene is how many boomers (including me) wanted to use it to become famous. Demographically, the scene became overrun with highly educated and well-heeled professionals from academia and even medicine and the law. You might not be able to discover a cure for cancer, but you can brag to your pals about winning a ribbon by playing "Cluck Old Hen," on the banjo—not really a significant accomplishment. But then, many of us will never be able to do even that.

Most people were less serious than Stan. When the South went hip, they did so with a characteristic enthusiasm and lack of restraint. One of the hotbeds was Blacksburg, Virginia, home of Virginia Tech.

Moon, a jeweler, came from there, and set up at Union Grove for a few years. He was a tall thin guy, set up on the Jewish Jesus school of hippies, like Tuli Kufelberg. He was a silversmith, but his moneymakers were the spoon rings made of Victorian silverware. He had a sales technique unique unto himself; he would strip naked, except for cowboy hat, sandals and a .457 Blackhawk revolver strapped to his hip. The gun belt had a money pouch on it, as I remember. He was rather well endowed, and decorated his unit with a large silver slip-on penis ring. He bore himself with the utmost decorum, and no one dared comment on his garb.

His old lady was similarly dressed, but the visual impact of Moon was so overwhelming, that most people never noticed this perfectly nice naked woman next to him. She had a smaller pistol, a .380 or something, carefully holstered to not obscure the view. They sold a lot of damn jewelry, buddy. Women would walk up, all unaware, and take one look at this package, and start shelling out the bucks. One might have thought that the older folks might have objected, but even Uncle Dave had only admiration for this enterprising entrepreneur. He might even have been a little jealous.

If Dave had a flaw as a luthier, it was that his active mind could always see another way to do something, and he always preferred his own idea. This is par for the course in lutherie which attracts idiosyncratic thinkers. I cite Orville Gibson, Lloyd Loar, Semie Moseley, and the Dopera brothers as the prime examples. A flip through the pages of an illustrated history of American guitars will validate my assertion. Only success can confer orthodoxy.

However, Dave was trying to sell to the most reactionary market in America. Old time players don't want new, they want a vintage 1927 Gibson for $30.00 in some pawnshop. The Bluegrassers are worse; they want a pearl-inlaid Martin for free. And neither field is making any money at all. With a total fan base approaching a hundred thousand, there is no money to be made. But it was all Dave knew. He had no appreciation of the money to be made in Rock. He really wanted to make guitars for Johnny Cash, like he had been doing at Grammer.

Instead of taking the Gallagher or Henderson path of making superior copies of pre-war Martins, Dave was trying to make the loudest, most powerful instruments on the planet. He was, like most engineers, absorbed with problem solving.

When he set out to make a monster Bluegrass banjo, he carved patterns and cast his own tone rings and flanges, and modified his South Bend lathe to turn the rough castings and the laminated hoops smooth. Typically, he made the tone ring extra heavy; solid brass. The flange—the part that mounts the resonator to the hoop—was really striking, with a pattern of pierced hearts.

He tried to cast these parts himself, but the first set turned out with small pits in the brass, and couldn't be chrome plated. He farmed out the casting and kept the pitted parts around as demos. Eventually, I induced Johnny to assemble these parts on the theory that pure brass might have a better tone than the plated parts.

And in any case, we could keep this one around as a sample. This banjo is documented in the "Foxfire 3" book. (Plate 150)[29]

My theory was right; this banjo sounded great, and a legendary North Carolina hippie musician, John B. showed up with $820.00 in twenties and took the brass monster off to Chapel Hill. I won't guess what he did to get the money, but it was evident that every twenty had once been folded a different way.

The next Union Grove, John B. showed up with a different banjo, claiming that at fifteen pounds, the brass monster was killing his back. He fed me some massive overload of windowpane acid, and we decided to talk it over. Sturgills had no money, nor did I, but I wanted that banjo. We walked and talked all night long, oblivious to all the craziness around us, making big laps of the festival, and sucking down Drummond Brother's kingers with no appreciable effect. At dawn, I had the banjo, and John B. had a promise to pay.

Years later I had hitchhiked back to North Carolina, and ran into John B at Galax. The banjo had gone through a car wreck and several necks, and was in Tennessee, in any case. All I owned at the time was a rosewood mandolin I had made. It was pretty nice, with an inlaid dragon on the neck, and I gave it to John B. in trade. He was most gracious. The banjo eventually wound up with collector and uber-banjo player David Ball. It is documented, after all.

The last year I went to Union Grove there was a shooting, and we were on the fringe of it. My brother's Connecticut friends had set up a primo campsite, just in back of the new permanent stage, and had even improvised a long table. For no real reason we were celebrating with a half-gallon of wine dosed with acid. Mike Weaver, the soul of the group, was decked out in a gorilla mask and a patchwork bathrobe, and was expounding some silliness and trying to suck down the last of the acid through the mask when shots exploded a few yards from us. Most of the dozen people around the table thought it was fireworks, but gunfire has a sharper, more focused tone, and I immediately decided to investigate the geology of the area, with an emphasis on declines and gullies.

The eventual story was that the volunteer security patrol, some motorcycle gang, had decided to demand a refund from a moonshine dealer and had filled him so full of holes "he couldn't contain his principles". No lie, there were a lot of shots fired. I hear he lived, but it was a miracle. I saw him on the stretcher and he was less than chipper. It was only the advanced stage of inebriation of all concerned that kept the death count low. God only knows why no bystanders were hurt.

The thing that killed Union Grove was not only it's own excesses; those could have been ignored as long as the money came in. After all, it never got as crazy as Jackson, Mississippi on a Saturday night, per capita. The killer was that when it ended—midnight, "Holy Saturday" as it were—all the wretched refuse woke up Easter Sunday and set off for home.

The festival was only a few hundred yards from the Interstate, but the feeder road led right past the biggest Baptist church in the county. The local gentry, in pink and blue, gathered on the lawn to bask in the Holy Glow of the Resurrection, while the hung-over (what an understatement) hordes of the unwashed filed past on their way to their native dens. It resembled the Retreat of the Goths, only not so organized. It is not past imagining that bodily fluids were decanted on the roadside, or that vulgar displays were made.

Eventually, enough was had and Union Grove came to an end. I was in Tennessee and didn't get the word. I had actually prepared, had bought a hundred one-shot bottles of Jim Beam, and was prepared to make a few bucks. I got all the way there, only to find nothing happening except the VFD polishing the new fire trucks they had bought with the beer money. I drove to a friend's house in Boone with my last few dollars, and he kindly bought enough of the booze for me to get home on. I passed out a lot of free airline bottles of bonded liquor to astounded hitchhikers all the way home.

Union Grove led to many imitations, most of which ended badly. There were the three Max' Parties in Vermont, which ended in an International Incident, The Love Valley Festival, that was peaceful, but changed the demographics of Western North Carolina for years, and Stompin' '76, which led to vicious Letters to the Editor of the Galax Gazette, and a flurry of haircuts among the Yankee settlers of Grayson County.

Stompin' '76.

There was some attempt to cash in on the Great Old Timey Boom, proving that irrational hope is irrepressible in the hearts of the not-too-bright. Some guy bought or rented a mountaintop near Galax and set up to produce festivals. The first one was a straight-ahead Fiddle Fest, that was set up to go head to head with Galax in 1975. I would give more details, but I have forgotten them, and Google is silent.

All I really remember was that Dave Sturgill tried to vend at both this "New River Jam" and Galax Old Fiddler's and we all ran back and forth like maniacs.

Our band, whatever it was named, was at the peak of its powers and we actually won band, or came close. Kyle Creed was judge and sound guy and Privileged Character. He gave me First Place Banjo, which helped cripple my relationship with Dave Sturgill. He also set up a recording session with the winning bands, but I had a head full of myself, and ran back to Galax to play in the banjo contest ... futilely.

And any case, there was an album produced, without me, and that is the only trace of the festival remaining, except perhaps a few old tee shirts. I think my band was called "The New River Jammers".

A year later, some sharpies convinced the landowner to put on a large scale "Bluegrass" Concert and festival. Booked acts included; Bonnie Raitt, Nitty Gritty Dirt Band, Earl Scruggs Revue, Vassar Clements, John Prine, Lester Flatt & Nashville Grass, David Bromberg, Ry Cooder, Papa John Creach, Eric Weisberg & Deliverance, The Rowans, The Dillards, Doc & Merle Watson, Osborne Bros., New Grass Revival, Star Spangled Washboard Band, Grass On The Rocks, Good Ol' Boys, Hickory Wind, New Grass Revival, John Hartford, Red, White & Bluegrass, and Joe & Bing (Who?).

Vendors were booked, and security hired. There were only three flaws in the ointment. The Moose Lodge was not about to take this lying down, nobody had cleared it with the county, and there was no money. I can only tell what I saw, and there is a Stompin' 76 website, if you want to see the official version.[30]

My first inkling that something was wrong came when we were talking to some of the honchos about an Old Time Contest that was supposed to happen in the afternoons. Vast prizes had been hinted at, and all the rowdies were lined up to play. The Sturgills were supposed to liaison with the Old Time community, but it was obvious that the honchos had greater concerns than a bunch of hip-billies.

The guy we were talking to was a dapper Italianate gentleman, resplendent in paisley shirt, designer jeans, fringed buckskin vest and perhaps a headband. I happened to look at his feet and flashed on his shoes; black, exotic leather, tasseled loafers, with soles as thin as vellum. It was obvious that those shoes cost more than any vehicle Sturgills had in their fleet, and my Connecticut street brain went; "Who is this Mafooch turkey trying to kid?" It was Sonny Bono drag, totally inappropriate for country wear .

We had come early to set up and had reached some sort of apogee in the annals of Sturgill. Johnny and Danny had resurrected a big blue step van, and had constructed a booth/stockade sort of deal, that was eight foot high and perhaps sixteen feet square, made of 4 x 8 plywood panels on 2 x 4's. A tarp went over the whole thing, providing a secure shelter for the guitars.

A year or so before, a Galax thunderstorm had filled a rack of guitars with water, and that was a bit much even for us. The booth panels fitted into the back of the step van, leaving room for a bunk bed, and all was well, except for the step van's stubborn refusal to possess any brakes at all.

We had, at this time, made friends with a couple from Memphis, who printed tee shirts on site at festivals. They would bring a 1950 Studebaker with a few silk screen frames in the back and get a bale of shirts and cut a stencil and print shirts. They made a mint.

Nobody can remember their names, so call them "Phil and Minnie." They were a beautiful couple, but were perhaps too fond of Valium. Nevertheless, they had come early and were camped nearby. They had lots of ink, and everything was ready to go. What could happen?

What happened was that about a quarter million freaks showed up. The county panicked, and blocked the roads, and the freaks shouldered their coolers and hoofed it up the mountain. We were stuck, we could leave but not come back, and still held to the hope that we could sell all this overstock.

The people who made it up to the site brought only beer and dope, no guitar strings needed. The site was jammed, and the sanitation, food supply, beer, and dope networks immediately broke down. There was great music, but there was nothing to drink, nothing to eat but very bad pizza, no pot, and no cigarettes. Cousin

Larry Sturgill gifted the hippies with a carton of Menthol Light Dorals, and we sucked those down in desperation. Woodstock it weren't.

I remember great sets by Ry Cooder, Bonnie Raitt and The Earl Scruggs Revue, but the bands soon discovered that they were not going to get paid, and what little money existed was spent on helicopter flights in and out of the grounds. Phil and Minnie were sitting on a gold mine, to the extent that the audience had nothing else to spend money on, and Phil flew in bales of tee shirts. When they ran out of shirts, they silk screened peoples' backs.

We sold one set of strings, and I traded another set for a joint. Don't tell the Sturgills. The people who had dope, Valiums and Quaaludes mostly, ate them all so they couldn't get busted, and stumbled around in a litter of white pizza circles getting uglier and uglier. The obligatory motorcycle gang led the way down the devolutionary chain to shambling anthropoid behavior. No one noticed.

I went out on reconnaissance, and cut through a woods to the main road, which resembled Desolation Road. Overweight beerheads were sweating up the hill and collapsing in windrows at the last steep portion. I scoped out the drifts of discarded coolers and salvaged a few cases of partially cool beers to help wile away the time until liberation.

I think we were due some money, and Danny was not about to leave while there was a glimmer of hope. This was just as they were planning to open the ill fated Harptone guitar factory in Independence, and every dime was precious. We didn't make one. Mr. Cool Shoes had split with the gate receipts on the last helicopter from Saigon.

And the next week, in Galax, the mood was ugly, and the Powers That Be were un-enchanted with hippies, Sturgills, and riff raff in general. There was no joy in Mudville, and the big Harptone deal was off to a bad start.

Sociology and other Delusions

Pete Stampfel was shocked that I hadn't ever studied the Smith Anthology, and I was shocked that he hadn't heard of Tommy Jarrell. I never needed to study records; I had Kerner, Glover and Ray, Jim Kweskin and the whole Even Dozen Jug Band doing all that for me. Plus $80.00 was a chunk of money, especially for a doper.

And it would have been a waste, because the scene is so small. For example, one night I had a fight with a wife, and went over to a friend's house in Hartford to pick a little. He had company from North Carolina, Steve and Merle. We fooled around and played blues and I was obviously outclassed, so I just noodled around with a bottleneck. This Merle guy had never seen slide guitar but after a quick lesson, he got the idea, and sounded great. Turned out he was Merle Watson.

So Merle Watson was two steps away from Clarence Tom Ashley, who was on the Smith Anthology several times. And one of Dave Sturgill's picking buddies was Art Wooten, who had got fired by Charlie and Bill Monroe, and lost the chance of being the world's first bluegrass fiddler. It was, and remains a very small scene and a very unpretentious one, at least among the "real" mountain people.

You could never tell what you would find at a fiddle fest; back in the old days, it was strictly "run what you brung". And some pretty odd people brought some pretty odd ideas. At the Independence Virginia Festival in the mid-seventies, a band showed up from Northern Virginia—"Merle Swinette and the Mountain Oysters." Muriel ("Merle") was short and cute, and the band had a guy playing flute and a red-headed dulcimer and autoharp player—one Lenora Fox, who was planning to move to Grayson, her favorite place on earth and the birthplace of her mother. About the time the sun sank in the west, Len and Muriel and our resident commie, Claudine, discovered that they wanted to sing "Molly Malone". Aided, perhaps, by several beers, they did so, and quite well. That accomplished, they dived into "Danny Boy", "Banks of the Ohio" and Claudine's favorite song, "Mad Tom of Bedlam." The "Yee-haw Factor" dived to record low levels and I dug into the blues bag for "Nobody Knows You When You're Down and Out."

Suddenly, out of nowhere, a sax player showed up, on key and in tune. He could play as good as the girls could sing, and jazz reared its ugly head. We were jamming. After a few hours of song-belting, near dawn, we heard applause. We had been so focused that we had forgotten where we were at, which was rural Virginia. Nobody applauds at fiddle fests, and there wasn't a fiddle in sight. We turned to discover the entire African-American population of Grayson County sitting on the bank behind us, gratefully soaking up what was probably the only live jazz in Grayson County history. There they were, all five of them.

And some people warped in from other planets, it being the Sixties and all....

Jeremiah Skarie Interview

I was living in a hippie farm in the Ozarks, called "River Mandicado", a commune. And I used to go to Key West, Florida during the winter. I met some people who thought highly about the fiddler's convention, Union Grove. And I knew some people who lived in Love Valley, and I came up for the festival, in my VW Microbus ...

Full of computer parts ...

And then I went to Love Valley and met Andy Barker.[31] *I wanted to use his woodshop to make banjos. He said, "Go up and apprentice to Dave Sturgill first and then talk to me." He set it up; I went up and apprenticed under Dave Sturgill.*

What did you care about banjos?

Because I played banjos for a couple of years. And I made a banjo. It was a little crude, but I still have it. The only thing that was really crude was ... I made the neck out of oak. And then I had to use black lacquer to make it look normal. And then my pot fell apart, so I had to buy a used pot, but the neck is original. Gibson peghead, lot of inlay.

So somehow you weirded Dave out, and he suggested you go to …

Independence, Virginia and work for Dave Hoffman. It was basically Dave and me and Sherry Hoffman. And their thing was piano restoration and dulcimer making. I did the sanding. That was my little niche. Then I eventually borrowed enough tools to start building my own dulcimers. And did it with borrowed tools at first, living on Fox Creek. Twenty dollar a month cabin on the creek.

That was the cardboard cabin.

Yeah. I put cardboard on the walls to keep the snow out.

He was so cold, and says, "What can I do? I don't have any money, how can I make this cabin a little bit tighter?" And I said, "Get a stapling gun and start stealing cardboard from the back of a supermarket or something …"

The dump.

Tack that on the walls and keep the wind out.

And I also got potato sacks and I used them on the ceiling to hide the cardboard … I had a wood stove, a little tin wood stove that got red hot occasionally. And had a fireplace. But it was a pretty funky cabin. It was used for hanging tobacco.

Did it have electricity?

Yes, but no running water.

No plumbing.

No plumbing. I had an outhouse but I didn't have a house over it so I always had a great view out there and I used to hang the toilet seat behind the wood stove so I'd have a warm place to sit when I got out there. And I used to do my showers in the creek.

Icy cold Fox Creek. I spent two weeks in Fox Creek building a bridge, and it was cold.

Well, it wasn't too bad in the middle of summer. And I did go, usually, to Florida in the winter. So it was tolerable.

Somewhere in there you sold a dulcimer to Peter Fonda?

In Key West. I was camped out on an island across from Key West called Christmas Tree Island, camped in a jungle hammock about twenty feet up in a tree. I had like five dulcimers with me that I made, and I got word that a friend of mine was looking for me, and I had this canoe type thing that I paddled back and forth … it was about half an hour. So I went over there and met him and then I met Peter Fonda, and I just knew him by the name of Pete, and he had this movie star looking girl friend with him that was like … wow! So I sold him a dulcimer and he told me to come by and visit any time, but I never did. But he was a nice guy. I still go to Florida in the winter.

You bought a place in Sparta in '84? You bought a building and were going to make instruments and furniture parts?

Not instruments. I was doing furniture components, sample building, and mockups and then I got into trolleys. Making trolleys for a Florida-based company for twelve years. The kind that are on a truck frame … tourist transportation type.

So when did you start winning dulcimer contests?

I don't know, it's been a while.

Describe your style. You don't play like everybody else does.

I play guitar style, because I was used to playing the banjo. And I started playing the dulcimer guitar style. Everybody else was playing on their laps. At first it was difficult, because it was a big reach. It was a stretch and a strain, but I got used to it. Now it works good for me. In one tuning I can play in three major keys and two minor keys. I got two dulcimers, one's in D, my favorite, and the other one's in G. I can hit most keys with those two dulcimers, that you run into at these festivals.

Did you have any problem being accepted by the more traditional dulcimer people?

When I started, there wasn't any dulcimer people. At a festival there might be a couple-three of them. They wouldn't even have a category unless there were three or more. Back then there were hardly nobody playing dulcimer. Back in 1978, is when I started playing festivals. I play so different ... but a lot of people didn't even know what a dulcimer was. I often times would get "What is that?" Because they never saw one before.

So why dulcimers?

I was sanding dulcimers ... And in that process I really took a liking to the dulcimers. And then when I started making them ... I don't remember if I was playing them before I started making them ... I put down the banjo and played dulcimer. I knew the dulcimer had a lot of potential. I'm still working on it.

So you still make a few dulcimers every year?

Make a few, fill orders, and stuff. I would like to make more. Got the parts cut out for a bunch. All different woods. I just love building them. One thing I'm good at. And I keep getting better at playing them. I'm still learning. There is so much potential in the instrument. I ain't close to where I want to be as far as playing.

You didn't study any records?

Back then I didn't even have a record player or a radio. Didn't have a TV, didn't have any of that stuff. Had my old car and had a dulcimer to play. Drank a lot of beer. The good old days.

I know some people have learned from you.

A little hard for them to learn from me since I play such a different style. I've never taught classes. My own playing isn't being copied. I really haven't had that big an influence. But I have had an influence as far as helping to create respectability for the instrument with Old Time and Bluegrass musicians. They see the potential in it. They like that style ... You know, they used to think of it as a toy; now they more see it as a real instrument. And so the respect for the instrument is getting better, people are playing it better. These new styles ... a lot of people are chording and playing the melody. They're doing some really fancy stuff. It's wonderful.

I learned to follow the fiddle, and now I can just listen to the melody, hear the melody in my head, or follow the fiddle, I hear the chord changes. That makes it so much easier ... play along to songs you never even heard before, or just get the gist of the melody.

Why don't you just talk about getting accepted? You were pretty spaced out for a hippie.

I wasn't very accepted at first.

How did you get people to like you? People like you a lot now.

My music improved a lot. So I get a lot of respect now for my playing ability. I think it's all in the playing. That's probably where I've gained so much respect and gained so many friends ... socializing and playing music. I got a lot of respect for my woodworking in earlier days, dulcimer building, and then the wood shop. I was quite the hippie back then. Barefooted ...

Those damn pedal pushers ... clam-digger pants ... pirate shirt ... barefoot ... Independence, Virginia ... middle of the winter.

I was a wild man. I've been around these parts since '75 and everybody pretty much knows me and I got a good reputation. So people are pretty nice to me. Now that the Mexicans have moved in, us old hippies are now very accepted. Now they're the foreigners.

In 1976 or so, the Sturgills invested all they had in two defunct guitar factories from up north, and moved a few truckloads of defunct guitars, tooling and machinery to Independence, Virginia. The two companies were the Microfrets Company of Frederick, Maryland, and Harptone Guitars of Newark, New Jersey.

Microfrets was the brainchild of an engineer named Jones, and he invented many guitar refinements that were later adopted by the industry such as the roller nut, a tremolo that stayed in tune, an improved fretting system, the first wireless guitar and many others. He also had the aesthetic sense of the guy that designs the Florida license plates, and disdain for rock and roll. He made great guitars, but they would not distort or feed back. His big endorser was the guitar player on the Lawrence Welk Show.

Harptones and Sturgills and Grammers and Guilds all had something to do with each other, but it's probably lost in history. All had solid spruce tops and laminated back and sides. The Harptones and Guilds were somehow descendents from the Epiphone Company.

The Sturgills, who had lived in Maryland, found out that the Microfret company was being auctioned off and they went up and bought two U-Hauls worth of guitar parts and machines for a few thousand dollars and dragged them back to a dead supermarket in Independence, VA, and started trying to assemble a few of the electrics. I was foreman, and Bud Russell and a few others helped out. Larry Sturgill, a cousin, came down to keep the books, and Tommy Sturgill, the youngest brother, came up from Florida to be the electronics wiz.

Then we all trucked up to Newark, New Jersey to pillage the Harptone factory. Harptone had a good business making cases, and the guitar stuff was just clutter. We got two semi-trailers worth of stuff for a pittance and took it back to the supermarket, and unloaded it with only minor casualties.[32]

So for the rest of that winter, we tried to sort out all this junk and produce some instruments, at least enough to pay the rent. Danny Sturgill, the oldest brother, was in charge and history demands that I state that he had no idea what to do, and no inclination to learn. The inevitable soon happened. I saw the handwriting on the wall, and made plans to split.

In an equally futile sub-plot my mother, who was from Alabama, had formed a cabal with her mother's sister, Lizzie, to find a piece of land to retire on. Lizzie had found a scabby hillside with shack in the most backward county in Middle Tennessee. My brother who has, as they say, sobriety issues, had moved to this shack and was working on being a remittance man, Dogpatch style. I had visited this place in the summer, and figured it was the proverbial any port in a storm. Had I mentioned that this was the coldest winter for ten years?

I knew I had no chance of employment in Allegheny County; a new crop of hippies had invaded the Sturgill shop. In fact, I hadn't been paid for a month anyway. They offered me a stack of guitar parts if I would just go away and stop being sarcastic about Danny's lack of resemblance to C.F. Martin. So long-suffering Bud Russell loaded me and a bunch of half-made guitars, a basset hound puppy and half a deer into an old (Bud only has old) air-cooled Saab, and off we went to the promised land.

The Independence shop lasted until spring. There was an auction; SBA got a few cents on the dollar. Gibson got the high tech Harptone side bender, and the hippies used Microfret bodies for firewood for years. To be fair, Larry Sturgill brought me the guitar parts they owed me the next time they went to Tennessee. I was in business ... and trouble.

I was embarked on a learning experience and we all know how painful those might be. I learned the difference between hillbillies and rednecks; the county I was in was next door to Buford Pusser-land,[33] only not as progressive.

I had assumed that as Belfast, Tennessee was two thousand feet lower than Piney Creek, and a hundred miles further south, the weather would be more moderate. That was until the wind blew from the north and I noticed all those hats with Saskatewan labels rolling past. Chicago was only five hundred miles north, and there was not a hill, mountain or barbed wire fence between to break the wind. There was also not a bookstore for several counties in any direction, not even bible ones. Nashville prints more books than any city in the south, but if they had a used bookstore, I never found it.

My brother soon split for Key West, and I stayed, studying losing. I got a job in a lumberyard and met a bunch of grown men who averaged ten or twenty thousand miles a year "running the roads", and had never left the county they were born in. They had names like "Coon" and "Toad" and "Fungus Dog". The local music was pretty lame. Anybody who ever learned their third chord had gone to Gnashville, and been eaten all up. The ones that stayed not only sang George Jones songs, they lived them. In a small town, everybody eventually slept with everybody else, no outsiders need apply. I did learn to distinguish hardwoods apart and how to tell real rednecks from liberal ones. Liberal rednecks only want to kill all the n—s in America, and consider it un-Christian to travel to Africa to kill the ones there. If it makes you feel better to think I am kidding, please do so.

I did meet the Gallagher Guitar people in Wartrace. They had a festival, and there was "Uncle Dave Macon Days" in Murphreesboro so that only left fifty weekends a year to get drunk in. My brother had made friends with the dregs of society, so I had all the drunks with guns I could stand until I ran them off in self-preservation.

Eventually, I got the worst job of my life at a huge air conditioner plant. I needed ninety days to get full time and join the union, my father's union, as a matter of fact, but got the flu and got laid off after eighty-nine days and five hours. So I loaded up Leroy the wonder dog and my Sturgill banjo into a '68 Chevy C-10 and hit the road for Yankeeland with my last paycheck.

I got the flu because a front had come through and the temperature had dropped fifty degrees in a few hours while I getting nice and sweaty unloading firewood. As I left on this desperate flight, the storm chased me all the way up the Blue Ridge, up I-81. I drove all of Virginia in second gear, and when the road went over the hump into the Pennsylvania coal country, the weather got worse.

There was enough snow in the bed for traction, so I just gritted down and kept trucking, living on Pall Malls and coffee and a few joints I had picked up in Carolina. When I got to Hartford, I had enough money for a few beers at Mad Murphy's hippie bar. I found that the blizzard had collapsed the roof of the Hartford Civic Center, missing killing every body at a hockey game by an hour.[34]

So I got my beer. As it happened, all the action was at this primitive console video game, "Night Ride". There was a steering wheel, and an accelerator pedal and a shift lever, and it was whipping everybody. I put in my quarter, and threw it into second and maxed it out to the amazement of all and a few free beers. It was easy, considering.

When I made it to my folks' house, Leroy walked in, snubbing the family cockapoo, and lifted his leg right on the couch. Home again.

I could get unemployment in Connecticut, if they couldn't find me a job in my field. I didn't want to work in another air conditioner plant, so I made them look up the code number for "Foreman Guitar Factory." The computer wheezed and coughed up a number for a job referral for the Ovation plant in New Hartford. I had always wanted to work there, and thought to myself, "How bad can this be?" The answer? "Worse than you can possibly imagine."

The plant was an old three-story brick mill, with molten metal scarred into the oak floors from some previous industrial hell. They had seven kinds of epoxy in use, no air conditioning, and the windows had been sealed to prevent theft. The toxic environment seemed to affect most people sexually, with cases of either impotence or extreme horniness, and the management piped in incessant disco music to boost morale. There was also a 125% rework rate, the same as that disastrous air conditioner plant in Tennessee. I was assigned to the buffing room, and was responsible for putting an optically perfect finish on one hundred and twenty guitars, or "units" every day. That comes out to Four (4) handcrafted quality minutes per unit.

The management thought it best to ignore the fact that they were in the music business, and had only recently allowed guitar players to work there. The management had lots of MBA-grade ideas. One that really grated was that Nancy Wilson,[35] of "Heart" was dating the owner's son. She was interested in making guitars, and used to walk the factory floor observing. We lowly lackeys were forbidden to raise our eyes to ogle her, under penalty of immediate dismissal. That was almost as popular as the two ten-horsepower vacuum pumps in the men's room that produced an ungodly clatter in that echo-tiled space, our only break room.

But at least they had guitar players, and where there were guitar players, at least in 1978, there was dope. I reacquainted myself with James "Rick" Rickard, the Chief Engineer, old-line hippie Bluegrasser, and certified genius. He was always ready to waste a few minutes discussing the finer points of guitar design, and I wasted no time ingratiating myself with the design and testing staff.

My brother and I still went to Union Grove every Easter, even from Connecticut. I had made dumpster diving at Ovation into an art form, and liberated enough spruce, mahogany, and maple to start hacking together mandolins in the parents' basement, and would take a few down to Union Grove and trade them for dope and things. Union Grove was getting crazier and crazier, as Southern Rock hit its stride and Outlaw Country music became a religion. The moonshiners had pretty much transitioned into growing bud, and the South was rising to new heights. Some of my brother's Swamp Yankee hometown friends had become introduced to the joys of Union Grove and were making the pilgrimage every year, although none of them played.

One of them, Phil Weaver, carried a fiddle, and dubbed the group "The Strung Out String Band" with their hit song "Turkeys Rubble in the Stubble." You had to have been there, but if you had been, you probably wouldn't admit it.

One memorable trip involved Bud's '59 Chevy station wagon, and took us to Tennessee to pick up some wood and guitar parts and then back to Union Grove with a dead bass fiddle tied to the top of the wagon. We all made it, but the bass fiddle shed a few square feet of laminate on the way.

The New England Fiddle Contest came to Hartford about that time, and attracted a huge crowd. Ever since the Hippie Be-in days, an organization called Peace Train had been running concerts in the large park below the State Capitol building. The year I went, probably '78 or '79, they had, in their wisdom, decreed that each contestant should play a fast song, a waltz, and a mandatory tune, which in this case was "Orange Blossom Special". All well and good, but massive advertising had attracted large numbers of French Canadian, Polish, Yiddish, Scandinavian, and (probably) Martian fiddlers, none of whom had ever even heard of "OBS". Real Old Timey fiddlers refuse to play it, as it is a Bluegrass contest showoff piece. It's all one chord, and the idea is to make train sound-effects at max speed.

The back stage was soon an Orange Blossom Special Learning Clinic, and octogenarian fiddlers struggled to master vulgar choo-choo noises in ten languages. Of course, no fiddler will ever admit he can't play anything and everything, so the large and exquisitely stoned audience was treated to a hundred mutant versions of chugga-chugga/wooo-wooo, which they applauded uncritically. It might have been sociology, and it might have been cross-cultural interfaith bonding, and it might even have been jazz, but it sure wasn't traditional music. I wish I had the video.

In October of 1979, my father's retirement came through and we sold the family house and packed up forty years of crap and books and headed back to scenic Belfast, Tennessee for an extended, and in a majority of cases, terminal session of losing. My Ovation buddy Seth Hedu offered to let me stay with him and his wife and make guitars, but familial duty and stupidity called and off I went. Seth helped us move. His comment was "Nobody has that many books."

My brother helped the local carpenters build a huge house for Dad and Mom, and then split to the Florida Keys to get his Ph.D. in substance abuse. I stayed, driving Dad around and making mandolins, driving to Huntsville whenever I needed conversation with words in it. It took over a year for the toxins I had accumulated at Ovation to leach out of my system, but by that point I was growing pot and making wine, and so stayed pretty stupid. After Union Grove died, I just stayed at home and festered, except for a few small festivals a year.

There was a little Old Time music in Huntsville, Alabama, a very nice city full of rocket scientists and their new-age wives, but it was a little too far to commute. I did win First Place Banjo from Minnie Pearl's Festival at Grinderswitch Park, but that was about that. I also made guitars and basses and mandos from the Harptone and Ovation guitar parts and found that you can't even give a guitar away in Nashville unless George Gruhn gives the OK. He was still mad at Dave Sturgill, so I would have been on his fecal roster even if I made good instruments, which I didn't. But all this time, there was a revival going on. I always did have bad timing.

Chapter Six: Hippies, Hippies, Hippies

Sometimes you are influential and never even realize what the heck you are doing. In the early Sixties, under the influence of Jim Kweskin, almost everybody in America that wasn't Peter, Paul and Mary became a Jug Band. The one from the New York School of Music and Arts was "The Even Dozen Jug Band", which lists thirteen members. Here is a quote from the album jacket:

"The very beginning of the Even Dozen Jug Band is a dramatic example of the similarities of style between old-timey and jug band music. In the late spring of this year, Pete Siegel, an extremely able and winning performer of both bluegrass and old-timey music, brought a sizeable group of his musician friends over to swap ideas and perform with an equal number of Stefan Grossman's blues singers. The group, after a few nights of playing together, found that the two forms of music complemented each other perfectly, and the Even Dozen Jug Band was born. Now, usually once or twice in every concert, they'll quip, this next one's from the album "Mountain Music Jug Band Style", or announce an upcoming "jug-grass" tune.[36]

John Sebastian is still almost famous, Stephen Grossman has dozens of blues guitar methods, David Grisman is the pre-imminent mandolinist in America, Joshua Rifkin is "the" authority on Ragtime piano, and Maria Muldaur does alright for herself. She once moved to North Carolina for a while to study Appalachian-style fiddle with Doc Watson.

The first "Hip" Old Time Band was probably "Highwoods Stringband", which will show up here and there in this discourse. In Hartford, Connecticut, there was an experimental theater, "The Image", and it became, on Tuesdays, "The Quiet Collage of an Image Coffeehouse". This was all the brainchild of Robert Matthew Lewis, a part time teacher, window dresser, and producer. The Unkind suggested that Bob ran the coffeehouse to attract sexual partners, but if he wasn't there to get laid, he was the only one. The two Bluegrass stalwarts at this coffeehouse were "Rick" Rickard, Chief Engineer for Ovation Guitars, and Doug Dorschug, a long drink of water who was the Hartford Symphony's utility infielder. As I heard it, he played about a dozen instruments and was on call to fill in for whoever on whatever.

There were a few other people who played frailing banjo: Don "Moose" Sineti, Denny Clifford, Robert Elliot Hardin but there were no fiddlers until Will Welling showed up.

There had been a Folk Rock Band in the latter coffeehouse days, "Some Dead Bears" and when they blew up, the bass player, Bill Wallach, who was tired of lugging amps, got a Suzuki mandolin and formed "Coster, Welling and Wallach", an energetic acoustic ensemble with the motto, "Never Turn Down a Gig". That was after our "Forum Coffeehouse" closed in '69 or thereabouts. They were sounding pretty good. Coster wrote songs and played guitar and so it was guitar, fiddle, and mando with vocals.

Welling had a party, and I was there because Coster had left the band and Wallach, The "Mando Troll of Connecticut", had offered me a spot in the band solely so the band could be "Wishnevsky, Welling, and Wallach". But my wife wanted to move to Vermont and get back to nature, so we did that. Nature won. Kicked our asses.

I met the "Highwoods" right after Doug joined them. It was the night of the Watergate Saturday Night Massacre, which was October 20th, 1973. They had a party at Will Welling's house. Everybody was tripping their brains out. Some girl was having hysterics because the TV was blaring, "They just fired Archibald Cox, and it is a Constitutional Crisis." And this girl was convinced that we would all be locked up immediately for smoking pot and playing music.

But "Highwoods" were hot. Connecticut had but one fiddler; Will Welling, a mannered, Yankee-style guy. And here were these two mad men, Walt and Bob, who would face off, hovering over each other, and it was a wonder that they never poked anybody's eyes out with their flying bows.

Their big break had come when they appeared at the Smithsonian Folk Life Festival in Washington, DC in 1971. The metamorphosis from "Fat City" to "Highwoods String Band" took place when a friend of mine, Marianne Mylet, pointed out that John Denver's Band was called "Fat City" too. They added a rhythm section consisting of guitarist Doug Dorschug and bassist Jenny Cleland. Dorschug's playing contained an element of ragtime and blues that added even more punch to their hot sound. Cleland's upright bass was perhaps a first in Old Time Hippie circles, as most bands had only a washtub, if that. And as most bands were made of five guitar players, nobody wanted to lug around the "Doghouse". It really wasn't fair. But it sounded great.

Jim Stanko Letter

One of my most memorable events came in 1980 when Steve Uhrik asked if I'd be interested in traveling to go to Tommy Jarrell's 80th birthday party. Well, for a working stiff, that seemed like a pretty fun idea, so we packed up on a Friday afternoon and hit the road. We arrived in Meat Camp, NC, at the home of host Andy Cahan, about mid-morning after driving through the night. With a few other early arrivers, we helped Andy prepare and by afternoon we sat down to play some tunes. I was thrilled because one of my favorite younger fiddlers, Pete Sutherland, had arrived and I had a chance to jam with him for several hours. As dinnertime arrived so did a whole ton of people, and we milled about eating and socializing with the steady stream of people arriving from all parts of the country.

But at the time, the excitement of seeing Tommy close up and personal for the first time was starting to reach a peak. And, what a wonderful person—the reality was more than I had imagined! I was fortunate enough to be sitting on the floor at his side for the rest of the evening while he played for the assembled crowd, and was that house packed! Hardly room for a fly to squeeze in! Tommy kept inviting his friends to come join him and play, but many of them demurred, as they didn't want to interfere with people's enjoyment of Tommy's playing on this special occasion. Of course, the fiddle cries out for a banjo and a guitar for backup so Andy and a couple of others gracefully took turns providing the setting for Tommy. Tommy was in fine voice and spirits as he, Andy and others interspersed bantering jokes with a wide range of tunes and songs. From the very first tune Tommy started out—"Why don't we whup a little Piney Woods Gal?"—to the last song of the evening—"Stay All Night", after which Tommy said "I cain't sing no more"—Tommy entertained his disciples, friends, and admirers with the unique fiddling style and singing that have made him a legend.

Tommy was so gracious to those who wanted to learn his playing style. If you brought a ham and a bottle of I. W. Harper, you were welcome to hang out with Tommy for days on end. As Tommy's energy and health waned, some of his close friends needed to protect Tommy from the affects of his own generosity to prolong his ability to play and enjoy life. And indeed, a sad day came just a few short years later, when I heard Tommy had passed away to join so many others before him. What a privilege to have gotten to hear him that night!

The music industry may well have deemed his music not to have commercial value. But to me, one of the most noteworthy characteristics of the old-time Appalachian music experience has always been the infectious graciousness of the old timers to share the heritage they cherish so intensely with anyone who demonstrated an interest. I believe that this attitude of sharing is almost inseparable from the music, and is the main reason why this music, more than commercial music, will be preserved far beyond the time when the last living link has departed.

Henry the Fiddler

Henry started life as Henry Tarrson in Evanston, Illinois. He took up the violin at age 9. In 1971, after serving in the United States Army during the Vietnam era, Henry took on the stage name Henry the Fiddler. He began an odyssey of traveling and fiddling across the United States and Canada. In the past two decades Henry has earned a reputation as A Minstrel in Our Time. In his travels Henry has learned 30 styles of music from around the world.

In 1976, Henry was honored as one of the United States' top 20 fiddle players at the National Oldtime Fiddlers' Contest held in Weiser, Idaho. He has also won awards at the Union Grove Fiddlers' Convention and the Jazz and Heritage Festival, New Orleans, Louisiana.

In 1980, Henry changed his name legally to Henry the Fiddler to avoid "the endless hassles of having two names—nobody knew the old one anymore anyway," he says

In 1992 Henry's love of the minstrel traveling life overtook him and he once again hit the open road. During 1994 and 1995 Henry traveled extensively abroad. The Holland America Line hired him to entertain in the theaters aboard four of its luxury cruise ships. So, in 1995 he booked a round-the-world airline ticket and spent over 5 months minstreling while circumnavigating the globe. This once-in-a-lifetime adventure took Henry to 8 countries: the Czech Republic, Germany, England, Spain, Italy, Thailand, Australia and New Zealand.[37]

One of the standards of Union Grove in the Hippie days was Henry the Fiddler. No lie, he fiddles a lot. If you get his first cassette, you can hear typical hippie Old Time music, including Larry Poole and Claudine Langille, friends of mine, who traveled the country selling limberjack dancing dolls and playing music.

A limberjack is a loosely jointed wooden doll that dances on a springy plank as you tap out a rhythm on the plank. It is somewhere between a Folk Art toy and a percussion instrument.

Larry was some kin to Charlie Poole, and Claudine later became a member of "Touchstone", one of the first successful Celtic bands in America. She had to go to Europe for people in America recognize her large talent. She and Larry would come by Dave Sturgill's shop and run off a few dozen limberjacks and throw them in a backpack and hit the road again. There are lots of Claudine stories, all outrageous and all true. She was from Connecticut too.

She and Larry rented, for a lick and a promise, a house high on Briarpatch Mountain, which led to their band name, "The Briarpatch Mountain Backscratchers". They were too sorry to dig an outhouse, probably didn't own a shovel, and one day Larry found a ground hog hole and decided to use that for a latrine.

Then a day later, they returned home to find a neat pile of ground hog crap on their doorstep.

Henry "Hank" Sapoznik Interview Excerpt by Mark Rubin

Being with Tommy was great. We were equally exotic to one another. Tommy couldn't understand how these northern city boys would want to play their music. He was actually pretty sophisticated for a guy from around there; he was no Aborigine, and he knew that we were Jews and all. We had this long relationship of trying to puzzle each other out. At one point he had been making breakfast, and I was a vegetarian at the time and he was making, bacon, eggs fried in bacon fat and probably the coffee had a bacon base. I wasn't eating any of this stuff and Tommy is pushing it on me, "Come on Hank! Eat up", more like a Jewish mother than a southern fiddler.

And I wasn't eating this stuff and at one point he goes "Come on Hank, what are you? A damn Jew?!!" I was so totally taken aback, I couldn't tell if I was more taken aback at the statement or the fact that he understood enough to know what Jews eat. Well, that got us started. "Well yes, Tommy I AM a damn Jew."

And he asked me "Don't your people got none of your own music?" But once we were talking about it, I tucked it away in the back of my head, but at that point all I wanted to do was play old time music and banjo specifically.[38]

Jacki Spector Interview

Jacki is the banjo player for Nancy Sluys' "Pilot Mt. Bobcats". She makes her living in Primary Music Education.

My sister and brother in law in Middletown, New Jersey, in the early Seventies—for seventeen years they ran a little Folk Festival for their town recreation department—Marlene and Dick Levine. Dick had been on the board of "Sing Out!" for a number of years.

Were your parents musicians?

My parents had a record player. And about four records. They had recordings from Musical Shows they'd gone to see. They had one recording of Jewish music and one or two children's records for me. That was the extent of my musical background from my family. However, my sister is fourteen years older than me; they had bought a piano when she was young, so I grew up with a piano in the house. I was musical. Nobody else really was. My sister's interest in music was from a Folklore perspective. She basically studied English Literature and is into the literature of folklore and songs. Mostly songs.

Her husband grew up in New York, and his mother was a concert pianist. So he grew up playing piano. He went to Music and Art High School, played trombone or something silly like that. So when they got together, she was a student at Penn and she had gotten involved with the folklorist there, perhaps Charles Wolfe.

Whoever it was, she took lessons and got interested, and because her husband was a musician he said, "OK, that sounds good to me." And he started playing guitar, and over the years it evolved—he being an instrumentalist, he plays concertina really, really well. He's a dentist and he set up a practice and they met a few people through his practice that had a similar interest in Folk Music. They started with two other couples, and so they started having monthly hootenannies.

Musically they are very influenced by Pete Seeger and Woody and the Weavers and all that stuff. They had these monthly singing sessions where they would sit around in a circle and everybody would sing something for each other. They would do that for a couple of hours and then they would have refreshments, and then a few people would sort of jam at the end.

I started going to that when I was fourteen. My mother had just died that spring before, so we started going to my sister's house a lot ... my dad and me. They got me a guitar for my fourteenth birthday. I started learning to play the guitar, and got a little book and started going to the sings ... And the thing about the sings is that you had a forum; once a month you knew you were going to sing for people. So all month long you would practice a new song. It would encourage you to learn a new song, to learn something new on the guitar, and I used to do that. I used to go throughout high school. Then I went away to college in Boston—1964 to 1968—where I used to go to all the folk clubs, where I used to see people like Mississippi John Hurt, and the Kweskin Jug Band, and Muddy Waters and you name it. Bob Dylan, Joan Baez, I saw them up close and personal, at Club 47 in Cambridge, and

The Unicorn down in Boston. My sister and brother-in-law would take me to the Newport Folk Festival and Philadelphia Folk Festival. Because they were actively involved in Folk music, they dragged me along.

"The All-nighters" Galax 1991 Jacki Spector is center with ribbon on banjo. (Sluys)

The thing that shifted me from folkie to traditional music: in the Boston area, there was a lot of British Isles influence, a lot of singer-songwriter and some blues ... I was always intrigued with the banjo ... and by the mountain music stuff that I saw at the festivals.

I went to Pinewoods Camp, which is run by the County Dance and Song Society, out on Cape Cod. They had a Folk Music Week where I would spend the week singing and working with people like Bessie Jones and Jean Ritchie. And I got involved with dance. I learned about Country Dancing there. It started off with English Country Dancing and then brought in all kinds of American dancing.

The early years of Folk Music Week: it was the English people who were running the dances at night, and they were kind of boring. But then they started bringing in some local New England callers, who brought in a little of the Square Dancing, a little bit of Contra Dancing—all of it derived from English Country, but a little bit looser and a little bit more fun.

I, also, at Pinewoods Camp met Paul Brown.[39] *He grew up in Westchester County, but his mother was from Virginia. They traveled down to Virginia a lot. His mother had musical connections, and so Paul, although he lived in New York State, he really absorbed a lot of the traditional stuff through his mother's contacts in Virginia. I was already playing the banjo. I started about '72.*

I can remember I really wanted to play the banjo. I used to go to Fox Hollow Folk Festivals, and I was really scared that I wouldn't be able to [play], because I hadn't been much of an instrumental musician; I had been involved in singing. I had met a woman through the Folk Song Society in Boston who became my roommate. She is a wonderful musician. Her name is Sharia Jimeon. She got a fiddle and a banjo; she had signed up for these Adult Education courses. And all of a sudden one day, she came up and she goes, "I can't start two instruments at the same time!" She was a great guitar player. I said, "Well, I'll take your banjo and go to banjo class." So I went to this banjo class that was taught by this Bluegrass musician named Rich Hand. He was somebody that I knew from a co-operative house in Cambridge called "Old Joe Clark House". It had been started by a bunch of single men who were involved with the dance organization and some Old Time music stuff. They had this big house. This guy Sandy Sheehan lived there, and still has a music store, "Sandy's Music".

What was happening to me was, through my Folk Music in Boston connections, I was meeting the people in the community who were into Old Timey. And through going to Pinewoods, I was getting involved with the Dance aspects of it. Then I met Paul Brown, and all of these things started pulling themselves together. The dance music and the Old Time are very connected. I started hanging out with all these different people.

What was your first festival down here?

I went to Union Grove in 1965. It was pretty crazy. I came down with some friends from the singing group my sister was involved with ... a couple who lived in Brooklyn, who wanted to come down to Union Grove and convinced me to come down with them. I was a sophomore in college and I drove down with them to Union Grove. To me it was just a complete ... I had no idea what was going on, no idea what to expect. I was a complete observer; I didn't play anything at that time. A little guitar. I was there to see what it was like.

It was just like opening the door on a whole other world. And then, in '83, I came down to Galax. Paul Brown was living in Galax at the time, Cole Creek community, and I came down to go to the Galax Fiddler's Convention ... I played a Contra dance in Cambridge Thursday night, drove up to Mt. Vision, New York, to pick up my friend Kathy, drove all the way down to Galax, got here Friday night, was supposed to play in a band with Rena, and she thought I wasn't coming, and she arranged some other people to play in her band. So Kathy and I got hooked up with Debbie Gitlin, and we played one night. Debbie was very young and kinda wild, and we weren't and it didn't work at all. But that was 1983.

And we stayed at Paul's house. And Alice Gerrard took us over to Luther Davis', and we spent the day. Alice brought me down the mountain to Tommy Jarrell's house, and that summer was also when Rose Sinclair and Beverly Smith, and Maxine and Brenda all came from California. They were all staying at Paul's house. Beverly and Rose, they came to that Galax Festival and never went back to the West Coast. They moved to Philadelphia.

I met them a year later and they were part of Jamal's band, "OK Bayou String Band."

They were already hooked in. I wasn't very hooked in. And I come down, probably two years after that to Mt. Airy, when Paul was still living over here in White Plains. It might have been '85, and stayed down here the whole summer. And then two years later moved down here.

Nancy Banjo and I had met at Brandywine a couple of times. She was working horses in New York, and had come to the Middletown Folk Festival. She remembers meeting me at a party at my sister's house.

The summer that I stayed at Paul's—"85 or '86—that was the summer that Nancy and Bill had moved here from Greenville. But we didn't run in to each other until the weekend of Fries Fiddler Festival. We had driven up to Fries on Friday night. Paul had played with "The New River Ramblers" and we didn't get to go back up Saturday because it was rained out. And we ended up going to a party over at Nancy and Bill's house. And that's where I met Joe Thrift and Tory Casey.

The first time I met you was at one of those New Year's Eve Bobville parties.

I started coming down to those New Year's Eve parties right about then. The first time, I came down to see Paul and we went to the Earnest East party, it was so late by the time we got back, Paul didn't want to go anywhere and I drove down to the Rock House, Steve and Charlie Mason's.

Did you have to change your banjo style when you moved down south? People down here think Yankees play too pretty.

I didn't do any conscious changing of my banjo style. And in fact, the summer that I was here at Paul's—the summer before Tommy Jarrell died, and towards the end of the summer—I went over to Tommy's with my banjo and just visited him. We played for a long time, and his daughter had come around, and after a little while, he turned around and put his fiddle down, and leaned on one elbow and said to me, "Are you sure you learned to play the banjo in Boston?"

And Deanie goes, "He meant that honey; he wouldn't say that if he didn't mean it!" To me that is the highest compliment I have ever been paid, musically. And I don't recall ever trying to play any particular way. I just listen and what ever comes out is how I play.

Where did you get the Kyle Creed banjo?

I bought the Kyle Creed banjo in 1980. I had wanted a fretless for a while, and this one was owned by a guy who was taking lessons from Paul Brown. The story I was told was that these two guys, Dave and Ray, had gone down and contracted with Kyle to build them identical banjoes. And at any rate, they brought them home and decided that it wasn't what they wanted. Dave built a new neck for his. Ray sent his back to Kyle and Kyle put this neck on the old pot. Ray sold it to Howie Somebody and Howie sold it to me. This guy from the "Delaware Water Gap Band" wanted it, but he eventually forgave me. Hank Sopoznik was in that band.

Do you know if that's true that Tommy Jarrell asked Hank, "If you're a Jew, why don't you play your own music? Don't Jews have their own music?" And that led to the Klezmer Revival.

Yes, that's the story that I heard. He did say, "Well actually, we do have our own music." But from what I understand, Tommy did say that to Hank. For me, all these different streams converged, and filtered me through … American Folk, Mountain, Dance Music, North Carolina Mountains.

I don't know how you are about intuitive things, but I have a very strong psychic component to my life, and I … I mean I love this area. Interestingly enough, I was born and brought up in Bethlehem, Pennsylvania. Which is a Moravian community. And the Moravians moved from Bethlehem to Salem and started Winston Salem, North Carolina. I had no idea. The first time I was down here visiting Paul at Christmas, we drove down into Winston, and I see all of these Moravian stars hanging everywhere. I hadn't seen them since my childhood. And then I found out the Moravian connection.

I understand why people from that part of Pennsylvania felt comfortable in this part of North Carolina. A similarity in the feel of the land. So there is that connection.

And also, I bought this house; came down to Mt. Airy Fiddlers Convention, stayed for a week, found this house, put a down payment on it, came back in July, closed the deal. But I couldn't move in until August. Came back, pulled up, the keys were left for me, here I am. I open the door to this empty house, brutally hot and stuffy, no air, windows all closed up. I opened all the windows, brought what I had in the car down to the house … "What have I done?" "I've just moved to North Carolina!"

I went and was sitting on the front porch, and I was half dozing and meditating or something, and I got this overwhelming sense, sort of déjà vu, but not really, that I had been here before. This sense of coming home. It was very strong.

And here I are. Still here. That's my story. I know that the thing that has drawn me in and attracted me to it so strongly, is that basically they are just real people. They are not "musicians" in the sense of professional musicians, on the circuit, who make a living and see music as a career. They were just plain old people. Who were very musical, had a musical voice to them, and somebody had the good sense to find them and bring it out. And to allow other people to participate in it and share in it. But still, at the base, they are just plain folk.

Johnny Sturgill Interview

John Sturgill is David Sturgill's middle son. He is the artist of the family, paints, does fine inlay and makes superior instruments. He won the "World's Championship Bass Player" trophy one year at Union Grove—on a gutbucket.

When did you get involved in making musical instruments?

In 1967, I worked for Grammer Guitar Company, in Nashville Tennessee. That's where I started making musical instruments. Guitars. I was finishing foreman. I did all the finishing work, I did a lot of the assembly work, eventually learned every step of it.

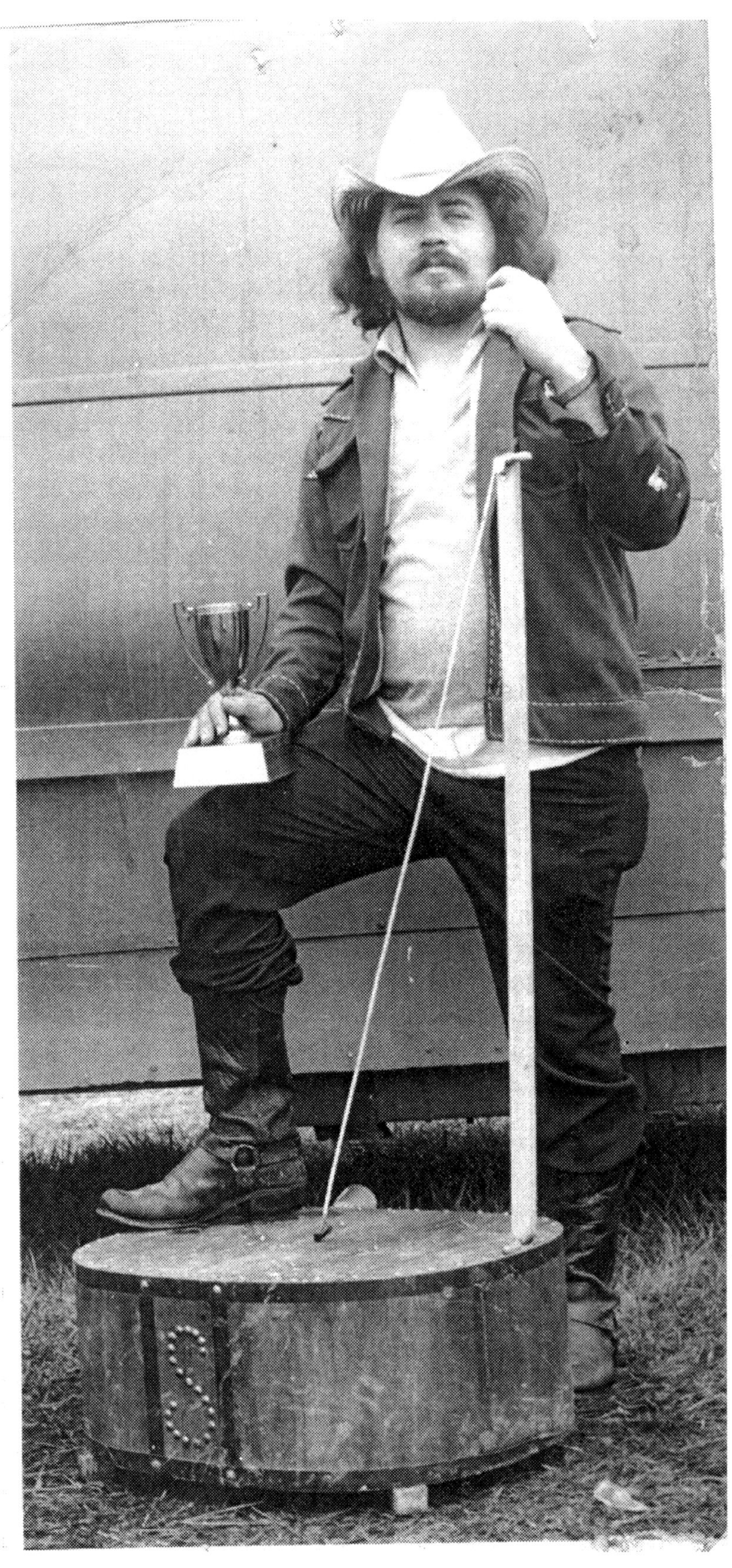

I had worked making computer trainers for the Navy, electronics plant in Maryland. I just needed a change. Dad was already associated with the company, I went down there and about a month later, he came down as president. Billy Grammer had known him for years. He had made some custom instruments for Billy before he ever started the guitar factory. He had been operating in the capacity of a company engineer ... He helped design the original instruments and everything for Grammer. So he was going back and forth. Then he went down full time.

Grammer Guitars, due to various uglinesses, closed down ...

It changed hands, it was bought out, and I left and it was bought out again after I left. I had a couple of different job offers ... Baldwin was wanting to open a guitar factory, and I had an offer for a job there as plant manager. And I had another offer for Emmons guitar to design an electric bass, and put it into production. So I took that job because it was closer to here, and this was where I wanted to end up. That was in Burlington, NC.

So I was there for a couple of years, and then the wife and I split up and I moved to Piney Creek with my (four) kids. My dad was back there by then and had the shop built, and I came to work in his shop making musical instruments.

And your brother Danny had been here all that time?

He was actually the first one in the family to come back to Piney Creek. He came several years before us. It was 1970 when I moved back. We made just about anything that had strings on it—dulcimers, hammered dulcimers—the main thing was the guitars and banjoes. We also made violins, mandolins ... I've built just about everything but a harp. I did rebuild a grand piano one time.

How did the apprentice program get started?

It just kind of happened. People approaching us. But at first it was me and Dad, and Danny and Smith Greer. I think the first couple were correspondents with Dad, and then we met several folks at Union Grove, and it just king of grew. It wasn't anything that was planned. I think we ended up with at least fifteen apprentices over the years. Some guy named Steve Wishnevsky, Steve Gendron, Sue Cahill ... Wayne Henderson[40] *used to come over to the shop quite a bit, that was when he first starting to make instruments and he would come over and get wood.*

His first wife was one of the apprentices.

Carol Seace. She played in our band for a while.

What was that story about your dad becoming "Uncle Dave"?

Well, we were coming back from a fiddler's convention one day, and he told me that he was going to grow a beard and become a character. I just looked at him and said, "What do you mean, 'become'?" But that kind of got to become his trademark. Which was funny, because up to that point, he used to make fun of my beard. Of course, mine is as white now as his was then.

He grew his beard and carried his banjo, and was probably one of the most photographed people 'ever been to fiddler's conventions. They couldn't do a write up in the paper that didn't have a picture of him sitting there with his beard and his banjo.

Your dad and George Pegam were a vanishing breed, "Banjo Wildmen"—more entertainers than say, Kyle Creed, who was so quiet.

As opposed, they were stage presences more than just musicians. Very much so, I think. I think Dad kind of cast himself in that vein, or tried to. I miss old George. I was just thinking about him just the other day.

You think Dave wanted to be a musician more than an instrument maker? He was such a complex person.

I think being a musician filled a need that he had. Instrument making did the same thing, but the gratification was more immediate with the applause than it is over a period of time; the recognition is more immediate and that was the thing with him and a lot of entertainers. They were equal, but ... unequal.

He was into so many things.

He was like that when we were growing up. I never knew what his next project would be. He did everything from building TV sets to telescopes in the basement. I think he would have built a nuclear reactor if he could have.

Sue Cahill with Sturgill mandolin. L-R Carol Seace, Sue, Ken Powers, Dave Sturgill. Circa 1975 (Sekerak)

I was always amazed that he would put up with hippies.

He enjoyed being a guru. And hippies were the people who were willing to listen to him. To sit at the Master's feet, more or less. That's the validation he was looking for. I remember he was talking to a biker, and the biker said, "You ought to get you a Harley". And Dave said, "I put a million miles on one of those before you were born. I've ridden across these United States twice." He had the scars to show for it.

Somebody told me he could do all those tricks, standing on the saddle and all that.

He did them all. He always told me, "That's when you get hurt, when you thought you knew it all." When you were first learning, and when you thought you knew it all—that's when motorcycles are dangerous

So what's the Johnny Sturgill story?

Well, I always wanted to play, I loved the music, I loved listening to it, and there would always be a jam session around, as a child I wanted to get into it so bad I couldn't stand it, and at a fiddlers convention in Independence, a jam session was going on, and I was literally playing the tent rope, like it was a bass. And a fellow name of Mike Crouse came up and set up a tub bass and started playing. I said, "Mind if I try it?" And he said no, and by golly I got a tune out of it. So I went home and built me one.

And then, they had some tapes there at the shop of the band, and I learned all the tunes that they played, and so then I started playing with the band. The first one I made was out of metal, and that didn't suit me. I had it a couple of weeks, never was happy with it and I thought I would try one out of wood. We had some curved plywood, chair backs and I used that to make the rim, and made a wooden tub bass that sounded more like a real upright bass. I played it with the band for about eight years.

Your dad wasn't afraid to use modern technology, furniture parts, whatever.

No, he always made a point of, and I always agreed, that as far as so-called tradition, I don't care who the instrument maker was. Stradivarius used the best technology in his time. So we basically did the same thing; if that meant using an electronic carver to pre-carve a top, and then finish it by hand, it was still a hand-made instrument. But we did use modern technologies, like using laminated woods, which even Martin is using now. When we first started, it wasn't common in an expensive instrument, but it is now. All of his designs were based on his research. We didn't build copies. Everything we did was an original design.

He was an engineer. He went to Bliss Electrical School. He was an electrical engineer, but his mind was an engineer's mind. No matter what the field was, he was constantly ... He designed so many things over the years. He designed a color TV tube, and never did do anything with the patent. Later an almost identical one came out, the Trinitron. He was always designing something. To a large degree I'm kind of the same way, so far as designing tools. That's what I've been doing for the last twenty-five years at the rug factory. Half the tools in there I designed.

I'm doing everything. I'm production manager, chief mechanic and bottle washer. We make high-end designer carpets and rugs. "New River Artisans"—n the old school building in Piney Creek. Right next door to Dad's house.

Did you feel any hostility between the people who stayed there, and you for moving back? Not to mention all the hippies.

I never did, personally. There was some resentment among people. I've been there for thirty years, and there are some people who are just now beginning to consider me a native again. I always did consider this area home. I tell people that being born in Maryland was an accident I couldn't help.

Led astray by evil companions at an early age.

That's just where my parents were when I was born. But when we came down here, which was several times a year, it wasn't a matter of, "let's go to the mountains", It was, "Let's go home." So I always grew up with this more my home than Maryland was.

Your Uncle Sidney stayed, except to go to Europe in W.W.II.

But most of the rest of that generation went to Maryland. And I think the hippies, to some degree, did fill those labor slots, particularly for farm labor; they could pick up work here and there for various farmers, and there wasn't that much of a local labor force. That niche now has been pretty much filled with migrant workers, but it wasn't in 1970.

Nancy Banjo said that the hippies, just by being here and being neutral, actually helped resolve some of the long-standing feuds among musicians. And because the hippies didn't know any better …

They would try to make friends with everybody. I think to some degree, they did. Just having outsiders who came in and showed a genuine interest in our music made a difference. Most of the people—your hard core natives, not the people who moved here since—have always felt a little xenophobic because a lot of their associations out of these mountains were not necessarily good. The exploitation was very real. And most people who came to this area, came to exploit, like the movie "Songcatcher". But the hippie wave musicians came for the music, came to join it, and there is a big difference.

They did get an acceptance that way. And a good musician, his accent makes no difference. It's how you play.

I see different waves … The very first wave was 78 collectors, that were trying to find Clarence Ashley, for example. And the next batch were more interested in learning from the people—the "Back to the Landers".

The first ones, before my time, were even before the 78's. Some of the stuff was recorded on cylinders. Old wire recorders. After the discovery, the Bristol Sessions, the whole world got to hear this music: Jimmie Rodgers and The Carter Family. Then there was a new wave of people coming and looking. And that's never really stopped.

And again in the Sixties, the Great Folk Scare—there were a lot of people scouring the country looking for songs. And a lot of them do go directly to the source. Did a lot of field recording and thank goodness they did, a lot of it is available now on CD. I've got t a lot of it myself.

When I first heard Old Time, when I came down here as a kid, a group of aunts and uncles—Charlie Cox, several people like that, Dick Finney sometimes, and they would get together and make music, and that's what it was: "music". Not Old Time or Mountain music, it was just music. And they might have done everything from "The Ballad of Jesse James" to "The Wreck of the Old 97", and might turn around and do "Barbry Allen". "Thunder Road" or something. They were just making music. And it was acoustic music.

I was thinking about "The Death of Fireball Roberts", probably the last pop song to have clawhammer banjo.

Middle sixties … Let's see. Outside of String Bean and Grandpa Jones, probably the last … Outside of Ronnie Stoneman, everybody in Nashville was doing Scruggs three finger roll. When I was a kid, I tried and tried to get Dad to teach me clawhammer, but he would never do it. "No, you have to learn Bluegrass, and I can't teach you that." So I never did learn to play the banjo. Dad did play drop thumb at a time when most people played the older two finger Charlie Poole style.

The modern revivalist Old Timey, they don't play two finger. There is a pretty limited repertoire, no singing …

There is a lot of things that are different in the revival music. It's like a lot of things: get back to the purist … a different speed, a different tempo. You can go to Texas, and you can hear the same song that is played at half the speed it is normally played here. Right through this area, the Old Time music, as well as Bluegrass, has a much more driving beat than it does in a lot of areas.

Most people down here can't stand Yankee Contra Dance music; it's too pretty. But I remember, Ken Powers, your dad's fiddler, was getting some flack, but also winning some contests, playing "Carroll County Blues".

"Lee Highway Blues".

And you and me were the only people who could back him up because we could play on 2 and 4, and everybody else was playing 1 and 3. Those were wild times, doing sometimes two and three fiddle fests a weekend.

I got out of it for so long, when I did quit, I just quit cold. Seemed like part of that was family and part of it was other things. It's just been the last two or three years I've been going back to festivals. After the Independence shop closed, and I got burned fire fighting,[41] I had to get a full time job, and that just about closed down both shops, the one in Piney Creek too. It was too hard working a full time job and making instruments too. And I was getting pressure from home about being away from home so many hours. And about then I got into painting pictures, and I just got into that. Lots of kids and lots of worrying about making it. My family had suffered for eight or nine years when I was trying to do my thing, and so I felt I owed it to them to try and make a steady income for a while. And Dave was slowing down too. Age catches up with everybody.

He went into to doing the judging thing at festivals, which he did up until a year before he died.

Do you think that if he played "Ye Olde Craftsman" more, he would have done better, or was it just his personality?

His personality was such that he needed what he got from being an entertainer. And as good an engineer, and good at designing, as good a craftsman he was, he wasn't that good a businessman. His needs weren't as monetary as they were emotional and the recognition that he needed. Which is true for all of us to some degree or another. There was a need for validation … that making music and being recognized as "Uncle Dave" gave him. It's kind of funny: Chris Sekerak, the day after Dad died, he came up and spent the night with us, and we had a long talk. Half the night. One of the things we talked about … we got a lot of things hashed out. Looking back in those days in the shop, Dad undoubtedly was the brains of the outfit, but in many ways, and this is going to sound egotistical, I was the heart.

Nobody makes an issue of it, but Old Time is the most sexually integrated genre in all of music. Perhaps only Classical Music has as many female practitioners as Old Time. This is, of course, mostly a modern phenomenon. Nancy Sluys is as well respected as any one in the field, and came up the hard way.

Fiddling Nancy Banjo Interview

Nancy Maurer Sluys has been a fixture in Old Time Music since the Seventies, and for years she supported herself making and selling "Spectrum Batiks" tee shirts at festivals and Dead shows. Her white Ford van was recognized as a center for music and information and the occasional cup of excellent coffee all over the Eastern United States. She and her bass-playing husband Bill live on a medium-sized farm near Mt. Airy, NC with horses and motorcycles. She is short, and he is tall.

Why don't you tell us your background?

Raised in Glastonbury Connecticut, that is where I started playing music when I was in Junior High School, and started playing the guitar in that era when everybody was sitting around on the school field singing folk songs and whatnot. I was quite the rebellious teen. Did a lot of school skipping and such. That's how I wound up being a guitar player, because that is what one did when skipping school.

In Glastonbury, the Youth Services Bureau started a coffeehouse. It was in the old post office. It was called "The Post", and we had this coffeehouse there and "Coster, Welling and Wallach" used to come and play there all the time and other acoustic acts. I started latching on to Old Time back then ... '72-'73.

I ran away from home when I was sixteen. I just wasn't understood. Actually my parents didn't pay a whole lot of attention to me; they were doing their own thing and I had had just enough. I set out on the road and hitchhiked to Washington State with some guy and I was gone for six months and then they traced me down and I got sent back home.

It was the summer I got back that I started going to Bluegrass festivals. In '73, I guess. The first one was in Escoheag, Rhode Island. I suppose I should talk a little about how I ended up at Bluegrass festivals. In high school, when everybody was into the Rolling Stones and Led Zeppelin I was more attracted to acoustic Grateful Dead and New Riders of the Purple Sage and other acoustic-oriented bands. And so that got my mind to hearing banjos and fiddles and stuff. I remember "Red Hot Burritos" that had Byron Berline fiddling on it.

Anyway, the other thing that turned me on to acoustic music, I had a little transistor radio and I used to be fascinated with getting in stations from distant places in the middle of the night. I could lie in my bed, I could tune it in, and I could get WSM in Nashville, and I could pick up the Grand Old Opry. That was more like when I was ten. That was my first magnetism towards that sort of music.

Fast forward to Bluegrass festivals ... I met a couple of people, Dave Steeg and Bob Dispenette—we used to call him "Cowboy Bob". And at the same time I met these two girls, Shelly and Val. And we all just got really tight. We started meeting at festivals that summer, around New England, then Shelly and I went down to Galax, I am unclear if it was '73 or '74, she had an old blue van, and we drove it down there and about ten miles away from Galax, the van burned up, the radiator blew and all this smoke went up and we ended up calling a tow truck and having it towed to the Galax Fiddlers' Convention, where we parked it, and that was my introduction to Galax.

That was right around when "Highwoods" and "Plank Road" were starting to go there. In fact, I remember you there. I didn't even play the banjo yet; I was playing the mandolin. Through all this, Shelly met this guy, Gary Joyner, who was a Green Grass Clogger. And she ended up marrying him the following year. And that's how I ended up in Greenville. I went to her wedding and I was like, "Oh, wow, this is such a cool party town!" I never left.

So anyway, after I got back from running away from home, the following year, after my summer of bluegrass, my parents sent me to an alternative school in Upstate New York, on a dairy farm. There were only half a dozen students, but one of the instructors built a Stewart MacDonald banjo from a kit. So the whole time he's building it, I'm watching him build it. I'm really intrigued, that was really cool. That was right when "May The Circle Be Unbroken" album came out. [42] *And so I'm starting to dial into all that stuff.*

Ok, so the guy makes the banjo, and he's got all the different books back then. And he tried this and tried that, and he latched on to Clawhammer. And right about then when I was hearing that tune on "Circle Be Unbroken", "Soldier's Joy", played with a Bluegrass and a Clawhammer banjo together, that was the coolest thing.

And so, one day I took his banjo and locked myself in a room and didn't come out until I learned it. And that summer I went back to Galax as a banjo player. That's when I really started connecting. The first year I went to Galax, I was just sort of viewing it all, taking it in, drinking a lot, partying, staying up all night … In fact, I remember it was a time when there was a difference between Old Time and Bluegrass, but nobody cared. In fact, that very first year, I was hanging around with these guys that I met and they invited me to play in their Bluegrass band. I had the mandolin. I don't remember even what we played or anything. It was really terrible. It was a money-back band, obviously.

Then I started playing the banjo, I came back to Galax as a banjo player, and that was when I really dialed into Old Time music. It just seemed like they were having a lot more fun. And it was also it was right in that era when "Highwoods" and "Plank Road" and "Swamproot" … That was Bob Naess, and Sandy Stark and some people from up North that had this kickass Old Time band. They used to come down to Greenville sometimes, and do gigs with the Green Grass Cloggers. That was '74.

Bill: Back in '74, I was graduating high school, my dad played trumpet in the NYC Police Band, I took up trumpet when I was probably about twelve years old, at the local grammar school. It was a way to have something to do during the summer, besides just ride my bicycle around. This was Long Island, where I was born and raised. And then I discovered, when I was about thirteen or fourteen, Rock and Roll, and got into listening to Hendrix and everything else. I decided I wanted to play guitar and my mother had an old Folk guitar where she had learned to play "Bill Bailey" on, it's still upstairs, that old beater, and I started learning to play that and took some lessons one summer and got into Rock and Roll and acoustic music and playing Folk music. I started hanging out with a bunch of people known as "The Jones Beach Bums".

Nancy: Hanging out and playing guitar was really big back then.

Bill: Just hanging out at the beach with a bunch of other ne'er-do-wells. Disaffected youth. Most of us just banged on guitars and played Crosby Stills and Nash tunes and that sort of … not gigging at all. Just learn how to play the basic chords. I was still banging on guitar when I moved to Florida in the late Seventies and was banging on a guitar when I met Nancy. We ended up going to a Bluegrass Festival the first day that I met her.

It was a mutual friend that worked with her at the harness track, said, "Oh there's this girl that plays banjo. She wants to go to the Bluegrass Festival." "Oh, cool, bring her along." So we went down there and that's when Nancy pulled out her Clawhammer banjo and everybody else was playing Bluegrass.

Nancy: What happened was, I had my banjo under a blanket, because I didn't want anybody to see it. It was like, "If I get this banjo out, they're going to ask me to play Foggy Mountain Breakdown!" This particular Bluegrass festival was a monthly thing and you just kind of went up and got in line. Whoever showed up got up on stage to play. And we were sitting there watching the show and all of a sudden, just in the back of my hearing, I hear Old Time fiddle coming out of the woods.

So I went over to check it out, and there were these guys, three fiddlers and a guitar player sitting in the woods. And they were all just playing their asses off. So I got my banjo and I started hammering on it. And they were like, "Oh, my god! We haven't seen a Clawhammer banjo player in Florida in forever!" The fiddlers were L.J. Slavin, Chuck Anton and some guy named Mike. And Chuck and L.J. ended up being in our band, which we started that very day.

Why were you in Florida?

Bill: I had gone to school in Upstate New York, and lived in Saratoga for a while. And winter was coming on, I lost my job and my sister lived in Ft. Lauderdale. And she said, "Well, you can't go back home and move back into mom and dad's house." I agreed with that, and she said, "Come on down to Ft. Lauderdale. There is plenty of work, my boyfriend's construction labor, he can get you work." So that's how I ended up down there.

Nancy: I was in Greenville, NC in '74. Really, I moved there in '75. In between the Upstate New York school, where I learned the banjo, and when I actually moved to Greenville, there was a year in between there where I was in this school in Vermont. It was called Sterling, all practical skills, almost like Outward Bound. And anyway, once again, I was part of the inaugural body of students. So, the other cool thing about that was in Craftsbury, Vermont, they had a big banjo contest. Right after I left there I wound up moving to Greenville. It was in Greenville where I started working with racehorses. That's how I ended up in Florida because that is one of the places where you can go work in the wintertime. .

When I was in Greenville, I was hanging with the Cloggers; in fact I was going to their practices every Wednesday and I would play the banjo. I would be the music. Believe it or not, I was kind of shy back then. But due to my kind of shyness, whenever I went to party or anything, I would just sit around and play the banjo, instead of socializing.

That's how I ended up getting the name "Nancy Banjo." And then I went to Florida, where I met Mr. Bill. It was that very day when we were jamming in the woods. And while we were jamming, the MC of the show came up and said, "You guys sound great! Want to get up on stage, and play a few?" So we did. And he asked, "What's the name of your band?" And we said, "Anything you want." And for that first gig, we were "Anything You Want."

It was so cool that we just decided to be a band. And the one guitar player, who was the legendary Scott Wise, was a kickass guitar player, and Bill was just sort of beating around with it. And it just became obvious that we really didn't need two guitar players and we really needed a bass, so I had the bright idea to make Bill a washtub bass.

Bill: So I came home from work one day and there was a washtub bass sitting in the middle of the living room. And I looked at it and said, "What's that?" And Nancy just said, "It's a washtub bass." And the wheels finally clicked in my brain and I said, "Oh, I should probably learn to play this ..." So I became the bass player.

Nancy: Which became the "Horsehair and Catgut String Band" who played for about four years in South Florida. .

I heard a tale where you had left the house and Nancy came back ...

Nancy: That was actually a few years later. When Bill was living in Durham. 'Cause I was working with the harness race horses still. And what that entailed was working in the winter in Florida and then come springtime, I would go on the road with the horses from April to October.

Bill: And that one spring time, I'd already come up and been to this big party ... and we had come up for a fiddler's convention or two, and decided to leave Florida and move up to North Carolina. Nancy was on the road with the horses. Scott moved out to Asheville, I think. Nancy and Scott and I had been sharing a house at that point for a year or two. I moved up to Durham with Keith Guile and Tom Riccio, at first.

Keith had lined up a house, we started a band with Keith and Tom and another fiddle player named Phil MacDonald. "The Muddy Mountain String Band." And we played a couple of gigs that summer. I was living in Durham in this funky old farmhouse off in the middle of nowhere. It was decrepit, and I was fixing it up for rent. I came home from work one day and the front door was locked, but the curtain was blowing out of the window, like the window was open and I could hear a voice inside.

And I was like, "Hello?" And I went to grab a stick, and went up toward the house. There was no cars or anything. I didn't know what I was going to find and all of a sudden the curtain blew open a little bit and I could see Nancy in there talking to somebody on the phone.

I hadn't seen her in three or four months that summer so I was pretty surprised!

Nancy: More than that ...

Bill: I opened the front door, "Hey, what's going on?" And she said, "Oh, You know, my horse got sick and I'm done with horses for the summer and so here I am and ..." It was the week after Galax.

Nancy: The funny thing was, I was in Ohio at that point, when the horse that was under my care was injured in a race. So I was out for the year, and I was going to go back and find Bill so I left Ohio and I drove all night long. I was going to surprise the shit out of everybody at the Galax Fiddler's ... And I drove and drove all night and I got there, and I had miscalculated and missed the festival by a week!

I drove into Galax and drove into Felts Park, and all I saw was an empty field with all those yellow squares were all the people had their tents. And that's when I left there and drove to Durham. That was '80, and later that summer we went to Independence and Mountain City fiddler's conventions and Bill whipped all the basses with his washtub bass.

Bill: Yeah, I used to switch hands and do different rhythms, do slapping and stuff on it. Do a lot of different things ... expanded ... I figured out what I could do and then ... Nancy didn't like the house in Durham, Riccio was out in Marion, and he said, "Come on out here." And so Nancy and I went out there and tried to find work, but couldn't find anything in Black Mountain or Asheville or Marion or anything. We ended up moving back down to Florida ... Scott too. We were down to Scott pawning his guitar in Gainesville when we were most of the way down in Florida.

Nancy: I think we pawned all our instruments, then we had to go back to get them a week later.

Bill: We didn't have any money left, the three of us. And went back down to Fort Lauderdale and my sister was living in a trailer down there with her husband and two kids, at that point. I remember we got down there and I remember opening up the paper that night and there was like three or four columns of construction laborers. I would do anything at that point. And there wasn't any work to be had up around Asheville. And all of a sudden there was work to be had everywhere. Boom.

Asheville was non-hippie back then. They had had a poet once, but he died.

Bill: So Nancy and Scott and I rented a house together. Scott went back to aircraft maintenance, and I went back to sign work, and Nancy went back to the track. We stuck around there a few more years, the same thing, where she would go on the road in the summer. Then finally, in '83, I asked Nancy to marry me and we got married and decided to just get out of Florida and we moved up here. We had been coming up here for the fiddler's conventions for years.

Nancy: First we moved back to Greenville. We would come up to Galax every year from Florida so it seemed right.

Bill: After a while I took a job up here in Mt. Airy that was perfect. I was working for a sign company. I had had my own sign shop in Greenville for a year. At the end of that first year of having my own business, I figured I was working about sixty hours a week and I had a hundred dollars a week income. I said, "To hell with that". And that same day, I picked up the sign trade magazine, and they were looking for someone with experience in all phases of signage, fabrication, installation, and all. In Mt. Airy. And I called the guy up, he said, "If you can do everything you say, I'll hire you last week."

And so I came up here and took the job and as soon as I found a house, Nancy came up, and that's how we ended up here. I was living at Steve and Charlie Mason's house. Sleeping on their couch ... I would come home from work, and just go out driving around looking for old farmhouses. I couldn't find anything, and Steve finally said, "We know this old guy, Oscar Burge, and we might talk to him." And so, Steve set me up an appointment with Oscar and his wife, and I went over there and talked to Oscar for about four hours. We sat there for four hours taking about "kids today, and Old Time music, and tobacco" and all this stuff. They used to go to Galax, and he pulled out a Galax program, and Nancy said, "Oh, let me have it!" And she showed him her name and our band name and Oscar finally says, "So, want to take a look at that old farmhouse we got over across the street?" It's getting dark and we say, "Yeah." And we took a look at it and it was this cool old farmhouse down a quarter mile dirt driveway, in the middle of nowhere. It had never had plumbing or anything. It had electric, but it was in rough shape.

Nancy: At that time it had the front room was full to the ceiling with tobacco sticks.

Bill: He said, "If you want to move in and fix it up, I won't charge you any rent. I'll provide the materials". So we lived there for a couple of years and then bought this land.

That's where I met you. Somehow I got invited to the New Year's Eve Party, and drove from Tennessee. I think that was the time you yelled at me for flat-picking the ceiling fan, and that was the night that S—M—sat on Richie Hartness' $1,500.00 fiddle bow, and won the "Be-a-Bob Tee Shirt.

I had been living in re-e-e-e-dneck heaven. And then to come out and see people get drunk without shooting each other was cool.

Bill: We had a big time in that old house.

How did you meet Chuck and Steve Mason?

Nancy: We met them back in Greenville. They were both dancing in the Green Grass Cloggers. We were the house band for the Cloggers at the time. Then, the year before we moved up here, Steve and Charlie had moved up here. And Riccio also was living up here. Riccio and Sherri lived in Winston Salem, and we were coming up visiting them, Steve and Charlie were also visiting them, and when they decided to leave Greenville, they chose to move up here to be near Tom.

And Joe Thrift and Tory Casey lived up here anyway.

Nancy: Joe had property in Devotion. In fact I remember going to a party there in the Seventies, when Joe lived in a cabin. Where Cheri fell off the porch and broke her arm. Back when he was known as Red Joe

I was there. Rick Dolinger fell off that same porch and cursed all the way down. No railing on the porch and kerosene lanterns and drugs. I smoked up their roommate's lamp chimney and got thoroughly cursed out, as if that was the worst thing that happened that night. She sent me down that hill to another cabin, a half mile with a kerosene lamp, and I turned it up too high and got soot on the glass chimney. That was a hell of a party.

Bill: I think Joe and Tory got together about the time we got married in '83.

I visited Joe in Winston about '83, when he had a violin-making studio on Wachovia Street. He must have told me about the New Year's Eve Party.

Nancy: The New Years Eve party started the first year Steve and Charlie lived here and we all came up from Greenville. It wasn't even called Bobville yet. That happened when we were all starting to form a community in those stalls at the Galax Fiddler's Convention and it kind of gravitated towards that lower corner of the stalls and we all tried to get camping in there. It was kind of funny, because we showed up a day late that year, because our truck had broken down.

That was '84, the year before we actually moved to Mt. Airy. We were coming from Greenville. So, sometime that night it became Bobville. It started off with this lady from Boston and this guitar pick, and I don't really know the exact details of it, because we weren't actually there till the next day because of the broken truck, but it had something to do with joking about a pick that said "Pick Bob". And the next thing you knew, they were calling everybody "Joe Bob" and "This Bob" and "That Bob". And by the time we got there, everybody was Bob, and we were Bobs too.

My favorite was Riccio being "Plumb Bob" for being a surveyor.

Nancy: When I first started going to Galax, in '73-'74, the stalls were there, of course, but there wasn't a real community in the stalls. The stalls were just a place where, if you didn't bring your tent, and it got to be four or five in the morning, you just flopped down in one of them and fell asleep. It was a little shady; for instance, Dave Steeg—the first year we were at Galax—he fell asleep and had his Martin twelve string ripped off from right next to his body. So those first few years, I would wander around all night and then when it got to be four or five in the morning I would flop down in one of those stalls ... I would take a piece of string and tie my banjo to my arm.

Was this that Stewmac kit banjo?

Nancy: Same one I lent you for years.

Did you go to Stompin' 76?

Nancy: Oh, yeah. I didn't go to New River Jam, but I did go to Stompin' 76. That was wild. This was when I was living in Greenville. And there was this girlfriend of mine,

Annie Dickens. And we both wanted to go in the worst way, and we were broke. So we, being our artistic selves, a friend of ours had purchased a ticket. The tickets were red, white and blue and had printing on them. We took that ticket and some watercolors and magic markers and we made our own tickets to look exactly like them. The funny thing was, you know we hitchhiked there, and by the time we got there, the whole scene was pandemonium

anyway, and we just walked right through the gate and never had to give anybody our tickets. I still have that ticket.

When we moved to Greenville, after we got married, Bill started his sign business, I didn't know what I was going to do, so I ended up opening a batik shop with Judy Cate in Greenville. I just kept doing it, and it got big.

When did you start winning contests?

Nancy: Actually, back up to that school in Vermont, just a year after I had started playing banjo. I was at that school, and the summer after I left that school, at that point I had been playing the banjo for about a year and a half, but I was rabid. I was eating it up. Anyway I came back to visit and it was the weekend of the Craftsbury Banjo Contest, so I entered, and won third place. And it was huge, the banjo contest was huge. It was astounding. I played "Mississippi Sawyer". That got me interested in going to contests, it's fun.

Were you listening to a lot of records, and finding a style to play in?

When I first got the banjo, I did gravitate directly to Clawhammer. But I was just a happy-go-lucky banjo player; I was out there eating up all the music. And I wasn't one of the scholarly ones that went down to study with Tommy Jarrell, or anything like that. Any of those old guys that I met, that I bumped into at festivals, I did learn from. Like Kyle Creed; I kind of latched on to him way back in the early seventies when I first ran into him at Galax, and was intrigued with his style. I would dog him at festivals and learn stuff. And after Stompin' 76, I went to Galax and then I was getting a ride home with Doug Baker, who was in the Cloggers, and he said, "Well, I was going to stop by and see Kyle Creed ... "I'm like, "Yeah!"

So we stopped by Kyle's house, and visited him there for the day. And that was pretty cool. I was more into just playing, and I didn't really care whose tune it was. I was just into the festival aspect of it, and the playing and I would just want to learn every tune I could and I didn't care whose version it was.

Did you ever feel there was a time that you were getting accepted by the people down here? Or was that never an issue?

Nancy: I think it was in issue in my mind, for a long time. We felt like there was definitely an "Us Versus Them" feeling when we first got here. I think when we first started the Bobcats, we were not that accepted as a quote-unquote, local band and it had to do with something about the beat.

In other words, we played places and nobody would dance. And then all those local dancers would dance like mad to Richard Bowman and all those other bands. Whatever we were doing was not inspiring them. But then, after a year or two of just absorbing the music and not really trying to, you just end up sounding more and more like a Round Peak band. After a couple of years, people started dancing to our music. And that's when I realized that we were accepted.

There is a thing in the music which I heard one Galax, and went around boring everybody with it. And none of the Yankees knew what I was talking about, and all the country people understood. I called it "being on the step"—like a speedboat starts planing. There is one place in a song, where it stops laboring, and nothing changes; it's all the same, nothing has ever changed, but at that point, it swings.

Nancy: It locks in. I know exactly what you are talking about.

It blew my mind. I was walking around going; "Do you hear that?" "Hear what?" "What are you talking about?" But country people, even grandmothers, I would say, "You were really on the step" and they would say, "Yeah, that's right."

Nancy: When we got on the step, was when we got accepted. It was pretty profound, really. I even remember, this one dance years ago, where Claudine, a local dancer, came up to us one time specifically saying that we got it. That we had finally had gotten it. And that we were OK. Also it was really interesting with the whole Galax judging thing, I played at that contest for twenty years before I ever won anything there. The year I played "Darling Nellie Gray" like Kyle Creed, it was the year Jerry Garcia died, and I think I had so much emotion in me, that particular day, that I played the living shit out of it, and won first place!

I don't think it had as much to do with discrimination against the hippie types ... It wasn't that at all. It was exactly what you just said. We weren't "on the step" yet. It's like, we weren't in their particular groove that they ... I mean, it has everything to with there being a certain sound, a Galax sound, and you're playing at the Galax Fiddler's Convention, that's the sound that they like to hear. That's their Old Time Music and if you're playing at the Galax Old Fiddler's Convention, then that's the sound that they want to hear. So, unless you're playing that sound, you could be Bruce Molsky, you're never going to win a thing unless you're getting to that sound.

Alan Freeman, that dulcimer maniac, he told me that he knew one of the judges, and the judge told him that when Alan played "Limehouse Blues", the next judge over wrote down all zeros.

"What did you do that for?"

"It's not a dulcimer song."

"It is now. He's a genius."

"Oh, yeah, you're right!" And wrote down 100's.

And he said, that what they wanted to do was not to pick the best performers, because you can't do that. It's too subjective. They wanted to reward the people that they wanted to come back. And that was their criteria. The knew everybody, and if somebody was having a hard time, the wife died or something, they'd give him a few hundred bucks. And if they knew that somebody was getting old, and had never won, they would give it to them. They wanted them to come back.

Remember that Japanese band that bowed to the judges?

Nancy: They gave them Thirteenth Place.

They laid down their instruments and bowed to the judges. "Fine. Here's a hundred bucks."

I do know that some of the judges judge from music and some judge for other things, I've known many of them over the years.

Sure, but to say it's the aesthetics ... "Oh, I played 64th notes", or "I played like Bascom Lunsford", that don't cut it. The Moose wants what they want, and that's it. It's their ball and their bat and their field and they set the rules to their game.

So when did you start playing fiddle?

Nancy: In 1979—when I went up to Augusta that year, my main focus was to learn fiddle. I went there and totally immersed myself for the two weeks I was up there. And then went from there to Galax with it, and by the time I left the several events, I had probably learned fifty tunes. And was pretty well on it. I was a fairly quick study at that time. Once I got the shuffle; before that, I didn't quite get it, it was hell for Bill, I'm sure.

Bill, when did you graduate to upright?

Bill: About five years after I started playing washtub bass. In Florida.

You're the observer, the strong silent type. What do you see in all this? What's the most important thing I should put in the book?

Bill: There are a whole lot of people around here, like Riccio and us, people who came to it from wherever they came from and lived a lifestyle that is more "Hippie-like", people who came to Old Time music from a different slant than most people. But if it has that groove, it's Old Time Music.

Nancy: Not long ago I had a conversation with Chester MacMillian. He is ten or fifteen years older than me. So for me, he's like partway in between us and the Old Timers. And that's where he lays in the scene. Like, when we were all first coming up, he was only in his thirties, but he grew up here and by right of family and tradition he was a pure Old Time musician. He was playing with Tommy and all those guys.

Now to me, hippies are just free thinkers but in this conversation, fairly recently, I was saying something about how I was just a hippie chick and he said, "But, ya'll aren't hippies!" It was the funniest thing, because to him, we weren't hippies, which was a negative thing to him. We were just folks who moved to the area and became local Old Time musicians. My feeling is he didn't differentiate between us and the other Old Time musicians in the area, be it Verlin Clifton or Benton Flippen or anybody. And we were right there, the same as any of those guys, in Chester's eyes, old time musicians. It was a cool feeling.

In the Eighties, every time I would go to Galax, I would run into these two old guys, nicely dressed, khakis and collar shirts, and they would talk about how the hippies were walking around barefoot in the horse mush in the stalls. And they were all upset about that. But they would be right there, watching. I kind of had the idea that they were checking out to see who was wearing a bra ... But I heard this rap two or three years in a row. But that's kind of a way of assimilating this stuff too.

And some of the hippies are still mad about tearing the stalls down.

Nancy: I loved the stalls but in actuality, the social scene at Galax improved greatly for me after the stalls were taken down. Because you were out there with everybody else. We met more people ... I think the stalls were just a way for the Yankees to insulate themselves from the real culture of the area. I was never the intellectual type. My whole reason for being here was that I was rabid for the music. And it was on a pure love-gut level. So it wasn't like I was down here to learn from this person or that person, I was just down here playing the music, because this was where it was played the most, more than anywhere else.

What about the music grabbed you?

Nancy: The Step. The Groove. It was like, yes they played Appalachian music in New England, but it was tinkley and weenie. It had no meat to it. There was just something about this area's music, that had the meat, that had the groove.

The French Canadians swang.

Nancy: They did! They were great, I enjoyed that music, but it just didn't get me. But when I came to Galax and heard "That". The Birchfields and Kyle Creed and Tommy Jarrell there was just something they had that was just so pure, it just knocked me out. When I saw the Birchfields it was just, "Oh my gosh. I have landed." Someplace, I didn't know where, but I had landed.

How far up the hill are they from?

Nancy: Way up there in Tennessee.

It's kind of interesting, but when we moved here half the musicians around here weren't talking much to each other. There was a lot of jealousy and competition. I actually think that we, the so-called hippies, had a lot to do with bringing those people back together as friends. About ten years ago, when Jackie and I had a birthday—turned forty and she turned fifty—we had a party and we invited everybody … we were always very inclusive … we always invited everybody. And most of the time the locals never came, but we invited them. We sent out invitations. We would invite everybody.

This particular party, a lot the local musicians came. A few of them hadn't spoken in years. But everybody came together, and there was one point during the party where somebody came over to me and said, "You gotta come see this!" They brought me out to Bill's shop, and there was one big jam session with all of them, these guys who hadn't been speaking for years all in the same jam session in our garage. Like cool. That's what it's all about!

What do you think about Dave Grant and that modern reggae hell Old Timey stuff?

Bill: It's another off-shoot. It's got a neat groove. I like that kind of music in a number of aspects, I enjoy it …

Nancy: Being the Deadheads we are, we like all those kind of crossover musics. It's definitely not Old Time Music, and yet at the same time it can use aspects of it. It's the groove.

Bill: It's the same thing, in their music. You could dance to it. We enjoy Donna the Buffalo too. When I say dance, generally I'm talking, in my range, there has to be some kind of a heartbeat in there. You can clog to it, dance with that clogging beat. And that's what makes something danceable in a lot of ways. It's just in 4/4 time on the four thing. It gets my feet and gets my soul. Garcia used to frail a banjo.

Nancy: So there was a lot in their music that was very akin to Old Time. The Rock and Roll music that was born out of acoustic music. We have some ancient bootleg tapes of Jerry Garcia's Old Time band, "The Sleepy Hollow Hog Stompers". That was back in the Sixties.

There is this Harvard Doctoral Thesis, "Jewgrass", about how everybody that played Bluegrass in New York City was Jewish. In 1959, including Roger Sprung.

Nancy: When I first met Roger Sprung, I met him at the Canaan Valley Bluegrass Festival in Connecticut.

I was there! I was drunk. Were you drunk? We showed up one time in a 1950 BMW R-50 with a sidecar. Playing harmonica and wearing a World War I army helmet with a peace sign painted on it. Me and Bud. People applauded when we drove in.

Nancy: I think it is interesting, that whole "us and them" impression thing. I don't know when it was that we became "Us" instead of "Them." It's interesting. Like definitely, after we came down, I think it had a lot to do with, like I mentioned about the stalls being torn down at Galax. That pissed a lot of people off who didn't come back, but the people who did come back, suddenly the people who used to be isolated in the stalls were just thrown out in to the general public. And within a couple of years, all the people who used to label us as "The Hippies" and be really apprehensive, got to know all these people who used to be the hippies, and suddenly it wasn't "us" anymore, it was some dirty longhairs from long ago that were the hippies.

All of us are coming to Old Timey for like totally different reasons. Everybody is a genius, everybody is whacked out, and they all come from different places. Like you're in Old Time for no particular reason, right?

Bill: No particular reason. It's something I fell into when I met Nancy.

But, at the same time, you are one of the best bass players in Old Time Music. I had no desire to play Old Time Music; I wound up here because Johnny Sturgill saw one of my fancy dope pipes and said, "Hey, you want to make guitars?"

And so I was down here, and I never did care much about Old Time Music, but I got to really like the people.

Nancy: I guess that's just what it's all about.

Bill: Part of the thing is that Old Time Music around here had survived a lot, in the mountains. When you look at a map of this area, from like 1972, there wasn't any I-77, just Route 52.

Nancy: That first year I came to Galax, it was pretty darn hard to get there, like you had to come down Rt. 100 … to Pulaski, and almost kill yourself over the mountains, let alone Fancy Gap. That was the main highway, and I-77 didn't get built until the '80's.

Bill: And like you say about the mountain people, the mountain people are different than city people. There is something about the isolation in the mountains, and the way people are around here.

A lot of people up around this community, they will take you at face value. And won't pre-judge you, unless you prove yourself by being a jerk. If you come on by being a jerk, you might be treated like one. If you come on and treat them with respect, that's what you get back.

It's My Story and I'm Sticking With it.
Joe Thrift

So it's 1967 and I'm a senior in high school living in Winston-Salem. I had seen "The Grand Ole Opry" and the "Arthur Smith Show" for several years. Not that I liked the music, but in the early days of TV there weren't that many shows to watch. One Friday night some buddies and I drove an hour to Elkin and happened on a fiddler's convention going on in the football stadium. I remember seeing a hillbilly band on stage and someone clogging on the side of the stage. I thought it was the funniest thing I'd ever seen.

A few years later I went to the state fair in Raleigh, NC. I remember walking through one of the exhibit tents and seeing an old mountain man (probably my age now, so not so old, right?) with a beard like one of the guys in "ZZ Top", and he was making dulcimers. I had really never done much in the way of woodworking and was immediately taken by the process. I went home and made a couple of dulcimers that weighed about 50 lbs. each. They were really rough.

I decided to try and learn to do a finer job with the woodwork, so I visited a guy I knew from school named Michael Byrd to get a few pointers. He had a violin shop in Winston-Salem. I started hanging out there and he showed me how to use and sharpen hand tools. Michael was getting ready to go to a violin making school in England, so I only worked in his shop for a couple of months. Working on dulcimers led to playing the guitar, mostly Neil Young. In 1975 I was living in Surry County and building a log cabin. I got the bug to learn to make a guitar and heard about Dave Sturgill and his apprentice program in Piney Creek, NC. I went to check his shop out and ended up working for him. I can't say I learned very much about making a guitar but I did do a lot of water sanding and made a few dulcimers. The best thing that came out of that experience was the people I met and my introduction to old time music. All the apprentices there had a money-back-band to get in free at the fiddler's conventions and display the instruments for Sturgill's. My first experience in a band was playing the mandolin, Steve Wishnevsky on banjo, Rob Mangum, on guitar, and Chris Sekerak on fiddle. We called ourselves "The Hungry Holler High Steppers". I learned the chords to "Soldiers Joy" waiting in line behind the stage. At this point we weren't a very good band.[43]

Around the same time I drove with a friend to British Columbia for his wedding. He brought along his father's half-sized fiddle and I started noodling on it, playing tunes I'd heard at fiddler's conventions. When I returned to NC I began twin fiddling in the band. Our money-back-band, now called "The Cricket Pickers", somehow ended up playing for the Greengrass Cloggers at a couple of fiddler's conventions. Soon after I decided to move to Greenville, NC to dance with the cloggers. While dancing I got to hear and dance to "Highwoods Stringband" and "Plank Road" which made me really start loving old time music. I also started listening to Tommy Jarrell, a neighbor of mine from Surry County. At a Clogger party I met a guy named Rich Hartness who was also just learning fiddle. He helped me with my new appetite for the music. We were both enthusiastic and Rich had tons of recordings. Playing so much, I started learning to "adjust" my instrument and wouldn't you know it … I became interested in learning to make violins.

I started hanging out at Albert Hash's shop and learned what I could about violin making, when I heard about a guy in Wilson, NC named William Walls who made nice violins, I called him up and went to visit. I wanted to apprentice with someone like him. He said if he were my age he'd go to this school in England and pulled out a copy of the Strad magazine with an article about the Newark School of Violin Making. I suddenly realized that's where my friend Michael Byrd had gone. I contacted Michael to find out more about the school. Next thing you know there I was in England interviewing for a place in the school. They accepted me and 3 months later I was living in England going to violin making school. Don't ask me.

After the first year of school I came home and danced with the cloggers at Wolftrap and Philadelphia Folk Festival. "Highwoods Stringband" played for us both times. Tommy Jarrell and Fred Cockerham were on the bill so I heard a lot of them as well. I went back to England for two more years playing only minimally, but did listen to lots of old time music while I worked. In 1980 after finishing school I came back to Winston-Salem and opened a violin shop.

Rich Hartness sent me a tape of his band and I was totally freaked. I wanted to play in an old time band in the worst way. I ended up playing some gigs with Rich and Earl White's band "Too Wet To Plough". This led to playing more and more. The summer of 1982 Rich and I formed The "Wild Goose Chasers" with Rich and I fiddling, Brian DeMarcus (a friend from The Greengrass Cloggers) on banjo, and Carol Mallet (also an ex-Clogger) on guitar. That same summer I also met Tom Riccio and Alvin Baugus (Riley). In the summer of 1983 we formed "The Red Hots" which was myself and Rich Hartness on fiddles, Tom Riccio on banjo, Riley Baugus on guitar, and Jerry Ray Weinert on bass. We only played a couple of times in this configuration. Rich ended up going back to school and moving away. We became a four-piece band and toured all over the east coast from Florida to upstate NY. Later Jerry Ray was replaced by Steve Mason on bass. We've now been playing almost 23 years together.

At this time I had started going to Tommy Jarrell on a weekly basis. We didn't always play. Sometimes we just hung out, drank beer, and watched TV. He was an entertaining guy. We played twin fiddles and sometimes he'd play banjo. I loved it. One of the great things Tommy taught me was to play the way I play. When he was younger he learned tunes but couldn't play them the way the person taught it so he played it his way. I never really tried to learn his technique. I learned lots of other great things from Tommy. He was a very gracious host.

Playing in "The Red Hots" led to meeting Jeff Claus and Judy Hyman from "The Horse Flies". "The Red Hots" first road trip as a band was to Ithaca to play some gigs Jeff helped set up. We started meeting more northern musicians at Mt. Airy and Galax fiddler's conventions. At the time there were only a few touring bands so it was really exciting when we'd roll into town. People were eager for the music. We got to know Keith Brand, Beverly Smith, and Rose Sinclair in Philadelphia and started playing the dance there when we headed north.

At Richie Stearns' wedding we met two brothers from upstate NY.... Jeb and Jordan Puryear. They had a band called "Bubba George Stringband". Through them I met Tara Nevins and Jim Miller. Tara soon after was playing with "The Heartbeats", which was a really powerful all-woman string band. We played lots of fiddle music with each other any time they came south for a fiddler's convention. They started a rock band called "Donna the Buffalo" and in 1991 I joined and became the keyboard player. We always took time off for Mt. Airy and Galax fiddler's convention. I stayed with that band for 9 years playing with "The Red Hots" when I could.

After quitting the Buffalo band I started a band called "Man Alive!" with good friends Bill and Nancy Sluys and David Long. A few years later "jimmyjohnnyjoe" formed with Mark Olitsky on banjo, Jason Sypher on bass, and Debra Clifford on guitar. Debra went on to play with the "Lonesome Sisters" full time and Charlie Pickford became the guitar player.

Today, 2006, I am making violins full time and playing with "The Red Hots" and "jimmyjohnnyjoe" any chance I get. I still love to go to the small fiddler's conventions to play with my friends and neighbors in the foothills. You hear the best old time music, and it's not commercial ... that's a beautiful thing.

Nancy Corey Interview

Nancy Cory is a quiet, friendly, comfortable woman with un-dyed hair. She is a very supportive player, not flashy, but always in your jam or the next one over.

How long have you been playing Old Time music, how did you get started?

I got interested in it when I was at Virginia Tech, in 1963-4-5. My first husband and I started a little coffee shop/bookstore/music store with live entertainment called "Books, Strings and Things". And I was there for about a year and then I just took off.

Were you playing music at this time?

No, I sort of let it go then. But I got interested in the Old Time and Bluegrass then. When I left, we were open seven days a week, from ten to midnight, maybe noon to midnight on Sunday. When we closed the store, we locked ourselves in, and lived in a tiny little room that even I couldn't stand up in. It was in a big warehouse space, right in downtown Blacksburg. Just a big open space and we had a little kitchen room and over it hung a room sus-

pended that was five feet high and we lived in that. It was kind of claustrophobic. And anyway, I just moved in and out of that scene pretty fast. And then I took off and was hanging out with cavers for the next twenty-five years.

I was more interested in the social scene, caving was secondary.

This was in the Folk Music era. I was interested. My second husband and I, we used to go to Bluegrass Festivals; we went to Berryville back in the '70's, and Bean Blossom, Indiana, and listen to music, but I didn't really start playing it 'til I moved back up to Virginia in '86. And started hanging out with the Blacksburg crew. I had a banjo and a guitar all these years. I had several nice guitars that I never played. I just never got into it until I got back to Blacksburg and found the Old Time people—"The Hooraw Cloggers", Bill Blevins, Tina Liza Jones, that whole crew and a bunch more. There's always people coming and going, because it's a college town. I had a banjo for years, and I never got it working 'til I came back up here.

In '87 I went to Rockbridge, in the fall, and in '88 I went to about half a dozen things and it built from there. I'll be a sub. I used to sub for Steve Mason, every once in a while, when he couldn't get his regular banjo player. I just play three minutes and get my money back. I play at midnight jams.

So why does Old Time matter …?

Because it's fun.

Why don't you play Rock and Roll, like God wants you to?

I don't know. When I was in college, I fell in love with acoustic music … I have an electric guitar and an amp, and I never even had them connected to each other. I'm not an academician by any stretch of the imagination. I just like the music and I like the people who play, and it's fun. There is something about playing with people that's lots of fun. It connects you. It's another way to get a buzz, really. Everybody knows that.

Rock and Roll was always just background music for my dysfunctional life. I didn't know what I was listening to. It was always there. But the only kind of music I ever tried to play, or wanted to try to play was acoustic String music. And now I play banjo, and guitar, and I have a couple of fiddles. I have a very nice mandolin, I never touch it. I had a bass. I gave it away. I thought my son might want to play it, but he never did.

Chapter Seven: Middle and West Coasts

Ken Bloom Interview

Ken Bloom is one of the most amazing craftsmen I know. You walk into his cluttered music room and it looks like the basement of a museum. There are so many odd uncharted things there, one longs for a guide. He makes bagpipes, flintlock muskets, hardanger fiddles, is the American expert on the Ukrainian bandura, wins Celtic Harp Contests, makes and plays minstrel banjoes, and is starting a one-man revival of the Bowed Dulcimer. He can play three songs at once on the fretted Orchestra Zither. I have three of his albums; "Mapamundi", "That Banjo >From Hell" and "The Bowed? Dulcimer". All are full of humor, quirks and unparalleled musicianship.

What's your story?

Too many world-weary experiences? Born June 12th, 1945, Santa Monica, California. Mostly raised in the quiet, sleepy little community of Beverly Hills. Started playing music when I was ten, on flute, clarinet, saxophone, did that through High School. Did a European tour when I was sixteen with a big band … And then got interested in string instruments right at the end of high school when I started playing banjo, hanging out at the Ash Grove. 1962-3.

The first concert of old time that I ever saw was at the Ash Grove was in April of '63. Mother Maybelle Carter was opening the show for "The New Lost City Ramblers". I remember that gig very, very well.

Before that, I didn't have a clue. I knew about old time Jazz. I was a horn player. I remembered seeing some of what were then called the "Hillbilly Shows" on television. The "Barn Dance" from Louisiana was on once in a while, and every now and again, I would be flipping around the tube and see one of the country shows, you know. The "Ernest Tubb Show" and some of that stuff. That was the early days of TV.

Mostly I listened to the jazz station. I was seriously into Sonny Rawlins and Coltrane, Benny Goodman, Sidney Bechet, all that early New Orleans stuff. Used to pore over pictures of the old New Orleans stuff.

This was the hardest music in America, so what attracted you to Old Timey?

The spirit of it, I guess. I fell into playing string instruments almost by accident. My father took a class at the high school on how to play guitar. And he went out and bought an inexpensive nylon strung guitar. He brought the handouts from class home and I looked at them and said, "Oh! How hard can this be?" So he took the classes and I practiced.

And then my best friend at the time was this guitar player who was studying jazz. And we had been playing all this Dixieland stuff, so we said to each other, "Whoever gets the money first, we'll get a banjo. Because we should really have a banjo to play Dixieland." And at the time, I didn't have a clue that there was more than one kind of banjo. So I had this old tenor, that my father had, it was a Washburn, in terrible shape. And in my senior year of high school, I got some extra money around Christmas time, and I took that tenor and the cash I had down to McCabe's Guitar Shop, and said, "I want to trade all this for a banjo." And they did it, and I got it, a Harmony five string, with the plastic rim, and the mystery wood neck, and skin head. In those days, cheap banjoes didn't deserve the new plastic head.

And I got the only book available, which was the Pete Seeger book.

Which, parenthetically, has done more damage than Chairman Mao's Red Book.

From the standpoint of people who play clawhammer, it's pretty useless. But what it did for me, it had the tablature but he had the stuff written down in regular score notation, and I could read that. Of course, as soon as I got that, "The Beverly Hillbillies" was a big show then. And I would be listening to the theme, every week, attempting to decipher what was going on with the banjo.

Well, here was some of Scruggs stuff, written out in notes. I went, "Great! I can learn this. How hard can this be?" I went my way through the book, and I was doing that for a couple of months and then there was a group of people at my high school who played old time. Dick Greene was amongst them. Richard Greene. He later ended up playing fiddle with Bill Monroe. And he's done a lot of Rock and Roll fiddle.

"Seatrain".

But I knew him from high school. He had a band. He played with Dave Lindley and a lot of the West Coast people ... Some sort of Ramblers ... I forget now. (The Mad Mountain Ramblers)

Was Dave Lindley in your school?

He lived out around Pasadena somewhere. I met him ... There was a band called "The Dry City Scat Band." And that was Dick Greene and Lindley and a couple other people.[44] *I met all those folks the next year, hanging out at the Ash Grove.*

Somebody who was part of this little group of folkies at Beverly High came up to me, and said, "Hey, you play the banjo, "The New Lost City Ramblers" are playing at the Ash Grove. You should go see them." I really though this was the most peculiar name for a band I had ever heard. I was used to "Red Nichols and his Red Hots" that kind of thing. "New Lost what? This is weird, this is bizarre. OK, I'll go check it out." 'Go down to the Ash Grove, hear the stuff, and I'm watching these guys do this all night. The music's great ... This was after Paley left, but they were tight, they were great, they were having a real good time up there.

And the music had this incredible life to it. And I'm looking at them up there, and they are like switching instruments every song, and I'm going, "Oh, that's right, that's what I do!" This is good because this time I had gone through the instrument room in the orchestra in California. So I see them, everybody's playing, switching from banjo to mandolin to guitar to Dobro, back and forth and on and on. I'm going, "This is pretty neat, I could do this." I just loved it. So I went out and bought every record I could find, and that was the first time I had really heard traditional. And listening to those records, I'm hearing the clawhammer, but I was also hearing the various finger picking styles. Charlie Poole and all that. And about a month later, the brother of a friend of mine in the orchestra, named Mike Bass, knocks on my door one night and says, "Hi, you don't know me, but I'm here to show you frailing."

God sent him?

I guess his brother had said, "You know, there's this friend of mine in the high school orchestra and he's interested in the stuff ..." So he just showed up at my door one night. He showed me the basics of doing clawhammer. And he was a record collector. He had 78's. But he didn't have a very good ear. So, after I had played for a while, I would go over to his place and he would play me a record and say, "Well, tell me what tuning the guy is in." And I could hear pretty clearly which notes were fretted and which weren't and all that. That summer, this was still '63, in June, they had a Folk Music Camp up in Idlewild, which was kind of an arts camp up in the mountains of California. And the teachers in the camp were Pete Seeger, Guy Carawan and most importantly, Stu Jamison.

Stu is one of the finest old time banjo players you will ever hear. A lot of the stuff he learned from Rufus Crisp. Excellent player—at the time I think he used something like eighteen or nineteen different tunings. Well, the two weeks that I spent at that music camp with Stu Jamison showing us all these different things, differentiating between the styles of Clarence Ashley and Roscoe Holcomb, and then what Rufus Crisp did, this one and that one—it was all new to me. It was like I had never heard of any of these people. Until the following fall, when the Ash Grove started bringing all these people into town, and here's Roscoe Holcomb. He does a week, and Clarence Ashley does a week. And the way the club is set up, you could go and hang out with them, and they were just really friendly people. And they would sit and show you stuff.

And we were the Young Turks, gobbling it all up, in a pretty obnoxious fashion. Most of what I learned, I either got from listening to my friends' 78's, or from watching and spending time with the people who came through. In that period of the early and middle '60's, traditional old time music was like big business. The first UCLA Folk Festival, which was in the fall of 1964, one of the first people they booked was Eck Robertson, Uncle Eck, a little goat-like guy, like five foot four tall or something. Looked exactly like that famous picture of him with the American flag hanging from his fiddle. From Amarillo. He made the first country music record ever made. December 1922. His very famous playing of "Sally Goodin". It's not a typical record, I mean he's playing all over the fiddle, man, he's up in fourth and fifth position and he's all over the thing. Some people say it's not the most typical country music record ever made, but it may be the best.

So what did you get from him?

I went out the next day and bought a fiddle. I just said, "That's great. I want to be able to do that!" So I went down to Wallachy's Music, which was down in Westwood at the time, and I knew nothing about fiddles, Fred Wallachy was the one who ran it, and I said, "Ok, Fred, pull out all the fifty dollar fiddles and let me kind of go through them", and I just plunked on strings and the one that sounded the clearest, "I'll get this one." And then I called up Dick Greene and he gave me a quick lesson, "Here's how you hold it, here's how you hold the bow, here's some basics of bowing ..." And stuff like that. And sat down with my records and proceeded to spend the next thirty years attempting to play the fiddle. Which I never really did succeed ... I'm what you call fiddleistically challenged. But banjo I could play. I was really fortunate. There were all these players came through LA that you could hang out and spend time with.

We had picking parties every Friday and Saturday night at somebody's house. During the week, it would always be the buzz of, "Where's it gonna be this time?" There was always somebody's house where we could do it. It may be way out in the Valley, or sometimes it was down in Venice. Venice in those days was nothing like it is now. It was a real funky part of town where students and artists, people like that lived. And there was a core of maybe twenty-thirty-forty people … We just all got together to play. And some of it was bluegrass, and some of it was old time, and some of it was just Ian and Sylvia Folk Music. Nobody really differentiated a lot. There were a few music Nazis around, but mostly we were all just trying to learn how to play, as best we could, having such limited exposure to it.

Was there a coffeehouse scene?

Yeah. The Ash Grove was the main one. That was the big center of traditional stuff. The Troubadour, which is still there, booked some of the more commercially viable stuff. And the more traditionally oriented people, the hard core folks, hung out at the Ash Grove. It was in West Hollywood … at the time it was kind of a nice, middle-class, Jewish neighborhood. Beverly Hills, at the time, was the wealthy Jewish neighborhood, it wasn't like it is now … lots of lawyers and doctors and businessmen.

The movie people were there, but there was plenty of other stuff to offset all of that. The Troubadour was just outside of Beverly Hills. I could walk there from my house. The Ash Grove was about two or three miles farther down the road. And all that is plunked right in the middle of the area where all the recording studios are and the record companies and all that business stuff. So you had this very, at times, bizarre environment of industry people hanging around, trying to sniff out what the next trend's going to be, and sign somebody up, along with the serious scholars who are all centered around UCLA. Because we had Dr. Donald K. Wilgus there in the Folklore Department and that was the real serious study stuff. We would lovingly call him Dilgus Kilgus Wilgus. But they had an excellent Folklore Department and that big collection from Australia had just come to UCLA. I think its in Chapel Hill now.

Anyway all these Folklore students and majors there basically spent their lives cataloguing this monstrous collection, because it had never been catalogued. John Fahey was there, I knew him real well. There were a lot of things happening all at the same time.

Was there any effort to catch up with the migrants, the Okies? I imagine a lot of those were fiddlers too.

Ummm … My father owned a lumberyard … And the guy who was sort of the head guy in the lumberyard itself was from Oklahoma, and had come here during the Depression and all that … And he liked to sit out back when he had a break and play his harmonica … Harry Don't Remember His Last Name. But, I guess, I would have to say, he was my earliest exposure to old time music. And knowing him, I guess, it meant that I got to see other types of people that I would never have seen just in Beverly Hills. So, working at that lumberyard, from the time I was ten, was a real good experience.

I was in a bunch of little bands. There was a band with me, Dave Polechek, who is now in Austin; Herb Steiner, who is also in Austin, a pedal steel player, good one. A guy named Bob Zuckerman … The others all knew each other from Fairfax High. We did a lot of Uncle Dave Macon stuff and Polechek and I did a lot of that McGee Brothers/Uncle Dave Macon double banjo stuff, with one of us playing a six-string and one of us playing five. We worked up a lot of those things. None of us could sing worth a shit. We all sounded terrible, but we didn't care.

Uncle Dave Macon is an expressive singer. I'm talking about just the simple ability to hit the pitch. We were all pretty hopeless at that. I mean none of these bands were very serious. All the time I was doing this I was still making my money playing with bands for weddings and bar mitzvahs and stuff like that. Everything was going on all at the same time. It was the Sixties; I did my first recording session in '64, because they needed somebody to play jug for some New Christy Minstrel-type of group, whose name I forget.

On that session I met Glen Campbell, who had just come to town. He was the latest studio fair-haired boy. And I had my banjo there and I had learned a lot of the early Bill Keith stuff. And he had never seen any of that kind of stuff before, so I remember sitting out in the hall and in between takes, showing him how to play "Devil's Dream" on the banjo. Everything was happening at once.

You never became a pothead?

Well, no. Actually I didn't do any drugs when I was in college. When I was about eight or ten, I had read this book of biographies of famous people for kids. One of them was a little short biography of the Buddha. And I just sort of went ... "That's neat. I like that. Plus I've always been one of those people who's just naturally kind of healthy. I wake up in the morning and I'm perky. So all through the Sixties, when everybody was smoking dope and taking acid, I didn't touch any of it. I just figured that the center of my life was music, and I was really afraid that if I was going to do anything like that, I would lose whatever edge I might have had.

I was also doing a lot of stuff in the Ethnomusicology Department. That first semester at UCLA, Ravi Shankar was teaching this theory class and I was a freshman and it was an upper division class so I couldn't take the class, but I was interested, so I just went. And I began to realize after a while that Country music is about the same, no matter what country it comes from. People do things for the same reasons.

By the end of college, I had met Michael Martin Murphey in one of my English classes.

"Geronimo's Cadillac?"

Big points for that one. He kind of picked me out, because I was the only other person in the class that wore cowboy boots every day. So we got talking, and we started playing some music together, he introduced me to his partner and they put this band together, this sort of hip Country Western stuff. This was "The Lewis and Clark Expedition"

This was right at the end of college, and I took time off because the band was recording and we were touring, and because of that, the people at the Screen Gems office saw that I could play fairly well on a lot of different instruments. So I started playing all these demo sessions for them. They put me on staff doing that.

I started getting work, playing sitar on things and for Screen Gems I could go into the studio with a bass player and a drummer and put down a basic track and then I could do all the rest of it. When Carol King first came out to LA I did a lot of work with her with demos and stuff. She would go into the studio, put a thing down and a bass player and drummer and I'd put on horn parts and all that.

And meanwhile, I'm still getting together with my friends and playing old time and bluegrass. My wife and I had just gotten together, in '67, and we lived up in Beechwood Canyon. Up the street from where I lived, was this big group of buildings ... Doug Dillard lived down stairs, Linda Ronstadt lived upstairs, Harry Dean Stanton lived in the back, Byron Berline lived up the street. And we would all get together over at Doug's house and play.

We had a great time doing that. So there was this whole sort of Hollywood Bluegrass crowd. And I'd known Linda, because one of the guys in "The Stone Poneys" was an old friend of mine. Just like Ry Cooder and David Cohen and Taj Mahal and all these people who were part of that Ash Grove/McCabe's Guitar Shop scene. The first time I met Taj, he had just come out from Boston, he was there in McCabe's Guitar shop playing Dave Macon songs on the banjo. The first time I met Ry Cooder he was fifteen, and doing a gig at the Ash Grove with a singer.

When did you start making instruments?

I kind of dabbled in it when I moved to San Francisco in the early Seventies. But I didn't start really doing it seriously until about '74, '75, when I started wanting a bandura, could not find one to save my life. And so I figured, "I'll make one." I was living in Chicago by then. And I set up a workshop and started to first build them for me and then other people wanted them, so I started to build them for them.

Did you go to Chicago for a job?

The last year I was in San Francisco, which was '73, I was backing up this singer-songwriter, Jim Post. And up until this time, except for tours that I had done with Ronstadt and with this other Rock and Roll band I was in, I had no idea that somebody without an agent and a record and all that could actually go out and make a living playing music. And while I was on the road with Post, a guy told me about the Mariposa Folk Festival. "Bloom, you're perfect for Mariposa! Send them a tape, I know they will hire you." And my wife and I were talking about getting out of California. So we kind of looked at each other, and said, "OK."

I made this tape, sitting in front of a tape recorder, not quite the quality we are recording on today. ($29.00 Sony) *And I said, "Listen, I'll send this off, and if they hire me, let's move to the Midwest. We will take it as a sign.*

And if they don't we will just keep plugging away here." I sent off this terrible tape, and they thought it was a terrible tape, but they thought that this was something interesting, maybe. So they hired me. And we moved to Chicago.

There were all these acoustic music clubs. During Mariposa a lot of people came up and said, "We have a Folk Club in such and such a town, would you come and play. I was doing some of the stuff I had written, and some traditional stuff, I was playing concert zither by then. And I had taken quite a few Uncle Dave Macon Songs and was doing them bottleneck on the zither. Playing clarinet, doing some stuff on the dulcimer, a little bit on bandura ... I had sort of concocted a show, of sorts.

Backing up a few years, I was going to Law School in San Diego, from '68 to early '71 or so. I was working in this guitar shop, "The Blue Guitar", and at the time I was really making next to nothing, just giving lessons. And these folks called up the guitar shop and said, "Hi, this is Chuck's Steakhouse. The guy who was going to be playing here cancelled. We need somebody to come and fill in for a couple of weekends. You know anybody?" "I know some ... We know a guy who is great! He plays all these instruments. He's fabulous! We'll send him right over." Hung up the phone, threw every instrument I could find in the car, closed up the shop, ran over there, played at them for two hours, wouldn't let them get a word in edgewise ... Just speed-rapped it. Finally they said, "You got the job. Just stop!"

And I played there for three or four months until I moved back to LA. And that was sort of boot camp for the single performer. You're playing for people who ... they're hungry, they don't want to be there, in a bar where they don't want to drink, because they haven't eaten yet. If you can entertain those folks, you can entertain anybody.

What I would do is, there were all these traditional things that I really loved, and music that I thought was really neat, and so what I would try and do was to present stuff to people I really thought they needed to hear. I tried to do it in a way where they would hopefully pay some attention to it. So I would try and set it up well when I introduced it. Being an English Major I was always pretty verbal, able to put some reasonable phrases together, so after a while I figured out ways of doing it. The other thing that happened at this gig was that all these friends of mine from LA ... and they would come down to San Diego and they would be playing in various people's back-up bands and such. So they would get off the gig and they would come down and sit in. So, even if we hadn't had a lot of people in all night, the place would be packed for the last set, just to see who was going to float on in.

So there you are in Chicago, being a single performer. Were you still doing Old Time?

No, I really, after I left California I really didn't. I got very interested in Celtic music, because going to Mariposa was the first time I really heard a lot of Celtic stuff. And you know, at night back at the hotel all the Brits would get together and get in a room and bellow together. I heard pipers.

And I was looking through the records and found that old Topic record of Billy Pigg and Northumbrian pipes. And again, "Loved it, how can I get a set of these?"

I got hired to open the show for Doc Watson at the Bottom Line.... My first big New York gig as a solo. So I go to the New York Public Library and there in the reference section is a book titled "The Northumbrian Bagpipe" And what is it? It is plans to make your Northumbrian bagpipes. I Xerox the thing, went back to Chicago and make my first set of pipes.

I was playing a lot of that and immediately started playing the pipes in the show a lot. And I really didn't get back to playing old time at all, until about the middle Eighties, I was living in New York, and giving lessons at the New School for Social Research, part of the Guitar Study Center, and I was the only one on staff who taught traditional music of any kind. Everybody else was teaching you how to become the next Rock and Roll hit guy. So I got anybody who wanted to learn finger style guitar, any kind of banjo, any kind of traditional anything ... they immediately gave them to me and figured that I could figure it out. I had been doing this for a couple of years and realized I had lost a lot of stamina in playing.

Anyway, I heard there was an old time session going at this bar in New York City. And I thought, "You know, what better way to build up my stamina than to be going down with a bunch of guys who are playing A tunes, ninety miles an hour. And I have to sit there and beat an A chord for four hours. This is exactly what I need. So I went down there, and the first night down there, here's Harry Bolick and he's leading the session.

And they're playing a bunch of tunes I'm not familiar with at all. And he starts doing all these rhythmic things. Well, the next time around, I pick up on it. And he looked at me like, "Oh, cool. He gets it!" So we started playing together. And then with Harry, I started coming down here to North Carolina to Mt. Airy Festival and Galax and we put a band together, "Tunesmith". And one of the earliest editions of the band was me and Harry, Jim Garber, Sam Zygmuntowicz, who is a world class violin maker. I knew him first just playing old time. The original band had him and had Stephanie Winters playing cello. So we had five of us ... Two fiddles, cello, me playing guitar and banjo and Jim playing mandocello and mandolin and stuff like that.

Let me digress here. One of the questions I can't ever get answered is; every once in a while we get a wave of Classical trained violinists who come down, see Old Timey music, go bgugugugugugugugugug! And start playing it. So why?

I think probably it's the energy, it's the fun and there are enough players around whose chops are really good, that they go ... I think they are mystified by the fact that they've spent twenty years studying all this technique, and they can't immediately jump in and do this. That there is something else going on that is elusive to them. And some of them get it, and some of them don't. I had that experience in Swannanoa, just last week. I was sitting there a little bit and this young woman sat down next to me, with her violin, beautiful fiddle, the bow was ... ivory frog, ivory, you know, gorgeous thing ... classically trained, you know as soon as she assumes the posture, and puts the bow to the strings. I'm sitting there playing some D tune. And she's trying to play along. And rhythmically, she's not getting it. And so I stop and say, "OK, put all the accents ... you know all those eighth notes you're playing?" She says, "Yeah". "Accent on the third one.—Dat—dat—dat—" and she had a lot of trouble doing that. Because it wasn't ... that's not what you do in Classical music. They don't kick the back beat much. Or if they do, they don't do it for long. It's not integral in it.

Thou shall not swing?

Well, I wouldn't put it that way. It's a different way of doing things. The people who catch on to it the best are the ones who have a lot of experience playing Baroque stuff. If you play Baroque the music the way it was intended to be played, it's got a lot of kick to it. If you just read the notes off the page, it's about as deadly dull as playing a page full of scales. As soon as I told this girl to just accent every third one, she could do it, but she had to really con-

centrate hard, but immediately it was like I turned on a light bulb. "Oh, it's like this. OK ..." And then I had to go somewhere, and she was going somewhere, but at least it turned on a light bulb.

In an interview, they asked Ralph Stanley, "How come nobody can duplicate your style, Ralph?" And he said, "Because it's too simple." If you're going to play blues well, it's a very Zen thing, knowing what to leave out, and how little to play. The same thing for any good music. I don't care what it is. One of the things that makes Earl Scruggs great, is not the notes he plays, it's the stuff he leaves out. It's all the holes.

And Old Timey banjo can be such a sparse, open ...

It can be, or there are the guys who are just playing the typewriter ... going dagadadagada ... And it doesn't let up. Too many banjo players forget that they are the only one in the band with a drum. The rhythm guitar player is fine, but it is really the banjo player who is the timekeeper, because they are playing the smallest common denominator of the rhythm. And if they're locking in, and doing some nice little rhythmic pushes, and stuff ... if they're being the drummer, then the whole group is just lifted. Like one of the ways old time is very much like Baroque music, is that it is an ensemble thing. It's not a solo thing. Bands that work are ones where everybody is doing their part. And there isn't any grandstanding. It's a matter of making the whole sound best. Sometimes that's just drawing back so that just one thing can come out, and by the other token, if there is a hole, and its your turn to fill it, then go in and fill it. Don't be timid about it.

What about the Minstrel Old Time banjo?

I made my first Minstrel banjo in '88. Knowing Pat Conte, really is what ... I got kind of tickled, "Hell, I can make one of those." It's like the redneck's last words [45]*, with me it's "How hard can that be?" So I made my first one, and loved it, and that was a five-string, and played it for a couple of months, and somebody practically ripped it out of my hands, handed me money and said, "I want that now!"*

How do you see the flow from Anglo dance music to Minstrel to Old Time?

It's not too hard to put together. At least in the over-all. The particulars get a little fuzzy. Colonial period you have no identifiable American music. You have all these cultures coming together, mostly British Isles and German, fiddles, fifes, lots of wind instruments. You have some plucked instruments; you have the slave population with their banjoes, those old four-string gourd banjos, with the little short fourth one and three on the fingerboard. You got those documented back to the Seventeenth Century in the New World. And then you have out-of-date Western Art music. Because this country, in the Colonial period, was the outback. This was a backwater. After you get into the Nineteenth Century, and the country begins to get a sense of itself as a separate entity, by 1830 you're beginning to get what's called American music. You have these travelling shows which are called circuses, which travel around. There is a tradition of white guys imitating black guys going back to Restoration Drama in the 1670's.

The first music hall, opera house, in New York City, they had a blackface guy playing banjo in the 1780's.

Right. So you have an old tradition of this. Joe Sweeney had grown up on a plantation outside of Appomattox, Virginia, which was a hotbed of banjo players on the plantations. And had learned to play them from the slaves on his parents' plantation. I grew up seeing his banjo. It's in Southwestern Museum in LA.

So he started playing for these circuses. They would bring out the banjo player to entertain the crowd while they were changing the scenery. By 1840-41, you have the Virginia Minstrels formed, the first Minstrel troupe. These minstrel shows become fabulously popular. The banjo takes the country by storm. By 1850, there's like four factories cranking these things out as fast as they can crank them out. There's banjo clubs, the patent office is filling up with patents, and a huge amount of the material that we play today as old time music, you can find out exactly who wrote some of these tunes, because they came out of the old Minstrel tradition.

Uncle Dave Macon's parents ran a Minstrel hotel for Minstrel troupes. And that's where Uncle Dave learned to play banjo. All the tricks and all that stagecraft that he did. So you don't see frets on banjoes much before 1870. And you don't see steel strings much before 1900. By the time you get to W.W.I and then after the war ... and then you get this boiling pot of all these things coming together. You have the recording industry, and the mail order houses, making instruments available to people who had to make their own before or go without. You have more communication between the country and the city because of Prohibition.

A polite way of putting it.

But Prohibition was a major reason for guys from the city to come out to the country to get moonshine and run it back in. People were making a lot of money. Also helped entrench the Mafia. Thank you, Congress. [46]

Al Capone played the banjo.

But what struck me about old time music from the earlier period, was the variety that it had. Because bands were made up of whatever anybody could throw together to play together. What always struck me about the old time musicians that I spent any time with was the fact that they didn't think of music in categories. It was just music they liked. Period. The End.

All those pictures that you see of these old time bands and it's two fiddles, banjo, cello, and guy standing there with a clarinet. So when I go to a contest and they say, "An old time band must consist of banjo, guitar, and fiddle", t alk about music Nazis. I mean that's one of the things that impressed me about "The New Lost City Ramblers" when I first saw them—all the variety of the stuff they did. When I saw Clarence Ashley playing, and the variety of the stuff that he did.

Music doesn't stay in the same place. If it does, it dies. It's constantly changing. Just like you see at any fiddler's convention. You go there and it ain't what it was ten years ago. It's going to be changing. What's remarkable to me, is now people like you and I, we are becoming the Old Guys.

So why did you move down here?

We moved down in 1989. The short answer of why is cheap real estate. We wanted to get out of New York. My father-in-law was alone out in California, we knew we didn't want to go back to California. I had been coming down here to fiddler's conventions. One of my banjo students from New York had just started a real estate company in this area. And so we came down and then made a couple of trips down just to look around at houses. This house came up on the market. It was perfect for us. It needed a lot of work. Now it needs a lot of work again. You know how it is where sometimes things in your life, they work out? If it's the right thing, it just all falls together and you're there. And so, in a very short time, my father-in-law was here, we were here, socked in—badoom, badoom, badda-boom baddabing.

It's a small word out here, but what I find really amusing is I've played more Klezmer music in the last ten years with "Mapamundi", playing weddings and bar mitzvahs, than I have since I was a teenager in high school when I used to play that stuff every week.

Your music, I have three of your CD's. You do some Civil War tunes. I don't know if I'd call it Progressive Old Timey, but very broad … and the bowed dulcimer. Say something about "The Horse Flies" and all that.

I like good music. Whatever it is. That sort of Caribbean approach to old time music—some of it is great and some of it stinks.

Traditional music is real interesting; you won't know for about five years what things are going to stick. But the way traditions work, is they absorb certain things, and they throw other things off. Back in the '60's, amongst the bluegrass banjo players, there was the Scruggs camp and there was the melodic banjo camp. And people got into fist-fights over that stuff. When Newgrass came out people were just … There was that hippie music, and then there was the other stuff, and one side said, "Aww, they're just straight-laced assholes," and the other guys said, "Aww, they're just dope-smoking assholes." Everybody was an asshole. Now you go and you hear somebody like Doyle Lawson, and if you don't play a blend of the two, you're not working. Same thing with the old time bands.

The band I had in San Diego, "Buffalo Crotch", we would take all these rock and roll songs and make them bluegrass songs. Kenny Lordes was our banjo player; we used to do tons of that … 'course we did all of that album that "The Charles River Valley Boys" put out—"Beatle Country". They were all from Boston.

I first heard of Bill Keith and Richard Greene and being Boston people. And Peter Childs … They were friends of Jim Rickard.

The first time I saw Bill Keith was at that same Folk Festival in '64 that I saw Eck Robertson. He was playing with Bill Monroe, and of course Bill called him "Brad" Keith, because there was only one "Bill" in Bill Monroe's band. That's when all that melodic style banjo was quote, "brand new". Of course Classical banjo players in the 1870's had been doing the same thing, but nobody ever thought of that.

I saw this guy twenty years ago—could play melodic frailing. It was just the loveliest thing I ever heard. At the Wartrace Festival.

Ken Pearlman does that. The big flasho clawhammer banjo player in the '60's was David Lindley. I'll never forget at the Topanga Canyon Banjo and Fiddle Contest in '65. He got out there and played "Arkansas Traveler". The first minute and a half, he did not use his right hand. And when his right hand finally came crashing down on the banjo, the crowd just exploded. It was astounding.

You are helping the bowed dulcimer revival.

It was played with the bow up until about W.W.II. And then everybody kind of forgot about it. The bowed versions were around a lot. The Mercer Museum up in Doylestown, PA, has got four or five originals in there. I keep hearing more and more about the originals.

There are some in the Smithsonian. At Merlefest this year, Marsha Harris was sitting there playing hers. And this guy from Kentucky come up to her and said, "You know, my Momma played the dulcimer just like you. I haven't seen anybody else play just like my Momma 'cept her." I started doing it, because I'm fiddleistically challenged. I can play upright and in that position, it just feels right to me. And I'm playing in an area that all the fiddles and banjoes are playing up high. And the bass players down low, and there is that kind of middle area down there that nobody is doing anything. So I'm kind of down there. So I can go and sit in with a group of people jamming, and it fill a hole and I already know the style and everything. So it's a welcome addition.

Instruments are just instruments. It's up to the people who play them to make them work in any particular context. At Mt. Airy, this year and last, there was this guy from Winston that plays tuba, you might have seen him.

Mike Teague.

He sits in with old time groups playing tuba and it's perfect! It's great! Nobody's covered up, the bottom's there, the runs are there, and it's got that extra little something that you don't get from a string bass.

If you've got people who kind of know what the boundaries are, the instruments themselves really don't matter. Otherwise, how else does the Greek bouzouki become a staple of Irish music. To the point now, where someone will say, "Oh, you play the bouzouki, You play Greek music?" And they go, "Gee, I didn't know they used it in that!"

Or banjoes in Ireland. I don't know if there's any Irish instruments left in Irish music.

Celtic is able to absorb a lot of different sounds. Instruments are just instruments. I know with my bowed dulcimer, I've been playing Klezmer on it, I've been playing old time on it. I've been playing Shephardic songs … I'm starting to be able to play some Swing songs on it … as my technique gets better, and I handle these things more. And to me an instrument is just a tool. It's just learning how to use the tool.

Letter From Chris Wig

In 1969 I bought a Bacon bluegrass banjo that came with a Pete Seeger Song Book. Soon I had that resonator off and was practicing all the different styles in the book. I had played guitar before—Country and Folk, and by '70 I was into the popular folk music of the protest variety. I began playing at local coffeehouses and joined the Canton Area Peace Movement.

About this time I got an album of Art Rosenbaum, an old-time banjo player who played clawhammer style. I wanted to play like that, but couldn't figure it out. One day in 1972 my cousin from West Virginia, who was attending the University of Michigan at Ann Arbor, invited me up and took me to meet his friend, Stan Werbin, then also a young student already immersed in the old-time traditional music scene. Stan, later to become the owner of Elderly Instruments in East Lansing, MI, showed me "drop-thumb frailing" and I was hooked. I worked in a bowling alley then and between calls of "ball on lane 5" and "out of range ..." I would practice the arrangements in John Burke's book Old Time Fiddle Tunes for the Banjo.

The next year I met Dave Neff, a banjo player from Uniontown, OH, and soon I was a member of the "Blue Eagle String Band," along with Dave and Diana Neff, Bob and Carolyn Riley, and a fiddler named Ed Courier. We played local venues including workshops at the Kent State Folk Festival, which is where I met Wil Bremmer. Wil owned a music store and instrument repair shop in Spicertown, a section of Akron near the university. I visited him many times, played banjo tunes and sang U. Utah Phillips songs. We'd go to the Byrth Coffee House near by and hear ... a countless array of folk and traditional musicians. I remember wishing I had a place that would do it all, i.e. instrument repair and coffeehouse—a real folk music center.

Well, you gotta be careful what you wish for, because you may actually get it. In 1976 I apprenticed with Scott Antes to build Appalachian lap dulcimers at his shop in Uniontown, Ohio called "Boulder Junction". We sold at the arts and craft shows. He also ran a coffeehouse. Then one day Scott announced he was selling the business and, to make a very long story short, I bought it. After awhile Dave Neff and I became partners (Dave and Scott were the original founders), thereby adding his vintage instrument connections, as well as considerably more business acumen than I had. Our "success" with instrument building and repair/restoration subsidized the coffeehouse through which we met many wonderful folk and traditional musicians. Most played at the Kent Folk Festival.

Well, being a banjo player, I was often around fiddlers and took advantage of free lessons and pointers ... from whoever ... would take the time. Another early influence was Columbus fiddler, Charlie Williams. I was in a band, "South Forty," with Charlie, Roger Phillips, John Sherman and Richard Colb. By 1980 that band had disbanded and Roger and I were asked to play with the "North Fork Rounders," then down to two members, Les Powers and Mike Hopper. With a 5th member, Tom Atwood, we played together for 20 years and still occasionally coalesce for a job or party.

In 1991 Dan Levenson asked me to play fiddle for the "Boiled Buzzards" with his wife Ruth on bass and Annie Trimble on guitar. It was then I renewed my journey into Southern Appalachian fiddle and dance tunes, a pursuit in which I'm still engaged. From being a buzzard, I next spent some time with the "Mustel House Muskrats", the Mustel House being a tavern on the Ohio and Erie Canal in Akron back in the 1830's. Of course we played canal songs and fiddle tunes—always fiddle tunes!

For the past 10 years I have concentrated on attending Mt Airy Fiddle Convention, Mt Airy, NC and Clifftop Old Time Music Festival, Clifftop WV, learning the fiddle, making friends and playing tunes. In 2003 I began recording with Mark Olitsky, one of the best clawhammer banjoists around, and Dave Rice, a seasoned guitarist ... That CD entitled "Gate to Go Through" contains many tunes I learned from WV fiddler Melvin Wine, who shared his treasures freely with whomever would learn. And that stream of consciousness into the past suits my sensibilities as I pursue more of those fiddlers of the older styles.

John "Doc" Holliday
Telephone Interview

I got a phone call from John Holliday early in this process, and tried to scribble down some notes about the reincarnation of Illinois Style Old Time Music during the period 1973-83. There seems to have been a certain disdain for the Easterners and the more academic style of Old Time Revival; Holliday and his mates wanted their music to be more German and French influenced. Much faster, for faster dancing. The word was "steppy". Keep it steppy, play both ways on the bow.

This was similar in some ways to the Long Bow style from Mississippi, what the locals called "Nigger Style". One of the earliest bands was the "Indian Creek Delta Boys", which merged into the "Volo Bogtrotters". The fiddler was Lynne William Byron "Chirps" Smith who doubled on mandolin. Another fiddler was Garry Harrison, fiddler and researcher of Illinois fiddle. Holliday called him, "Best fiddler you never heard". He was the son and grandson of Illinois fiddlers, and usually played with his twin brother, Terry. The Harrison brothers had a hobby of creating hot air balloons with candles and garbage bags, in the hopes of igniting UFO reports, if not the woods.

The Illinois style was a conscious alternative to the "shuffle style" of Round Peak Style. Truer to the tune, more melodic, and using the long bow. They seemed to be pretty proud of their local style and called "Highwoods" "bouncers", which was not a complimentary term. Garry thought he was more authentic than "Highwoods" and Holliday called him "very opinionated"

They were friends of Bob Carlin's and Pete Sutherland, who learned from Harrison, as Holliday remembered. Harrison was called "eccentric but important, with a perfect memory, can remember pictures on wall of recording studio." Harrison is also a ukelin virtuoso and maintains a Dolceola page on the web.[48]

Both bands are featured on "The Young Fogies II"—"The Indian Creek Delta Boys" with Harrison playing "The Devil in the Haystack" and "The Volo Bogtrotters" with Chirps Smith on mando playing "The Crow Song"

Holliday remembered that they recorded their third album in "a drunken brawl". Drinking 509 beer, and recording all first takes … "It was "about putting out tunes no one had ever heard". They made a "point of playing the most obscure tunes". At the time they were all in their twenties, mostly factory workers. Somebody, my notes aren't clear, worked in a sewage plant, another in a furniture store.

There was a strong anti-academic bent from Garry, who would never do vocals to aggravate academics, seeing it as an "us and them situation." Their avowed goal was to "lighten up Old Time."

They played in the Battleground festival with "Miles Crassen who wrote Old Time fiddle books with Bruce Molsky". They played tunes like "Wild Horses" and "Stony Point" in march time to aggravate people, "trying to be unpolitically correct". Garry and Terry's older brother, Steve "Scurve" Harrison, the banjo player, would pick fights with promoters and then try to blow them away with technique.

Their finest hour was when they got so drunk Bill Monroe tried to throw them out of Beanblossom, and they laughed him out of camp. And now some of them are members of Academia. Somehow, it figures.

Todd H. Cleave

Todd Cleave is on a few of the mail lists I subscribe to, and I gleaned a few fragments from his emails.

In 1956 I was 16, and I talked mom into taking me and my sister to Marine Hall Auditorium, San Francisco, to a Pete Seeger concert. Mom, a REPUBLICAN, noticed skin headed guys in gray flannel suits taking down license numbers. She called one of the young spooks over, wiped off the license plate of our 54 VW with handkerchief, and said, "Be sure you get it right young man!" I was never so proud! My Mom was a real Republican!

Six years later, I got Top Secret-Crypto Clearance from ASA. And then, years later, local politicians called me a bearded, commie pinko Berkeley "red"! I left, in hysterics! Six generations, and counting, of career service in US Army and Navy, and he calls me a "red"!

Traditional (AKA "Folk") music has long been a subject of scholarly, academic study—parallel and in conjunction with academics on your side of the pond. 'Hope you include the spread of traditional tunes, instruments via the Old Left, often with new, political words and overtones in the Thirties. It was revived in the late Fifties in New York, Boston, various college towns across this country.

During all this, the "Folk" carried on being the "Folk", sometimes bemused, sometimes irritated, by earnest young college kids—collectors wanting to "collect" in the field, sort of like entomologists. God forgive me, I was one, working in Kern City, CA around Bakersfield in summer of '58, '59 looking for Dust Bowl refugees to learn tunes, playing styles. I was delivering Agricultural bug poisons to remote air strips, 80 plus hours a week, left hand on the steering wheel, banjo in my lap, practicing rolls, living on A&W chili-dogs, orange freezes!

Grandpa Jack Rollin taught me 1890's finger picking on banjo, including the "Spanish Fandango". He was 96; his family lived in the middle of a 20-acre pig farm ... in intimate association. When I visited, 'nose burned out after 20 minutes or so ... He came out in the early Thirties from Paul's Valley, Oklahoma, and told me, from direct personal experience, about being driven out of camps at gun point when their usefulness was over, by sheriffs, ranchers, farmers, etc. 'Sure made Steinbeck's books come real!—I was 18, I learned a lot from him after I realized he was a treasure trove of classical banjo and traditional mountain music! After my nose burned out, I could really learn from him. I used to have to bathe, wash clothes after a session at his place so I wouldn't lose my job driving truck. Count your blessings; wheat smells better than pigs!

When I think now of the nature of the stuff I was delivering on an old bobtail truck, I get cold shivers! When I'd get to the strips, crop-dusters were waiting to pour the stuff in tanks ... by mid-summer, their eyes were pinpoints. Chem companies were making nerve gas derivatives; never any warning to field workers living nearby to clear the area. Got sprayed a few times myself driving past a field being sprayed. Nowadays they have to post fields, move people out, close roads when they spray some of that stuff ...

Chapter Eight: Movin' South

One of the things you need to understand about the Old Time aesthetic is that there is none. There is a tradition, but it varies place to place and person to person. This valley sings "Sally Ann" this way, and the next town over doesn't sing while playing "Sally Ann" that way. The traditional people are way too smart and individualistic to follow any rules. And the revivalists are almost as bad.

Every person I dealt with in this research is a genius, and every one of them has a different vision of what Old Timey is. The collectors and the ethnomusicologists can talk to each other, sometimes, but the punksters and the hippies and the feminists and the academics have little to say to each other. And so they just play together. The songs are simple, and the rules are self-evident. You can play music with somebody for decades, once or twice a year, and have no idea what their names are, or where they come from. Fanatics are like that. Tom Mylet is not a fanatic, but somehow he knows them all. He was into Old Time real early, and unlike me, he knew what he was doing. Tom is an affable man, modest and comfortable. His wife Marianne is a mural painter, and they have two daughters.

Tom Mylet Deposition

I was brought up in the Philadelphia suburbs of South Jersey: Camden, Pennsauken and Westmont. I got into folk music without really knowing what it was. I was an insomniac with an old tube AM radio in the headboard of my bed. I'd lay awake all night tuning in all sorts of weird, funny stuff: Lee Moore, the Coffee Drinking Nighthawk on WWVA, Wheeling, West Virginia after the Wheeling Jamboree. He'd broadcast all night, mostly for truck drivers. Sometimes he'd sing and play guitar live; stuff like "The Cat Came Back." He also had great commercials for The New Piano Method: "imagine the joy of sitting down to your piano, or your neighbor's piano and playing the hits that are so popular today ..." I can still remember writing down the address for the baby chicks. "Happy, Healthy Red Top Chicks, earn good money, big money in your spare time, 10, 20, 30 dollars a month."

It was my plan to send them to the lady next door and watch when they arrived. I can still picture my vision of Mrs. Steinberg arguing with the mailman. Of course it never happened. The station always seemed to fade out at the key moment. But it didn't matter. There was plenty of other funny stuff just up the dial: John R. on WLAC, Nashville, playing nothing but the down home blues; Wayne Rainey on WLCKY, Cincinnati, one Oh Hi Oh. He played a lot of Stanley Brothers and sold his harmonica method along with the Miracle Picture of Jesus.

A few things happen around the same time that pushed me further in that direction. I first heard Folk Music with Gene Shay—a Philadelphia institution. The first hour was records and the second hour was live music and interviews with whoever was playing the coffeehouses in Philadelphia. Here I first heard Dave Von Ronk and people like that.

About the same time I read a review of the first Philly Folk Festival. I talked about it so much that the next year my parents closed our little grocery store early on Saturday and we went. Man, that was a whole new world for me. I especially remember John Hurt. By then I had a guitar and was learning from my Aunt Ella. She had taken an adult course at a local high school and was getting together with her old classmates once a week to play and sing stuff

like "Five Foot Two, Eyes of Blue". At the time it seemed corny, but it gave me a pretty good foundation in chords and playing with others.

I eventually found the first John Hurt album and started trying to figure that stuff out. I was also trying to learn from records by Dave Von Ronk, Patrick Sky, Tom Rush, Phil Ochs, anybody I could find. I kept going back to the Philly Folk Fest and got to see Son House, Skip James, Gary Davis and Fred McDowell. I also saw and liked the instrumental side of Bill Monroe and the "Stanley Brothers". At that time the singing was a little too much for me. I was also really into Jim Kweskin, and especially Leadbelly on record. I eventually found the Harry Smith Anthology too. A high school friend, Jeff Murza and I tried to be the white version of Sonny Terry and Brownie McGee around then.

By then I was at a two-year college in Philadelphia and transferred to Western Kentucky University in Bowling Green. I started playing at the folk music club and the local coffeehouse. I wound up in a local band called "The Squeeky Clean Jug Band" and met a teacher there named Bill Koon. He ran the folk club and offered to trade me home cooked meals for Brownie McGee-type guitar lessons. It turned out to be a good deal and another real eye opener. He had a Ph.D. in Folklore and had done his thesis on Frank Profitt. He also had what appeared to me to be a wall of records, a wall of instruments and a wife who not only could cook but sing harmony too. This became my dream.

He took me to one of the first Tennessee Valley Fiddler's Conventions in Athens, Alabama. That was like entering another world. We camped out by the fair grounds. The fair was in full swing and I thought I'd check it out. An old guy who was there for the fiddler's convention stopped me and said I couldn't go over there. "It's nigger night at the fair, no whites allowed." I was a dumb kid from New Jersey who had never even heard of something like that.

I wound up backing Bill Koon on guitar in the banjo contest. I didn't realize it at the time but it was really something. Sid Harkreader, who had played with Uncle Dave Macon on the Opry played in the contest and didn't even place. I remember seeing George Gruhn there with some banjos on a card table.

It was at this time that I heard of the Union Grove Fiddler's Convention. I hitchhiked from Bowling Green to Union Grove during Easter break to meet up with Jeff Murza, my friend from New Jersey. This would have been '68 or '69. At that time you played in a gym, the auditorium and a fair size tent. I remember seeing Little Jimmy Edmonds and Wade Ward and Kyle Creed. I know it was Kyle because he was wearing a cowboy shirt with his name across the back. The "New York Ramblers" were also there, but the hippies hadn't discovered it yet. I wound up going every year until it was closed down and went from wide-eyed observer to winning the old time banjo category.

After I got out of college I wound up working as a social worker in Camden. This kept me out of Vietnam as long as I stayed there. It also gave me time to play and look for instruments. By now I was into the banjo and would plan my client visits around junk stores and antique shops. At one time I had thirty some banjos. Great stuff too, mostly Fairbanks. I got to hear a lot of great music around Philadelphia at the time too. One time I went to a bluegrass festival in rural Pennsylvania and met the "Morris Brothers" (the ones who gave Earl Scruggs his start) and the "Blue Sky Boys". I also met Jerry Milnes there. He went on to be a musical partner for the next few years.

Jerry lived a couple miles from me and was learning to play the fiddle. I was playing banjo, guitar and mandolin by then. Along with Jeff and few others, we started playing regularly and went to the first Smithsonian Folk Festival. They had an old time string band contest. We came in third. A guy came up to us and asked if we could play for a dance. He was trying to break up some sort of rally or protest. It turned out to be David Peel and a pro-marijuana rally.[49] *I was really torn but went along with the band and played.*

The guy who called the dance turned out to be Stretch Pyott, then the president of the Philadelphia Folksong Society. When he realized that we were from the Philadelphia area, he suggested we do some dances around the Delaware Valley. This became a really steady gig, two or three nights a week. It seemed that anyone who wanted a square dance would call the Folksong Society for a recommendation. Stretch got the gig and called us. Jerry and I bought a sound system based almost entirely on the fact that it would fit in the back of our Volkswagons. We must have averaged a couple hundred dollars a week each.

Jerry and I were also going to West Virginia at this time. We met some of the great old timers there partly through Dwight Diller. He had just stumbled onto the Hammons family.

We were also going to Sunset Park in West Chester, PA on Sundays. All summer they had either a local bluegrass band opening for a big name country star or the opposite. There was lots of great music in the parking lot including some old fiddlers who had moved up north for work years before. We also hooked up with the only other old time stringband we knew of in the area: "The Brandywine Friends of Old Time Music". That was Carl Goldstein, Shel Sandler and a woman fiddler, Ann Yerpe. We used to go down to Carl's house one night a week and play with them. I wound up getting a couple of interesting things out of that.

One, the fiddler was more interested in European folkdance than playing fiddle and the Brandywine Friends went from being a band to putting on concerts and eventually festivals. I was lucky enough to be involved with planning some of the first events. At that time I was also looking to play music with a little more punch and Carl was forming a bluegrass band and asked me to join. The band had a great hard-driving banjo player, Troy Spencer, who kept us progressive upstarts down to earth. I was trying to play hot guitar and listening to mostly Django and Charlie Christian but to be honest, I think it sounded more like very slow versions of bad Clarence White. It was a great situation though; I was able to know and play with a lot of the local older bluegrass guys.

During this time I was still playing old time with Jeff. We decided to open a music store: "Collingswood (NJ) Stringed Instruments". It seemed like a great idea and worked for a while but Jeff and I had different business philosophies and we were both just married. Jerry Correll, who I knew from the Brandywine Friends had moved to

Grayson County, VA and invited me down for a visit. Grayson County seemed like the answer to a couple of my dilemmas: moving could gracefully get me out of the music store with my friendship still intact with Jeff and the local stringbands were just what I was looking for: old time music with plenty of power.

Marianne and I moved down and started going to the local fiddler's conventions. It was a great scene. There were all these older guys still playing the old stuff plus a bunch of young outsiders like me who just showed up to learn from them. After a while, Dale Morris, one of the few local young guys who really appreciated the old time stuff came by and asked if Kyle Creed had called yet. He had seen Kyle and Kyle had mentioned that he thought he'd ask me if I'd like to play banjo in his band. Dale quoted him as saying I "seemed polite and kept good time." This was the ultimate complement . Kyle was and still is my all time favorite banjo player.

We not only played together but Kyle taught me all sorts of stuff: plumbing, horse-trading, cutting timber and dragging logs out with a horse. For someone from New Jersey this was really amazing. While Kyle had almost no education, he was one of the smartest people I've ever been around. He really took me under his wing like a son or grandson. Getting his approval really gave me the in with all the other old guys. I played banjo or mandolin with the "Shady Mountain Ramblers", the "Pine Ridge Boys" and the "Smoky Valley Boys" as well as the young bunch.

At fiddler's conventions I'd be camped up on the hill partying with the young guys and Kyle would send someone up to get me so we could play in the contest. Kyle thought I was the best person to tune the instruments so I'd be there trying to act straight and tune up everyone: two guitars, a bass, a mandolin plus the fiddle and banjo. It was a real test.

If somebody asked, "How does Kyle play the banjo?" I would say, "Go to Kyle's house and go look at the bathroom". The door that closed the bathroom opening, also closed the linen closet ... So one door swung and closed two openings. Everything about Kyle did something like that. "Hey, you're inside and you want that door closed, but you might want something out of the closet. You don't need the linen closet closed when you're in the bathroom. And when you're not in the bathroom, you don't need the door closed, so just use one door". One door, two openings. He ran the water pipes in the ceiling so they wouldn't freeze.

I became great friends with Dick Tarrier and John Hilston. John is a great old time fiddler. We still get together from time to time. Dick passed away a few years ago. He was living next door to us at the time. Some of the "young" bands from then were the "Cork Likkers", the "Rebel Yellers" and the "Swamp Cats". The "Cork Likkers" are still together after more than thirty years

In 1981 Marianne's father died unexpectedly. She went up and stayed with her mother in New Jersey. I came up that spring. Some people up there wanted to form a band but I had been spoiled. It didn't seem as exciting or relevant playing up north so I passed. We were up there for about seven years before we moved to Winston-Salem. We moved here because it was close to our place in Grayson County and large enough to have a few city amenities and decent work.

Through Dick Tarrier I met Kirk Sutphin. He's a great fiddler and banjo player. He does all the styles of traditional music in a hundred-mile radius of this area, dead on right—Piedmont style, Round Peak, and so on. Kirk has been a real inspiration to play with. There's also a lot of music between here and Grayson County. I just counted up, that in the last year or two, I've played in bands with at least a dozen different fiddlers at dances, contests, street festivals and God knows where else. I've also played a smattering of blues and been in a jug band. And now my younger daughter Chloe is playing and dragging me to fiddler's conventions. There's no end in sight.

Stalking the Wild Bojo

At this point, I must introduce a figure of legend, the mythical Bojo. He was a Catholic kid from the DC area, who, for some incomprehensible reason, left his comfortable suburban home and his daddy's car dealership to come down and learn "authentic" banjo. He wound up with Dave Sturgill, and learned to make banjoes and play in the most pure style, and never once noticed that he was driving everybody around him to distraction. Bojo stories abound. He was the Pat and Mike, the very Rueben of the Old Time Revival. He was so sure that he was the True Vine, all 20 years of him, that he felt it was his duty to pass judgement on the real old timers.

He thought Kyle Creed was a little slack and Dave Sturgill was beneath contempt. The fact that Dave and Kyle gave him the run of their shops and kitchens never seemed to register. All in all, the hillbillies were a bit of a disappointment to him. They just didn't seem to be authentic enough.

Annie Nonomus: We knew Bojo well, we spent a lot of time with him … one hour … It always seemed a lot longer.

He was at Sturgill's when I got there … He's like this huge incredible walking-backwards machine … Dave decided that we were all going to go hunting … He had lots of old cheap war surplus guns, so he gave each of us a rifle, me and Pruney … and we go out there, and I actually saw a buck. But I drew a bead on it, and the scope was all fogged up, full of moisture. Pruney just went out and sat down and smoked cigarettes … We're freezing … it's raining … it was miserable … And Bojo had just spent all summer restoring an old pickup truck … And he hit a deer … A five point buck! And he's like "Look at this scratch I put in my truck!" … And there's a scratch three inches long in his new paint … "Bojo, what did you do with the deer?" … "I didn't want to put it in my new truck … It might bleed on the bed … I left it on the side of the road" … So they went back and got it, and it was the best buck anybody got all season … He had hit it on the antlers and broke its neck … Not a mark on it … And he was totally obsessed with the scratch on his new paint … And not thinking that he had done better than Dave and his brother Sid and all the other mighty hunter hippies, and had come up with two hundred pounds of burger! It's a wonder nobody killed him.

Annie Nonomus: We went over to Kyle's one time and his wife said, "You won't believe it … Bojo was here with that kid of his, and the kid was walking around and his diaper kept falling off, and finally he came in and he said, 'Percy, do you have a stapler?' And he staples the kid's diaper together. Because the sticky tab wasn't working."

Late in the Bojo years, he went over there and had Kyle help him finish a banjo. And I think they got snowed in, or his car wouldn't start, and Bojo spent the night. And before he left … it was a big deal … because he had a Tubaphone rim, and I wanted to trade him something … "No, no, I'm going to keep this rim." … Kyle wanted the rim too. He does all this work for Bojo, he puts him up for the night, he gives him breakfast, and then Bojo is ready to leave, and Kyle goes, "Hang on a second". Kyle gave him a bill! And Kyle wound up with the rim. I was about to give him like two hundred dollars for the rim, and he wound up giving Kyle the rim for helping him!

But on the other hand, Kyle and Percy would give you the shirt off their backs, if you weren't a pain in the ass …

I remember one time; he had the most obscure banjo record that could ever be. And some guy on there obviously made a mistake in the middle of a song. 'Sounded like he kicked over his drink, and he wound up putting nine and a quarter beats in a bar or something. And Bojo sat there for days …

Trying to figure it out …

Making us all listen … trying to get that to work. "Bojo, this is nuts … Either he's drunk or you're crazy … it's not happening." I was over at his place, one night after a festival … And there was no car. We got dropped off at his place, and it's way out in the woods, no phone, in Piney Creek someplace. And me and him and Pruney and Steve G—got dropped off there. We were drunk. Well, me and Pruney and Steve were hammered. And there we were.

And it was Sunday morning, and Steve hadn't bothered to tell us he had Juvenile Onset Diabetes. First thing in the morning, he wakes up and starts having diabetic convulsions on the kitchen floor. This is real. This is really happening. I'm going, "There is no way to get this guy to the hospital. There is no human way. The hospital is twenty miles away. Even if we had a phone …" Our choices are, walk a mile or so to Sid's house and wait for him to get out of church. Period.

So, Pruney was a doctor's son and he ran to his car, which didn't work, and groveled under the seats and found a few packets of Macdonald's sugar ... The only sugar in the place, and he's prying Steve's mouth open with the back of a spoon ...

I didn't like Steve; I was disgusted with him putting us in that position ... I was getting ready for him to die and for me to walk down to Sid's ... So Pruney is prying his mouth open and sticking the sugar in. And Steve is in total convulsions ... And Bojo is running around with a jar of honey and a wooden spoon ... I swear to god ... "Don't give him sugar, sugar is bad for you! You should have honey, it's organic!"

I can hear it now. I can see it happening. The guy is dying ...

Dying—Steve is—at that time, one of the leading lights of Old Time music, and he was turning blue and dying. Well, Pruney got enough sugar in him so save his life, and he got up and his ride showed up, and off he went, and he may have thanked Pruney, but I have no memory of it. And a few months later Steve pulled the same routine in a hotel room someplace, and there was nobody to save him. And he died. I doubt if he was thirty yet. He must have wanted death passionately. He was such a beautiful blonde boy and all the girls just loved him. And so, as they say, it goes.

Jerry Correll

Jerry started playing folk guitar in about 1970, in Wilmington Delaware. He was interested in "The Sound" and listened to Lee Moore. He moved to Southwest Virginia in 1974 after playing guitar and fiddle with OT jams in Wilmington and a "pseudo bluegrass" band in Cecil County, MD. In Virginia, he played with the "Cedar Springs Band", (Doug Young, Brian Yerman, and Dale Morris) and "The Wolfe Brothers", a long lasting band that has included Dale Morris, Brian Yerman, Casey Hash, Hogie Siebert, Roger Wilson, Jim Gehske, and others over the years. His fiddling has ranged from the Galax Sound to a more Ozark sound over time. He usually goes to the Galax and Independence festivals, and in fact was commissioned to write the Grayson County theme song "Oh, Grayson County".

He dryly notes that he "tried and failed" to live back-to-nature, and wound up working for the local Post Office.

He has four Wolfe Brothers CD's, noted for a lighthearted and eclectic approach to OT, aided and abetted by the lyrical gifts of Casey Hash. Jerry also has a solo fiddle CD. He doesn't study any styles but has a good collection of recordings from many regions. He is now retired from the Post Office and the Army, and says that 100% of his social life has resulted from OT music. His daughter plays horn in the high school band, and "fools around" with acoustic instruments. He sees "very little tension" between the Appalachian peopl, and the imports, and hosts a yearly party at his hand-made house during the Elk Creek Fiddle festival in June, that is a magnet for players of all ages. The setting is lovely, in a grove of tall trees, next to a large pond. There is a pot luck brunch and, in keeping with Jerry's Chesapeake heritage, crabs are devoured.

He thinks that competitions tend to "one dimensionalize" the music and relegate it to its most elemental level and also minimize fiddlers' "repertories". On the other hand, competitions foster interest in newer players.

"I was born in Northeastern Pennsylvania in 1947 and grew up in Wilmington, Delaware. There were no musical roots in my family other than an uncle that played saxophone in several professional Chicago based jazz "Big" bands.

I first heard the "Sound" quite by accident. Sometime in the early 60's I set my clock radio alarm to 4:00 am for a fishing trip with my dad. Somehow the tuner got set to WWVA in Wheeling, West Virginia and I woke up to "Wildwood Flower" played and sung live by all night DJ Lee Moore, The Coffee Drinking Nighthawk. 'Hadn't heard anything like that before and I loved it. What a great sound to start off a day of fishing! 'Bought a guitar while in high school and gravitated somewhat to the 60's folk style music of early Dylan and Ramblin' Jack Elliot. I just sort of folk-strummed along.

After graduating high school in 1965, I went away to the mountains of Eastern Kentucky, enrolling at Union College in Whitley County. There I first heard genuine mountain music picking. 'Met a banjo picking friend there—Ken Landreth of Marion, VA. Ken was very knowledgeable about bluegrass and traditional music. He taught me to correctly back up his banjo playing with my guitar (a Hagstrom!), took me to local shows and festivals and introduced me to the nearby Phipps family of Barbourville, KY, who played the Carter Family style of old country music. I remember one early bluegrass festival we trekked to with Ken laying on the floor of my Peugeot, working the accelerator cable with a pair of pliers while I steered and called for more or less gas.

Although I was learning more about the music, I wasn't too focused as a student and dropped out, got drafted by Tricky Dick. In May of '69 I got shot in Vietnam and was retired by the Army on a disability. While a physical therapy patient at the Veteran's Hospital, I met some genuine local Old Time Music revivalists who fostered and nurtured my interest in the music. Carl Goldstein, Sheldon Sandler, and Mike Hudak had become old time music aficionados, while Jerry Miches, Tom Mylet, and some friends would come over from New Jersey for weekly jams at Carl's house. This gang founded the "Brandywine Friends of Old Time Music" and I served as its first Treasurer.

Because of my "Nam" wrist wound I couldn't play the guitar anymore so I bought a fiddle and set out to learn how to play it. I also enrolled in the University of Delaware. I was able to parlay my music interest into an under graduate research grant to collect field recordings of traditional singers and musicians in Southeastern Kentucky.

In addition to the "Brandywine" OT group I began to interact and play some music with local Appalachian musicians whose families had migrated to the Maryland-Delaware area, particularly the Lundy family from the Galax area and Ola Belle Reed's family, rooted in Ashe County, NC. Fiddler Jerry Lundy, grandson of legendary Grayson County Fiddler Emmett J. Lundy, was especially helpful and encouraging to me with my fledgling fiddle playing. During the early 70's I also joined my first "band" "Fertile Dirt"; we played a longhaired, stoned, style of music that might be described as pseudo bluegrass.

I graduated from U. of Del in 1974 and with about one hundred dollars, a useless BA degree in Anthropology, a wife, a fiddle, and a VW bus, we headed to the Galax area of southwestern Virginia in pursuit of mountain music, a "back to the land" lifestyle as glorified in all the "Mother Earth News" magazines we had been reading (usually while stoned) and maybe even a job.

We found an old farmhouse to rent for $25 a month in the Saddle Creek Community of Grayson County near Buck Mountain. It had no hot water or indoor plumbing but enabled us to save some money and eventually buy a nice piece of property in the Elk Creek Valley of Grayson Co. to build on. I worked, briefly, at the local welfare department and local community college before taking a postal service job.

Musically, I was in heaven! I met local musicians and fiddlers, Bruce Mastin and Dean Ward, and numerous outlanders, and revival musicians, like myself, that had come to the area in pursuit of music. I felt very comfortable and well accepted by the local music scene and enjoyed the friendships with the "outlanders" also. There were festivals, competitions, jams, parties and dances, and concerts everywhere and I was a happy and improving fiddler.

In 1987 I remarried to a local girl, Donna. She soon became enthused with the old time music, began to play the string bass and we both play in the Wolfe Bros. Donna and Casey are local folk and I'm the outsider-OT Revivalist—a combination that has brought us a bunch of fun over the years."

Donna Correll Interview

Donna is a local girl, and is perhaps the most articulate and educated individual I interviewed for this project. She has strong opinions about the White Top Festival of the Thirties and has sharp observations of the Old Time scene.

So the White Top Festival was this elitist deal?

It became; "What do you do, how do you keep it pure?" And one of the guys, his big deal was that it was a big Anglo Saxon thing. I know Ralph Blevins, in White Top, who was a kid when that festival went on, and he was at that school that was run by John Thompson, and they taught them the Scots Sword Dance for that festival ... So they were teaching them, and the kids were proud to learn that, but here they were trying to act like the standard bearers of a culture that had never been there. And it wasn't even existing in England at that time. It was kind of bizarre.

But Ralph has very fond memories of it and the school. He was one of those who went away for his working life and came back. But just the whole idea, that once you put your hand on it, it's like Captain Kirk: "First, do no harm to those cultures you are coming into".

Jerry sometimes fusses that there is an approved list of tunes, and if you deviate from that, then you're wasting your time. But they had the same thing, back on White Top. The management didn't want people playing things they heard on the radio, being influenced by that. So the musicians were altering themselves to fit into a competitive mode to put on the show. The more things change the more they stay the same.

I'm not sure I like competition at all, but it provides enough of a budget to keep festivals going.

It's a necessary thing, as long as you don't get too bound up in it. I thought that it was really fascinating to read about the White Top Festival. My daughter is in the marching band at school, and the same issues come up when they have competitions.

I have heard that at Galax, they give the money to the people they want to see come back. And there is a certain amount of charity involved. If they know somebody's wife has died, they might be more inclined to award a prize.

I know of a band whose bass player died, and the Moose didn't want them to use an non-registered substitute. I know the people involved.

Don't know how important Galax is anymore, anyway.

To a lot of people, Galax is Mecca. I am involved in the Crooked Road Program, and you don't speak against Galax.

People who hate it say that there is a lot of money vanishing, but I did a little figuring, and I don't see than there is actually a lot of money there. The big money is the camping fees, and a lot of that goes right back out again to the musicians. I worked it out, and it's about fifteen cents an hour to camp there. It's a lot of money to the extent that the County budget is like forty million a year, but it comes in and goes out ... boom.. they stamp the state check with a rubber stamp and its gone. If somebody was to show up with the odd hundred thousand it would be a lot of money.

There is a sea of humanity that comes in and pays their admissions.

One night. Five dollars.

Two nights, and it costs more now. One year Jerry didn't get us registered, and like a lot of people, some friends had extra people registered and we played under those names. Well, they recognized Jerry, I guess, with binoculars, and they told us that we cost them money by walking across the stage. And even if they had given us a refund, how did we cost them money? It's like, you know, you took up time on the stage. But isn't the point to entertain the crowd? And the weird thing was, the next year, our contraband band's picture wound up in the program.

I see that happening. Sometimes a band will get into trouble, and the next year they will get into the program, or accidentally get hired to play for the cloggers or something.

That was a long time ago, and we haven't done anything like that since then, but you really feel like they have long memories for some things. But everybody does like that. The only thing I didn't realize that we would be so recognized, because this was a long time ago. But as a place to go and jam, to be around people, every one should go. And I like it for that, but not for the competition.

No. It's silly. When I was back with the Sturgills in the Seventies I was pretty consistently placing in banjo, and I didn't know anything. I had no idea what I was doing. And later when I knew what I was doing, I couldn't place. It may just have been that Kyle Creed liked me, or something.

That's the thing, these are human beings and they, of course have their preferences. And if they are not the same as yours, so what? They don't have to be yours. You want to have yours, have your own fest.

Sure. They have to eliminate 90 % of everybody immediately. And it doesn't really matter, who. I can remember when the "New River Ramblers" won every year. And they made all the hippies cringe, wearing those straw hats and the overalls with the patches. But those were the Galax guys, and they played what the judges wanted to hear.

And they went everywhere, representing Old Time Music to the world. As if standing up drunk, playing an instrument was the thing, in blue overalls with red patches.

I never could tell if they knew what they were doing, but now I think they knew exactly what they were doing.

They played for Liz Taylor, and they played for everything.

It wasn't too long ago before that, that Woody Guthrie and his uncle were a "Hillbilly Band" and they wore straw hats and overalls. What does that make you feel like, though?

There is no doubt that there is a package to crossover from being a musician to being an entertainer.

Bob Carlin's book[50] documents that up until the Sixties, Old Time Bands had Blackface comedians, even on television in Winston Salem. And Ronnie Stoneman, who is here at this festival today, as the grand old lady, was directly in the Minstrel tradition on "Hee Haw". That's pretty much of the package.

You know how it became popular? There was a band from Galax, actually, "Al Hopkins and the Buckle Busters". But they called themselves "Hillbillies". They went on the vaudeville circuit and popularized the term. In the late Twenties. And they were the first really popular band. And actually, at the music center today, they played part of a piece of footage, a film from that time. They actually did a short trailer for an Al Jolson movie. Overalls and real goofy ... They were real entertainers. When the camera was on them, they made sure they got their close up.

String Bean and Grandpa Jones.

And they made a good living out of being a caricature of themselves, and that's fine. A lot of people took exception with "O Brother" but I thought it was great fun. That's obvious caricature; nobody believes there are people like that; it's too over the top. But, on the other hand, there was another movie out the same time; it was trying to be a serious treatment of it. The misconceptions that it perpetuated were far wore. I did not like "Songcatcher".

I have an idea that the reason this area is so fertile with traditional music, is that it's just a little too far from Nashville to pick up "The Grand Ol' Opry". It's over the hill. Here there is no place to go, to "make it." There is a lot of Bluegrass in DC, but no money. No music scene in Atlanta, and it's a little too far to go to Nashville. So what you do, is stay home and play on the front porch. Which is actually the healthiest thing to do. Play for your neighbors, play with your neighbors.

They were talking about that at the Music Center too. There were actually four or more musical groups that come out of the cotton mill at Fries. The first one went to New York and got recorded, and then another one went, and another and another. In one way, it's just amazing that that many people of talent came out of such a tiny place, and even one place of employment.

I am from here, and now I claim that legacy. I was not part of music at all, growing up. I grew up one road over from Enoch Rutherford, knew him my whole life, he used to come over and put up hay for my grandpa, and never knew he played music. Not until I went to my first fiddle festival when I was grown, working for the Independence Declaration newspaper. When the fiddlers' convention was in Galax, we actually didn't even go to town. Now my parents come out to the festivals.

But on the other hand I knew E. C. and Orna Ball, I was in church singings, E. C. Ball gave me a quarter once to sing in church. But I didn't know that I was hearing anything different than what everybody else was doing. I hope it kind of got in there, even though it really went over my head, because I was like six. But the whole thing of it was, when I was growing up here, most people who had exposure to the rest of the world, i.e. Northern Virginia, were not too proud of where we come from. Like it was something to overcome. And now, with this celebration of the music, what it evolved into, and these hippies got older and assimilated into society, then I don't think that kids growing up today have that feeling of inferiority at all, which is a very good thing.

Chapter Eight and a Half: Henry Heckler Reminisces

So like in 1971 or 2, I was at Union Grove, trading instruments, setting up in my van. This guy brings over a banjo, it's a Little Wonder pot, Vega Little Wonder, a pretty good little pot, and it had a home-made neck on it, hard-shell case, five string, home-made left-handed neck, really poor quality. So I figured, I like an Old Timey banjo, I played just a little bit of Old Timey banjo, not much, so I'll take it, have a neck made for it. It was pretty cheap, 75.00. It was a fair amount of money then, but still cheap. So I take it home and of course I don't do anything with it. A couple of years later, I'm at this big Old Timey party, in Lexington, the "Breaking Up Christmas Party". With Odell McGuire and his whole crew, and this young college kid comes down, and he's a real good banjo player. Odell goes, "Man that kid has got real potential." It's David Woods, and he's still in college, come down from Oberlin. And he doesn't have a banjo. And I'm at this party for three nights, but I don't feel like driving home. I got cows. I say, "Listen, I got this banjo, you drive me down." So we drive up to my house, and I go across this board, to walk the creek, across the creek, and I feed my cows. And I grab this banjo, and I sold it to him for what I paid for it, which I think was about forty-five, fifty bucks. He takes it home and makes a real good neck on it. David turns out to be a real good banjo player. This was a twelve-inch pot, instead of the normal eleven, or ten and fifteen sixteenths. I talked to David about it, and the guy in "Highwoods String Band" also had a twelve-inch banjo. But ten or fifteen years later, here's all these kids scampering around because they need a twelve-inch pot, because David is playing one. So he started this whole trend, the most desirable banjoes are like twelve-inch pots. And that's the whole reason behind the twelve-inch pots.

Dave Sturgill had a twelve or thirteen-inch Orpheum that he loved because it was the same as Charlie Poole had.

After Charlie Poole died, I've got a whole bunch of people who came from around that area, Eden, North Carolina, I met at least ten people who had his original banjo that they got from his widow or his family member, you know. This Orpheum banjo. At least ten of them. And they got it from a family member. I'm pretty sure that banjo was destroyed in a fight. 'Cause Charlie used to womanize. And I think somebody took it and smashed it over his head.

Chapter Nine: Clogging the Electric Glide

It may once have been that the mountain folks held on to their own old ways because they didn't know any better, but that was long time gone. The railroad changed all that a century and a half ago. The Civil War made this one nation in more ways than one. The Union Army standardized rail gauges and telegraph conventions coast to coast; American always were an itchy foot bunch, but they got worse.

Dave Sturgill's father homesteaded a farm in Montana and got droughted out in 1910 or so. The story was they drove a Marmon automobile all the way there and back. The Marmon was one of the first cars that could make it up the mountain to Piney Creek. There were no Model T's that could pull the grade from Winston. They had to go up hills in reverse, because they didn't have fuel pumps. And Sparta didn't have a railhead. Galax did. Supposedly, the Marmon motor ran a sawmill until the Sixties ... I won't swear to that, but I have seen the motor in Herb Barr's junkyard. Dave Sturgill's father had both the money and the desire to leave Piney Creek due to his employment, which was as a Revenue Officer. That one fact will tell you quite a bit about the Sturgill family.

It is so easy for urban persons to assume they are the sophisticates and the rural person the rubes, but it takes a lot of knowledge, hard work and savvy to be a dairy farmer. No room for error there. It's not "Rebecca At Sunnybrook Farm."

And the mass culture is always available; the Sturgills treasured some early edition Tarzan books that were read transparent years gone by. If the mail could get there, you could get anything. The real issue was the cash. Once a year, they would sell their tobacco and that was what cash they had.

The W.W.II generation had all the options. If they played Old Time, or made instruments, it was a choice. And their grandchildren can do the Electric Glide or the Macarena to fiddle songs, or clog to "Achy Breaky Heart" if they so desire ... I've seen them do it. And you don't want to be on the dance floor when fifty kids are clogging and dancing the Electric Glide at the same time ... Miss a turn and you might get stompled.

Dave Sturgill, when he lived in Maryland, worked for Western Electric, as an engineer, although he had no degree. He played the rube, but actually he was a techno-geek. He was part of that generation of luthiers that included Semie Moseley of Mosrite and Paul Bigsby and Leo Fender.

It is frequently stated by liberal arts types, that engineers are defective people, lacking in depth and human emotion. However, engineers have one overwhelming advantage that makes them some of the happiest people on earth; they can turn their dreams into functioning hardware. Any dolt can make a sculpture, but it takes a lot of hard work and knowledge to make a sculpture that will do two hundred miles an hour and let you live through the ride. Correspondingly, it feels really good to do something like that and, even better, to have some sort of quantified measure of success.

Hot rodders and experimental aircraft builders do it every day, completely ignored by the Artistic Elite. Both Dave and I gave up entering craft shows and art exhibits. Making musical instruments is so much more complex than painting or pottery, that it's just silly. It requires serious woodworking skills, some metalworking, painting and finish work, design and more than a trace of acoustic intuition. What always happened was that we would win all the prizes, and sell not a thing. It seems odd that people will gladly spend thousands on a picture of a guitar, or a sculpture of a musician, and not be able to see that a hand-made instrument is an artwork too.

Another low down genius was Albert Hash. He had worked as a machinist, and did something at a secret tear gas factory in Southside Virginia during the Vietnam War. He settled into making fiddles, and started creating wonderfully unique instruments. They were varnished in bright colors, had parrots carved for the pegheads, and brightly colored mosaics inlaid into the backs. He used toothbrush handles for the inlay stock. Dave was no slouch as a machinist, but Albert was in a class of his own.

Somebody brought him a 300-year-old grandfather clock and asked him if he could fix it ... It required all new gears, which had been hand made out of brass. He analyzed the problem, made new machines to cut the gears on his trusty South Bend lathe, and while he was at it, figured out the wear patterns and upped the specs so that he could make clocks that would not wear out for a thousand years. He machined new bearings out of synthetic rubies from broken laser crystals; designed stronger casings to eliminate flex, and worked in a phase of the moon escapement. So, after a little work, he had tooled up to make grandfather clocks that were guaranteed to last a thousand years. "And if they don't last the full thousand years, you just bring them right back, and I'll fix them for free." Albert's daughter, Audrey Hash Hamm is still making fiddles in her father's style.

I have already mentioned Kyle Creed, and his views on efficiency. He was such an original thinker in everything. Unlike almost every other banjo player, he used a hand made pick on his index finger. After years of trial and experiment, he had determined than the best brass to use was from the reflector of a Model T Ford, and so he made sure he had a lifetime supply of Model T headlight reflectors.

Another thing the Yankees never grasped was that the Old Timers were, "Just Folks", not stars or outlaws or celebrities. They might have made a record or two, but they still had to make a living. Everybody played, and everybody had to work. There were nephews of Charlie Poole's fiddler, Posey Rorer, playing and scuffling just like everyone else. They had a saying in the mountains, when asked about the Depression; "We never heard of no Depression, times was hard, and they stayed hard." Similarly, there never was any "Old Time Music". There was music. You played what people wanted, and what you liked, and that was music.

Yankees, especially the academic Yankees, are so blinded by Category; they totally miss the economic and social realities of music making, north or south. And they all missed the point; I didn't have to listen to old records, I was getting drunk with the cousins of the people who made those records. Although that evident fact never seemed to penetrate the intellectual crust of some Yankees, who would bring down their treasured scratchy old 78's and listen to them while ignoring the live jam sessions right in the next room. Go figure.

Mountain people are amused rather than insulted by the "Beverly Hillbillies" and "Hee Haw" ... Hillbilly, to a certain extent, replaced Zip Coon as the comic stereotype, and people from Jimmy Rogers to Woody Guthrie to Tom Ashley to String Bean to Grandpa Jones made a buck or two playing the rube. I suppose Ronnie Stoneman is the last of the breed, or Leroy Troy, a younger man who does the Dave Macon schtick. An inherent part of the act is playing the fool, as per expectations ... But some times, as in the TV show "Green Acres", it's the city clicker that gets taken ... "Arkansas Traveler" probably goes back to Babylon. And there are whole genres of jokes, the Jonathan Slick and the Traveling Salesman stories, that flip these stereotypes like flapjacks. There are also families of jokes where the modern fool, "The Polack," meets the modern trickster, "The Nigger".

"So these two Polacks get a mule, and they decide to build a shed. And they measure the mule, but when they do, he had his ears laid down. When they get the shed finished, the mule has his ears up, and the Polacks see that he won't fit through the door. So they start fighting; one wants to cut the door bigger, and the other wants to just cut the mule's ears off.

While they are arguing, a Nigger comes by and listens for a while, and then he says, "All you have to do, is dig out the floor a few inches and the mule will walk right inside."

And one Polack says to the other, "Ain't that just like a damn Nigger! The mule's legs ain't too long, his damn ears are!"[51]

Your average grad student could get a whole book out of that joke, if he set his mind to it.

There is a constant thread in semi-academic Old Time commentary and debate, as to whether it is better to be "authentic", and use the word "Nigger", or to replace the offensive term with some other bi-syllabic designation. The same problem was being debated when I was in grammar school concerning Stephen Foster songs. That was resolved by vanishing the most melodic American composer down the Memory Hole. One Avant-Old Time band, The Cacaphones, solved that problem by changing the N-word to "Hippie", as in "Some folks say a Hippie won't steal ..." Older groups sang, "Preacher."

The Nigger, in Old Time iconography, was more of a mythical figure than a real oppressed person or race. This may have something to do with the Minstrel tradition, or just to the fact that black people are rare, if not unknown, in classical Appalachia. Tommy Jarrell sang, "Great big nigger lying on a log, finger on the trigger and eye on a hog."

The thrust of all the verses I know is that Nigger is a cagey character, ready to take advantage, but not actively malign. He—always he—might be in your cornfield or might be a poacher, might be Trickster.

All over the South, people of both races sang, "White man and a nigger playing seven-up, nigger won the money, afraid to pick it up."

Like blacks, moonshine has a certified place in Old Timey lore. Locally, the very best moonshine is "Peach Brandy" or simply "Peach", a slivovitz type distillate made from peaches in Ashe County, NC. Incidentally, the American Heritage Dictionary reveals that "the Slavic word for plum is sliva, which is related to Latin lividus, "bluish, bruise-colored," from which we get "livid", a word synonymous with our black-and-blue when used to describe the discoloration caused by a bruise." This is so appropriate.

Moonshine comes in three descending grades. There is the fine stuff the shiners drink, of which Peach is a good example. This is not the more common "flavored shine" where the liquid is drained from a Mason jar of peaches or cherries and refilled with white liquor. Peach is distilled from a mash made of peaches. The Yankees used to do something similar with apple and pears but they fermented cider and froze out the liquor. I have done this. It works. You could get hurt.

The next grade is corn likker, made from fermented corn and sugar, or in more modern times from the liquid that flows out from the bottom of a silo.

The bottom grade is "sugar pop", made from commercial sugar and yeast and water. All grades have been called Hillbilly LSD, and it was a common diversion in the early days to wind a hippie up on corn, and let him loose to see what he might do. The hippies sometimes turned hillbillies on to LSD to see what they would do. They both did all sorts of things.

I remember one old man I saw clogging and hollering, "Live and learn, die and forget!" No telling what he was on, but it was working.

Another guy I know vowed he would never drink shine again, because, "I come to, and I was dancing. With an *ugly* woman!"

A know-it-all swamp Yankee came down to see Fiddler's Grove one year, and was warned to not drink the moonshine that came in the jars with the green rubber rings; it was Bubba's shine and "weren't no good". Of course he suspiciously ignored this free advice and soon found himself puking between his legs, while sitting in the middle of the festival crowd. Which would have been embarrassing enough, but he was sitting flat on the ground. The same helpful local patted him on the back and said, "Don't worry about it, buddy,' happens in the best of families. You'll be a'ight."

My particular crowd never cultivated a moonshine connection, it was just as easy to ride to Sparta and get half gallons of Jim Beam for eleven dollars and change. That was enough trouble for any partially sane person. After all, we were potheads who had been saved from a life of shots and beers by Bob Dylan and Tim Leary. Alcohol hit us pretty hard, and some of us were smart enough to realize it. Some of us didn't.

One education major, the legendary Dick Tarrier, decided to make a still. Armed with a Foxfire book and a total lack of mechanical ability, he set forth on this noble quest. He had made friends with a certain fabled NASCAR garage, and whenever he was stumped, he would seek advice there. They were not fooled for a second, but invariably gave him sound advice, probably out of amusement. They also informed him that if he was to lift the top tank cover of the toilet, he would find a prize; the company quart of moonshine.

Dick is long gone, but I hear the still is still in action in an undisclosed location.

As we got established down south, we invited friends down to homestead and met other hippies from all over who were seeking the simple (hah!) life. Some of them were fellow refugees from Vermont, smart enough to realize that nine months of winter were sub-ideal for sustenance farming, and too dumb to quit and go back to the city.

One of Bud's friends, Pat Nash, moved down to Piney Creek and had enough survival skills to soon be counted on as a man of substance. He didn't play music, but loved it, and could split wood, cook beans, repair trucks, and do rough carpentry. I called him "Ramblin' Nash, the Classic American Rebel". He resembled a gremlin.[52]

He soon established a tradition of a Thanksgiving Party. All the freaks were invited, and came bearing pasta salads and bowls of beans. Pat had a semi-renovated farmhouse, and there were a few of the landlord's cattle out back. The landlord had inflicted on us a Border collie named Butch, who had a pathological hatred for cows. Butch had worked out a way to stampede a cow and then grab her nose and flip her right over on her back. This is not a recipe for contented cows.

Another classic Butch move was teaching the turkey to fly the day before Thanksgiving. It slowed down the proceedings until Bud and Pat could borrow a gun and harvest the turkey out of the tree.

All these threads would soon mesh.

Pat loved all that counter-culture-back-to-nature stuff, with his own whimsical twist, and had come up with an alternative way of cooking the turkey. This involved hanging the stuffed turkey by its legs on a string from the mantle of the fireplace. A twist on the string, and the turkey rotated slowly and evenly. Then a sheet of cardboard was covered with tin foil and used for a reflector. The turkey suspended between the fire and its reflection was soon cooking quite nicely.

A little too nicely, but Bud stapled a few strips of bacon to the bird with an Arrow stapling gun, and that moisturized the skin and produced a most enticing aroma. The drippings fell on the hearth, but a few more sheets of tin foil, (real hippies always had tin foil and Baggies) produced a drippings pan. All was well.

Guests arrived and substances were abused, and we set in for a long day and night of playing and eating and drinking and smoking. What could happen? Even the icy rain that started to fall seemed of little import.

And then the cow got her head stuck under the shed. Due to the backlog in the single bathroom, I went out to leak and noticed old cow, down on her knees, head under the shed. She had been probably licking ashes or salt from under the shed, and got caught. Cows are as dumb as Republicans, and never foresee the trouble their greed will lead to and never have an exit strategy. Even I could tell that this was trouble. So I told Bud, and Bud called up the landlord, and Landlord, who was watching a football game, deputized Bud to take care of the issue. The cow was over-age, and sickly, but was pregnant, and dosed with some medicine that made her meat inedible. If the cow could be kept alive a few months, the calf would be born and the meat sold, and Landlord could make a few bucks. Therefore …

So Bud and Pat ventured into the storm to free the cow, and the rest of us worked on getting a good buzz on and dancing in the drippings pan. With bumper jacks and come-alongs they lifted the shed and depressed the cow's head enough to free her. She lifted her head in gratitude, and slipped down the clay bank into a slimy red clay gully. Her limbs had stiffened with cold and she couldn't climb back out.

Bud ran for the tractor and some ropes and got the cow about half way up the slope before she collapsed onto the frozen mud. He raised an alarm, and we dropped our instruments, threw on coats and tried to push Poor Old Cow up the slope.

Cows weigh about 1,500 pounds and we were skinny back then. Ten 150-pound hippies do not equal one 1,500-pound cow. Bud would not give up, but his sorrowful looks availed him naught. He tried rigging "A" frames and all sorts of makeshifts to lift POC up and out, but to no avail. Eventually I convinced him that he was doing more harm than good, and we staked some hay bales to hold the cow where she was, and we went back in to disport ourselves in the classical manner.

Perhaps I overdid the Jim Beam, but in any case I was up at the crack of dawn, and went outside for a wizz and a breath of cold mountain air. The cow had managed to free herself from the hay bales and was now at the bottom of the creek with all four legs in the air. I didn't investigate farther, as Butch came around the house, wagging a guilty tail. I don't know if the calf had started to come out, or if Butch had gone in after it, but he was bloody past his shoulders, and swag-bellied to the point of pain. That was more information than I was ready for, so I just went back in and had a cup of tea and a joint.

I went home as soon as possible, and studiously ignored any reference to the great Thanksgiving Day Bovine Rescue Expedition from that day to this. But I did gain a different perspective on all this "Back To Nature" crap. Nature is a Bitch, and the farther away from her the better.

Sid Sturgill, Dave's brother, explained to me: "The good farmer is the cruel farmer." Time wasted on a sickly calf will endanger the entire herd. Sentiment is an emotion that only applies to people, and damn few of them. Culling the herd, disposing of genetically malformed lambs or calves and so on, is actually kinder than keeping hopeless cases alive for a few days.

Any farm needs a cat, and a dog, but they are not pets, they are tools—tools to keep the mice under control or to herd cattle. Sid, who had the charisma that Dave lacked, used a Honda Trail 90 to herd cattle. It was quite a sight, old Sid, ball cap on dead straight, yipping at the cows like a cowboy, putting around the herd on his yellow Honda.

He came into the shop one day, all biffed up, black eyes, road rash, scuffs and abrasions. He explained he had been riding his bike and a dog had run out in his path and he had wiped out at thirty.

"Next time, I'm going to hit that damn dog."

"You'll still wipe out."

"At least I'll take the damn dog with me." And he meant it. He had a great store of tales and stories, but you had to watch him. One day when we were chopping 'baccer, he had a bunch of hippies on the back of a wagon behind his tractor. After every trip to the barn, he would stop at a certain place in the field and tell us a tale. Eventually I figured that this was out of character, to waste daylight in such a way. I confronted him and he admitted that there was a huge sweat bee nest right there, and he had been stung the day before, and wanted to spread the wealth a little.

The best part about working for Sid was the breakfasts. The farm breakfasts had at least five kinds of meat: bacon, sausage, country-fried steak, sausage patties and souse, and every dish except the coffee had pork in it. And if you didn't clean your spoon, the coffee might have a little grease slick on it too. Everything was hand made and wonderful.

For lunch, dinner, all we had was a pack of Nab's and a coke, or perhaps a can of sardines, if it was cold. Sid liked to pour a tube of Tom's redskin peanuts into a RC Cola, and then shoot the whole mess down his throat. Lunch took him about two minutes of eating and a half-hour of telling lies.

TAKE A
724-7779

Chapter Ten: Meanwhile, Back in the Eighties

SAMURAI

SUBIO COMES ALL THE WAY FROM KYOTO TO THIS FIDDLE FESTIVAL IN SEARCH OF AMERICA. YOU SUSPECT IT HAS TO DO WITH HIS DADDY, AND HOW HE CAME HOME FROM BUNA IN AN ENVELOPE.

HE FEEDS YOU SASHIMI, AND YOU SHOW HIM THE SIGHTS, AND HE IS POLITELY DISAPPOINTED.

THE KONNAROCK KOUNTRY KRITTERS…. TOO YOUNG

THE HORSE FLIES…. TOO WEIRD

THE LAUGHING CRINOIDS…. TOO LEARNED

THE MUMBILLIES … TOO HIPPIE

HE HAS A THREE PERSON VIDEO CREW TAPING EVERY MOVE HE MAKES, AND YOU SCRATCH YOUR ASS EVERY TIME THE LENS POINTS AT YOU.

THE MANDOLIN MAFIA…. .TOO HAIRY

THE COOL AS GRITS STRING BAND … TOO URBAN

THE RED HOTS…. .TOO DRONEY

THE BHUDDA BELLIES…. TOO YUPPIE

ITS HARD TO FIND SOMETHING IF YOU DON'T KNOW WHAT IT IS, BUT ITS ALMOST V-J DAY, AND BANJO CONTEST AIN'T UNTIL DARK, AND YOU WONDER WHAT'S GOING ON BEHIND THOSE EYES. THEY'RE SLANTED BUT THEY'RE THE SAME COLOR GREEN AS YOURS, AND …

AND THE SLUTPUPPIES ARE SINGING ABOUT ANOTHER WAR.

"WHAT KIND OF SHOES DO THE ROUGH RIDERS WEAR?

BUTTON UP THE SIDE, TEN DOLLARS A PAIR.

IT WAS ALL ABOUT THAT BATTLESHIP CALLED MAINE."

TWO CLOGERINAS ARE BITCHING ABOUT DANCING BOOTS:

"WELL I'D EVEN WEAR COMBAT BOOTS IF THEY WERE SMALL ENOUGH, I'D HATE

TO WEAR OUT SOMEBODY'S GRANNY'S ANTIQUE SHOES."

"I KNOW JUST WHAT YOU MEAN, BUT IN "MOTHER EARTH NEWS", I FOUND AN AMISH CATALOG THAT HAS THOSE OLD…."

YOU HEAR YOUR DAD'S VOICE, "WE HAD THIS KID IN OUR OUTFIT, AND HE WAS KINDA DELICATE. HE WASN'T A QUEER, OR ANYTHING, DON'T GET ME WRONG, BUT HE HAD BEEN RAISED WELL AND WASN'T A ROUGHNECK

LIKE THE REST OF US. THE PROBLEM WAS HE HAD REAL SMALL FEET AND

WE DIDN'T HAVE ANY BOOTS TO FIT. WELL, NATURALLY HIS BOOTS ROTTED OFF IN THE JUNGLE, AND THERE WAS NO CHANCE OF SUPPLY. IF YOU HAD NO BOOTS YOU WERE DEAD, PERIOD. HE WAS CRIPPLED. SO HE WENT TO TAKE THE BOOTS OFF A JAP OFFICER WHO HAD NO FURTHER USE FOR THEM, AND WHEN HE TOOK THE BOOTS OFF, THE FEET CAME WITH THEM. I STILL REMEMBER HIM PICKING THE MEAT OUT OF THOSE BOOTS AND PUKING.

HE WORE THOSE BOOTS ALL THE WAY TO BUNA. GOOD MAN, GOOD BOOTS."

SUBIO WANTS TO MOVE ON, SO YOU TELL HIM YOU'LL FIND THE REAL OLD TIME MUSIC FOR HIM, AND REPORT BACK LATER.

SO YOU LOOK;

THE RAZOR LICKERS…. .NOPE

COUSIN CURTIS AND THE CASH REBATES … NOPE

NEE NINGY…. NO FUCKING WAY

WOLVES IN THE KITCHEN…. CLOSE, NO CIGAR

THE HUNGRY HOLLER HIGHSTEPPERS … ALMOST

FINALLY, YOU FIND THEM.

THE RABBIT HILL TAIL DRAGGERS. THE BASS PLAYER IS A HUNCHBACK, AND IS SITTING ON A RED VINYL KITCHEN STOOL. ONE OF THE FIDDLERS, THE KID, IS GROWN UP AROUND HIS FIDDLE LIKE A TREE AROUND A WROUGHT IRON FENCE. THE OTHER FIDDLER'S HIS PAW PAW, PROLLY. THE GUITAR PLAYER HAS A HERRINGBONE MARTIN WORTH AS MUCH AS ALL FOUR OF THE VANS THEY'RE PLAYING AT. IT'S GOT REFLECTIVE MAILBOX LETTERS STUCK ON IT SPELLING OUT HIS NAME; "RBjr". THE "j" AND THE "r" ARE A LOT NEWER THAN THE OTHER TWO LETTERS.

THE BANJO PLAYER HAS A CHEAP JAP BANJO, AND WHERE THE TRADEMARK WAS, IS STUCK A CONFEDERATE FLAG. HE'S GOT A PACK OF RED DOGS ROLLED UP IN HIS SHIRT SLEEVE AND IT EXPOSES A FADED BLUE TATTOO. YOU CAN JUST MAKE OUT WHERE IT SAYS "USMC" AND "TARAWA."

THEY'RE PLAYING THAT OLD STUFF WITH THE BARK ON IT.

"IF YOU WANT TO GET YOUR HEAD KNOCKED OFF,

IF YOU WANT TO GET YOUR KILLING,

IF YOU WANT TO GET YOUR EYE POKED OUT,

GO UP ON SUGAR HILL."

THERE'S A CHORUS LINE OF GRANNIES, DRESSED IN GINGAM, POLYESTER, AND TYE-DYED SWEATS, LEFT TO RIGHT. THEY'RE GONNA DANCE ALL NIGHT, COOK BREAKFAST FOR THE MEN FOLKS, NAP UNTIL DARK AND HIT IT AGAIN.

THE BAND SHIFTS GEARS, EMPTIES SPIT CUPS, FILLS DRINK CUPS, AND....

"GIRL ON CRIPPLE CREEK GETS HALF GROWN,

JUMPS ON A MAN LIKE A DOG ON A BONE."

SOME OLD GAL HITS THE CLOG BOARD, FEET FLYING. SHE'S GOT BLACK JEANS, A COWBOY SHIRT, AND YOU CAN TELL SHE'S A FLATLANDER, CAUSE SHE'S GOT MIXER IN HER DRINK CUP. SHE'S GOT A MOMMY-BUTT ON HER BUT SHE CAN REALLY HOOF IT.

IF SHE DON'T GET TOO DRUNK TO REMEMBER, SHE'LL GIVE SOME COWBOY A NIGHT HE'LL NEVER FORGET.

SHE'S GOT THE BAND ON THE STEP NOW, THEY'RE CLICKING LIKE KNITTING NEEDLES. THE BASS AND THE GUITAR PLAYERS HAVE THE DEADPAN

LOOKS OF MEN REACHING ORGASM, AND TARAWA'S PALL MALL IS ABOUT TO

BURN HIS LIPS. THE ACRID SMELL OF GRANNIE SWEAT MINGLES WITH MOONSHINE AND PALL MALLS. THE FIDDLE BOWS ARE FASTER THAN SEWING MACHINES, AND THE KID IS GRINNING LIKE A POSSUM. EVEN THE OLD MAN LOOKS LIKE HE MIGHT SMILE.... DIRECTLY.

"GIRL ON CRIPPLE CREEK LAYING ON A BED,

HAIR ON HER PUSSY STRAWBERRY RED."

THE GRANNIES NUDGE EACH OTHER, THEY'VE BEEN THERE, IT WAS. MOMMY BUTT'S OVERHET. YOU SHOULDN'T WEAR SATIN TO CLOG. SHE DRAINS

HER DRINK, BLOWS DOWN HER SHIRT AND SAYS, "DAMN, I'VE GOT SOME SWEATY TITTIES HERE."

TARAWA GIVES HER A LOOK THAT SUGGESTS HE'S GOT SOME HELPFUL IDEAS ON THE TITTIE FRONT. THE GRANNIES NUDGE EACH OTHER AGAIN, NEVER BREAKING STEP.

THE BAND PLAYS ANOTHER ROUND TO SHOW WHO'S BOSS, AND YOU GO FIND SUBIO.

"SUBIO, BUD, I FOUND WHAT YOU NEED. GO DOWN SPRUNG STREET TO BOBVILLE, GO LEFT AT THE CADILLAC CAMPER WITH THE COW HORNS, AND LOOK

FOR FOUR VANS WITH BONDO. WHEN YOU SEE THE RED HOT CHILE PEPPER LIGHTS, YOU'RE THERE. DON'T TAKE YOUR CAMERA CREW."

LATER I SEE HIM, HE'S NOT HAPPY.

"WATTSAMATTER, BUD?"

"I GO WHERE YOU SAY, BUT ALL I SEE WAS A BUNCH OF OLD DRUNKS.

I GO BACK TO JAPAN. AMERICA IS EXTINCT."

Eventually, in 1984, I quit smoking cigarettes, and what with the sudden rush of oxygen to the brain, decided to go to Galax Fiddlers' Festival. So I loaded up Dad's Plymouth Champ with a dozen funky mandolins and an old tent. For some reason unknown I threw my brother's conga drum in the back and took off.

When I got there, I found a scene of unparalleled debauchery, at least in a musical sense. When we had been there with Sturgill's, we stayed pretty much at their stand and answered dumb questions and tried to sell stuff. The last time I remember being there was in '76, and that was the week after the great "Stompin' '76" disaster. Galax was much stricter than Union Grove, and we didn't do much except play our song on stage and get our money back.

Felts Park, the venue for the Fiddler's, was a large fairgrounds, perhaps ten acres, a few blocks from downtown Galax. It is bordered by Main Street and on the other side by large and noisy furniture factories. It is a large rectangle, five city blocks long by one wide, and has a covered grandstand at the north end, and is split by a block of tennis courts in the middle.

Opposite the grandstand, back in the northeast corner, were several rows of tin-roofed stalls for the animals at the County Fair. The stalls, complete with assorted dung and straw, had been liberated by the hippies, much to the amusement of the locals. The hippies wanted a private place to smoke pot, and the stalls' tin roofs allowed a few more hours of sleep than could be gained in a tent in the field. The stalls were also wired for electricity.

Main Street was up a fifty-foot hill, and the park itself was famous for flooding. The Galax mud is beyond description. It is particularly foul, with a stench that is both organic and chemical. Perhaps it is the residue from the livestock, or some leachant from the furniture factories, but verily, it stinketh.

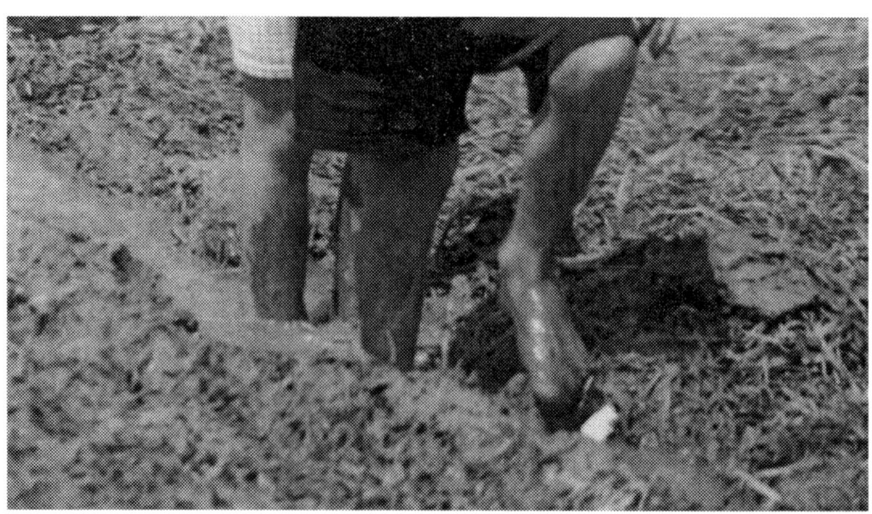

A pair of rubber boots is mandatory wear for Galax, and care must be taken that they don't get sucked right off your feet. I have heard a story of somebody losing a shoe in the mud and digging up two different ones before finding his own.

One year I ruined all my shoes in the deluge. I was down to a pair of flip-flops, and wore them in the rain until I got trench foot, which is blisters under your calluses. This hurts a lot.

I had only been away for five years or so, but the changes were immense. My old hippie buddies were well on their way to becoming the Establishment, and a new crowd had appeared and were breaking what few rules the hippies had left intact.

One of my old friends from Sturgill's was Dave Grant, who had had graduated from tub bass to "Slappin' on the Big Girl". He was in a band, "The Cacaphones", which included trumpet, accordion, glockenspiel, and other heresies. They were known for swapping instruments in mid song, anarchy, and genre crossing to the point of high art.

When first seen, he was imbibing heavily with divers odd companions, playing James Brown fatback riddim to ragtime songs and calling everybody "Rasta Debbil".

Chief Rasta Debbil was a demented-looking lad, with an ancient Dobson banjo and all his clothes on backwards. He was racing from jam to jam, frailing away like a man possessed, and playing the funkiest syncopations to everything. He broke strings as the day progressed, but kept playing until he finished the night frailing on a single string. I knew this was impossible, but I didn't say anything, for fear of unleashing demons.

That kid was Richie Stearns, and his band was "The Horse Flies". Other bands worthy of note were "Cousin Curtis and the Cash Rebates" from St. Louis, "Nee Ningy" and "Woodchucks from Babylon" from Chapel Hill and "The Mando Mafia" from Charlottesville, "The Laughing Crinoids" from parts unknown, as was a Cajun outfit, "OK Bayou". They were all nuts. It was obvious that I had been missing out on something.

One trippy note: when I set up my tent, I found a dope pipe and a Union Grove Bumper sticker, "I lost It At Union Grove".

This year, some hippies had taken over the stalls in the back of the festival ground, and there was jammage to the grotty max. Joe Thrift had a band, "The Bolo Bandits" with Tom Riccio on banjo and blind fiddler Rich Hartness. Nancy Banjo was no longer a waif, but was instead the head honcho of a new conspiracy, Bobville. Every body had a Bob name, Joe Bob, Plumb Bob, Chuck Bob, and so on. The jamming went on 24 hours a day, and there was a lot of reefer and other fun things on hand.

Joe Thrift and the "Bolo Bandits" had one of the corner stalls and were jamming non-stop. I would sit in on mando, playing as fast and as hard as I could, and when I would break a string, I would run up to my stall, and grab another mando and run back to play. The songs were so long; I never lost my place. I have a tape of them playing "Hangman's Reel" for sixteen minutes.

I managed to sell a few mandos, at least enough for beer and strings, and found a band to fall into. A very nice guy, Rick Friend[53], had brought a blender and was making Daiquiris as fast as the blender would run. He used up every banana and strawberry in Galax, and was down to Honeydew and Cantaloupe Daiquiris by Friday night. In any case, he needed a banjo player, or I thought he did, and we hooked up with a very small lady, Dea, who couldn't play, but could belt out the blues. We ran through our respective repertories and agreed on Maria Muldaur's "I'm A Woman" for our Old Timey Song. Everybody survived, and we got our money back. Dea even carried a fiddle on stage so we were sort of legal, at least trying to please.

Charlie Pickford tells a story of me offering a very drunk lad a cup of coffee so he could go on stage. It took a while for the water to boil, and we soon saw the guy eating instant coffee crystals right out of the jar, too drunk to wait for the water to boil. Probably true.

One of the landmarks of the New Galax was a kitchen in the end stall, decorated with Christmas lights and an eclectic selection of gimcracks and gewgaws. The signpost was the lifelike effigy of an Indian, seated in a lawn chair as if nodded out from excess. The kitchen featured a never-ending pot of volunteer soup, venison based, and hot water for coffee and tea. The proprietor was Mary Edna Thompson, who also runs the Galax Kazoo Contest. She is a tall blonde woman and sees the kitchen as her Ministry, I suspect.

Mary Edna Thompson

You have been coming to Galax for ...

Near is I can figure out about thirty years. Give or take a year or two. I keep thinking I need to go back and check my records. When I first came, I didn't play music. I just came and was up in the field watching and listening and realized there was more. The first two years I did that. Then I realized there was more than what was going on on stage.

Born and raised in Lynchburg. Probably lived half my life on this side of the Blue Ridge. And there was music in my family. And it was just one of the things I always wanted to do. And party was part of it, to be honest. I realize now there was more reasons than that for me to come down. What Galax was really all about, so I decided, "Well, I just need to play an instrument." So I got an autoharp and the Old Timeys took me in, and they started teaching me, and then years later, somebody gave me a fiddle, and that's when "Nee Ningy" showed me things.

I prefer to not call them hippies. It was the Old Time community. I don't like to label people, but they were the ones that played Old Time music. When I first started playing and got so enthusiastic about it—and you get so wrapped up in it—first thing you know it's three o'clock in the morning, and then you realize that you haven't eaten all day. And that was what happened to me and it was actually a prayer. And I said, "You know what, Lord? If somebody just had a pot of soup or a pot of beans, I bet it would help a lot of people." And I kind of heard Him chuckle, "Like, I knew that. Now you know it. So ... the next night I started making soup. That's twenty-eight years ago.

And when did you get the Indian?

He came around '85–'86. Made by Mark Cline, who's a sculptor-artist person. He brought him up here and decided it was something the "Kitchen" needed ... I had to commission him for a company I was working for. I told him, "You ought to check out Galax. If you've never been there, you ought to go."

We were "The Fountain City Frogstranglers"

Tell me how you smuggled a set of bagpipes on stage. .

We just walked up there. We were going to have a bagpipe in an Old Time band.

Tell me about the Kazoo Parade.

That was when Nee Ningy was here.

There was a certain amount of satire, I thought, with the rules.

It's complete paradox, well what happened was that "Nee Ningy", which was great—people loved them, would get disqualified. It was like the plague "Whoa, you're disqualified" But they would still get their money back. But we went up and talked to Oscar Hall about harmonicas being traditional and everything, and he said, "Yeah my daddy played it, but you got to draw the line somewhere." That's understandable. We were just walking back across the field, and it was like, "We just need to have a contest." So we played kazoos.

Everybody wins, everybody is Band Number Three.

And that kind of grew. But it was always a trophy. The very first year the trophy was a bag of Galax mud. Or straw from the stalls. Always the trophies are simple. So everybody wins.

I forget what rule is, "No Fun Not Allowed."

Number one.

Rule Number One. And sometimes they had this slightly raunchy bunch of skits.

It became that it was not child friendly. And I'm the biggest kid of all. So we kind of spread the word around and everything else, you got this very public ground—it's for the children and also to give the children an opportunity to do something in front of other people. And not being so afraid to go up on stage. A lot of people worked on it, and we spread the word around and talked to people and told them, "It just can't be … that's the best way to kill something".

It's about an hour, and then the parade. They do the Queen thing, which has nothing to do with sexual orientation … The Kazoo Queen. All of this stuff, it just grew. I never realized, twenty-three years ago, when we started the Kazoo Contest. And the same way with making soup. It's just something that the Good Lord blessed me with.

There are other things like the Mandolin Toss …

And the Fiddle In. Robby Wells, a fiddler out of Lynchburg started the Fiddle In. It's just an opportunity to for a big massive jam session. One change I've seen in Galax, there's not as many big open jams.

Tom Bailey

I actually started coming to Galax … my first and only time was about eight years ago. I was dragged here by a friend from England. Name of David Wright. Me and him and bunch of other guys were running around creating a terror. Playing Old Time String Band music. This is only my second time, actually.

I'm from Salem, Virginia. When I was young, I was learning how to play. I was playing with a bunch of folks that were my parent's age. And they came here all the time. And after I had been playing with their band for about a year or something, they were coming down here—this was 1979—so they asked my parents if they could take Tom to Galax with them. And they wouldn't have it, because they had heard about Stompin' '76. My mom and dad had heard about it. They said there was going to be bikers drinking moonshine and doing speed, and hippies smoking pot and doing acid, and being nekkid in public. From what I understand it wasn't too far from the truth.

Yep. And their little boy wasn't going to go do that. So. I was all of twelve, I think. No Galax for me until 1996 or something. I'm really sorry I haven't come. I love going to the smaller ones in the area. Like Grayson County. I try to go to that one as often as I can. I've been playing since I was ten.

Are your parents musicians?

No. They did everything they could to discourage it. I was playing all sorts of rock and roll. Hanging out with the bad kids and stuff, too. I don't know if it was the music so much as all the getting rowdy they were opposed to.

And I started playing Old Time music again, and I took a diversion plane to rock and roll for a long time. Ended up at Jazz Studies at VCU at Richmond.

A hotbed of strange music.

Of very strange music indeed. In '91 or '92, went up to Charlottesville to hang out, and wound up with a bunch of those guys in the Old Timey scene. In one night ... It was the debut performance of a band called, "The Free Will Savages".

Dave Grant and James Leva and Al Tharpe and Dirk Powell. So everybody within a two hundred mile radius came down to the bar. And a friend of mine had told me I would like this bar because they served Guinness. I ended up meeting all those guys and when I went home, I just threw all my stuff in the car and came back to Charlottesville. It was nice, but it wasn't all it was cracked up to be.

I have a fairly tame Dave Grant story. I had been helping Dave do some work, building Darlene's (Dave's wife) orchid hothouse, and it was the week before Rockbridge (Dance Festival in Buena Vista Va). And we had all been there and he had a whole bunch of other stuff going on, a gig with Robin and Linda Williams that weekend, and we were all ... got wrapped up on Thursday, and went up to Rockbridge on Friday and everybody was kinda, "Where's Dave?"

He had work work to do and had a couple of gigs he had to do. We stayed up about as late as we could on Friday night, and finally went to bed about 3:00. Come 4:30 in the morning, Dave come pulling in to our camp beeping his horn and flashing the lights on our tents, wakes us all up to shotgun beers. Which was the ritual at 5:00 in the morning. He had driven from his place out near Gordonsville, up to Lexington, back home to help Darlene do some stuff, then back up to Alexandria to do this other gig, then back to town to get his instruments and a case of beer, and then back up to Lexington. So he put in a lot of miles that day.

When I heard about his accident, we all ... I was living in New York City with a bunch of guys ... me and couple of other folks from the scene, when we heard about it, we just dropped everything and drove down for the wake. Very sad news.

I knew him when he first showed up. Even when he didn't know anything at all, he had a lot of flair, a lot of hell raising. He used to talk about some festival or party, the "Get Face Down Festival". Something about Bumpass, Virginia.

I know where Bumpass[54] *is. The first time I heard anything about the Old Time scene here at Galax, this fellow—Fiddly Davy—I was still living in Richmond. A bunch of other guys from Loudoun County came down under the auspices that they were a painting crew. They had all been down here, and they came back and reported a bunch of Old Time music in the stalls. They were all tripping out about one band called "The Horse Flies".*

"Man, you got to hear this! These guys are right up your alley." That was the first time I had ever heard about that. That would have been the summer of '86 or '87.

I must say that "Special Ed and the Shortbus" are well in the tradition of being whacked-out.

Oh, yeah. My dad still lives in Richmond. And I was down there in June helping him work on his house. I met Josh, the mandolin player, at this guitar shop he works at. He invited me to come down and have a tune with them. I had no idea what to expect. So I sat around and listened to the first set, and got excited about playing with them. The invitation was open, they kept asking if I had my fiddle in my car, which I usually always do. So I jumped in there in the second set, they kinda kept it sort of tame in the first set, and I was up there and had no idea what to expect ... I was laughing so hard I could barely play.

What were they doing?

The Special Ed Show. Making stuff up off the top of their head and they do like, traditional Bluegrass tunes right between the lines, and then do one of their own songs and they do like a Swing number, "Doing that Rag", play their armpits, tell really terrible dead baby jokes ... They got red-lighted last year.

Last year, they got inspired at the kazoo contest, and played kazoo right in the middle of their fiddle tune. And that red light came on so quick.

I think it was the "Mando Mafia" that came on stage and put down all their instruments and did a seven man Jew's Harp solo version of "Never Been Satisfied." So they yelled at them, and said, "You have to have a fiddle, banjo and guitar". So the next night they carried on a fiddle, banjo and guitar and played seven mandolins. Six mandolins and a mandocello. Whatever.

Mary Edna: Steve Parks was a Frogstrangler, and the fiddle player decided that he didn't like our attitude and he split the band. He took the banjo player and the guitar player, because he was going for the money. So the band split; that left an autoharp, a dulcimer, and a tater bug mandolin. So the first night we went up and did "Four Wet Pigs" acapella, and the crowd just loved it. So the next night I borrowed a fiddle, Peggy borrowed a banjo, and Steve had a guita;, we went up and hit the first chord, and then did acapella "Shortening Bread". I laid the fiddle down on the stage. Those were the stall days. They were very creative.

In the event, in '84, in spite of our worst efforts, none of the hippies won anything. A certain amount of grumbling was heard, and sardonic banjoist Bob Carlin, mentioned to a member of the "Cacaphones" that what they needed was a Second Line to mourn the disaster. (Shut up, Bob, this is my book) The Cacaphone, one L. Reed Dorsey, produced a trumpet from out of thin air, and Bob ran back to his car for his trusty clarinet. We were near my car, and the conga drum leapt into my hands. In a trice, whatever a trice might be, we had a marching band, with a few horns, a tenor banjo or two and a rowdy crowd of paraders. Dave Grant organized two short but sturdy women to hold his bass over their heads while he thumped out a backbeat.

I took about three swipes at the drum when a beautiful blond woman in a sarong appeared, and said, "You don't know how to do that, but I do!" So I held the drum while she frenzied upon it, and as quick as that we were blasting out "When the Saints Go Marching In". Banging on tambourines and wailing on kazoos we did a few laps of the fire lanes and eventually collapsed into a jazz jam in back of the stalls. I understand some people are still pissed.

Dave Grant Obituary
By REED WILLIAMS—Daily Progress staff writer

Guano Boys bass player and local radio host David Grant was remembered Wednesday as a gifted and versatile musician, a kind and gregarious lover of life.

"He was definitely a musician," said Charlie Pastorfield, a long-time friend of Grant's who plays guitar for Alligator and Big Circle and bass for Skip Castro Band. "That extended all the way into his personality. He sort of had a pirate quality in him. He really liked being alive."

Grant, 46, died Tuesday while working on a construction site in Buckingham County. He was testing soil in a six-foot-deep hole, probably crouching and recording information, when a bulldozer driver who thought the hole was empty began filling it, State Police said.

"He was literally buried alive," Trooper Danny Williams said. "By the time they got to him, he had already suffocated."

When the bulldozer operator, who police said worked for Palmyra-based Scott's Backhoe Service, noticed a rod sticking out of the dirt, he began suspecting something was wrong and ran to consult someone on the soil-testing team, Williams said. By the time they returned, 15 minutes had passed.

The workers tried digging. Then someone ran for a shovel. Next, they dug a trench and, after another 15 or 20 minutes, removed Grant's body, Williams said.

Officials from Scott's Backhoe could not be reached Wednesday.

Friends said Grant loved everything about nature, from trees to soil. He liked all types of music and has played with several local bands and, occasionally, with musicians from other countries.

Pastorfield called him a "have gun will travel stand-up bassist" whose "name had gotten around, [someone who was] able to play almost anything. He listened to everything, so he could play everything."

"He's just a guy who was wide awake and very much alive," Pastorfield added.

Ryan Hughes, a part-time member of Guano Boys, said: "He was, in my opinion, the best bass player in town. He was probably the most humble, but the best."

It was unclear Wednesday how Grant's death would affect the future of Guano Boys, which plays Caribbean and reggae music. The band's lead singer, Chris Leva, could not be reached for comment.

Grant also was co-host of a world music show called "Radio Tropicale" on the University of Virginia's station, WTJU-91.1 FM.

The station's general manager, Chuck Taylor described Grant as a "very laid back person, very friendly."

Grant is survived by his wife Darlene Crawford and son, 11-year-old Ryan Grant.

Susan Sterngold

I had always enjoyed Folk Music when I was in college, in about 1976; I was visiting my girlfriend Nancy who lived out on the Flathead Indian reservation in Montana for the summer. There is not much to do out there, and somebody said, "There's a Fiddler's Contest in Folsom, Montana, 'want to go?" I had never heard of a Fiddle Contest, but I fell in love with fiddling. And I bought this cheap fiddle and I started chasing the records. I went to the store and said, "I want to hear some deep fiddle." I got a bunch of Bluegrass records and that wasn't quite it. I ended up with "Doug Kershaw", and "Fenning's All Stars", and "Trapezoid", and none of them were it. Then I discovered a "Highwoods" record. And that was it. And "The New Lost City Ramblers". And then I went to a "Highwoods" concert in New York, and met people who told me about "The Skillet Lickers" and Tommy Jerrold. And that was really it.

Then I discovered Jay Unger's dances that were being held near me in Westchester County. There I found out about Ashokan Dance Camp and I met people up there who were talking about going to Galax. And so the next year I went to Galax and bought a dulcimer on the way there. That was 1983. I met the Bobville people, and some of them were even nice to me, even though I played the dulcimer.

Two years later, I got a banjo, and I went to Augusta. I just did a bunch of Camps and stuff. Just got in the scene and went around and played tunes.

I still live in New York, and I'm a Clinical Social Worker. And now I play banjo and guitar. I'm in a sort of part time occasional band. A couple of different bands. I play with Drew a lot.

Drew Smith

I live in Hohokus, New Jersey, which is only about twenty minutes maximum from Mike Resnick and Susan up in Suffern, New York. We get together every Wednesday and tickle tunes. Mike was the guy that first introduced me to Old Time music, way back in the early Seventies. In 1977 we came down for our first time at Galax, and we haven't missed on since that time. So that is twenty-nine years.

Before, I played a little guitar and then I picked up autoharp, I found I could do more on the autoharp and we found ourselves at all sorts or parties and get-togethers at social circles up near where we live. Roger Sprung was at many of these parties, and I aimed to play with him, so I developed a style on the autoharp, that led him to ask me, in 1976 he asked me to play in the band with him. "Roger Sprung, Hal Wylie and the Progressive Bluegrass". Roger just always happened to like Autoharp. So I learned his whole repertoire and played with him for seventeen, eighteen years. Different times at the Philadelphia Folk Festival, and various gigs all over the place. It's been a lot of fun.

Were you part of the great Folk Scare?

I started playing in 1965. I bought my first guitar and I took Adult Education lessons. In Teaneck, New Jersey. Then I wanted to learn fingerpicking, John Hurt, Elizabeth Cotton style, so I found another Adult Ed teacher named Bob Abram, from whom I learned a lot of picking styles. But, it's interesting where music takes you. Mike and Susan and I ended up about seventeen years ago getting together with a Russian Balalaika player, and we would go visit him once a month and we would learn a bunch of his Russian repertoire. And we were playing gigs with him; he was eighty years old when I first met him. He passed away at the age of ninety-two. And the interesting thing was, that he was as powerful at the age of ninety-two ... he would just floor us and build up to a crescendo. We got into Israeli music ...

Susan: There are a lot of New York Jews involved in Old Time music. There seems to be a connection there somewhere.

Drew: So many of the pickers down in Washington Square were all Jewish. Roger Sprung. We came down with him in '77, and we played with him on stage, and when the Roger Sprung band played, we were the only band ever that got a standing ovation and got to play another number on stage.

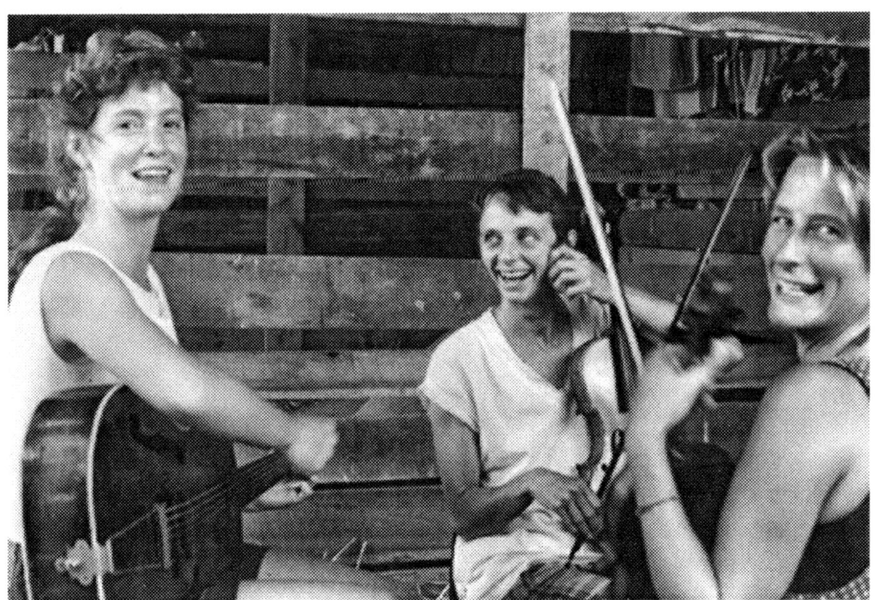

Kielbasa Bill

Kielbasa Bill is a bass player, attends every festival with a middle-aged school bus and always seems to be surrounded by women, music, food, and massage tables. He dresses in hog-washers and tie-dyes, and is always at the center of some craziness. He is our token Bluegrasser in this book.

My name is Kielbasa Bill Guthrie. I live in Danbury, North Carolina. My bank account number is seven. I am as old as dirt. My Social Security number is two. I remember when the Dead Sea got sick.

I don't know if you play Old Timey music, but you look like a damn hippie to me.

I play Bluegrass music. We're trying to keep it alive best we can. This is my thirty-first year at Galax. 1974. I grew up in Winston Salem, escaped in 1980.

Got as far as Danbury, ran out of gas?

Got as far as I needed to go. Property taxes were cheap. Got a river. Neighbors I can't see. Neighbors I can't hear. I'm a happy boy.

How long have you been playing bass?

I started with my formal training when I was twelve years old, played for five years with the Winston Salem Junior Symphony and laid it down and when the Moose moved the fence back, I picked it up back up. Tore the stalls down one year, and moved the fence back a year or two later.

And here we are, sitting under the last two or three trees left in Felts Park.

They are about 200 years old. Look how big they are.

You are Kielbasa Bill's Road Show?

We play Bluegrass, a lot of novelty tunes, some old hippie tunes. We play three or four weekends a month. Usually a hundred mile radius. Whoever books a gig. A lot of parties, store openings, restaurants like to have us in, "Oh Henry's" in East Bend—we play them a whole bunch, and the guitar player we had at the time made Henry real upset, and got us unbooked. He was running his mouth. He was from Michigan and didn't know how to act around people. Didn't know how to act in polite company.

You need to teach these hippies, that every song ever written has a beginning, a middle, <u>and an end</u>. I have heard some of these Old Time tunes go for hours and hours, and not have an end. They just get hung up on that A and E and they will play for days. And sometimes you feel they will change songs. My untrained ear can't tell the difference, because the banjo is still going "puckapuckapuckapucka" and the fiddler's going "eyeyeyeyeyeyeye". So, I like them to put their fingers down on the neck every now and then. Play a melody.

It would be great to sing one ... Nobody sings "John Henry", very few people sing "John Hardy" and I think me and Fred Stags are the only two people on the planet that still sing "Dear Old Dixie".

Somebody was telling me that there are a lot more Bluegrass bands here at Galax than Old Timey.

Quite a bit of Bluegrass here. Mt. Airy—there is a lot more Old Timey than there is Bluegrass. There are a lot of new people. I kind of like it. Anything to keep the music going. And the children are coming along.

Mark Rose Interview

The quickest way to describe Mark Rose is that he has been known to dress as Julius Caesar for Halloween. He is a ball of energy, the center of every scene. If there is not a scene, he can be counted on to start one. He makes his living as an architectural draftsman, and lives in a constantly rehabbed double log cabin with his wife, Lenora Fox Rose, in Mouth of Wilson, Virginia.

How did you get into Old Time Music?

A friend of mine, Boo Messer, brought me the first time to Galax. In 1971. And that was my first exposure to festival music. When I was younger, my uncle was a heavy drinker and would stop at the Holiday Inn in Lexington and have a cocktail—in the late evenings, and I would be driving around with him, and he would make me sit in the lobby. J. D. Crowe would be playing in the bar there. And so, it was kinda, at an early age I got a feel for good Bluegrass.

Your friend brought you to Galax for the party, because you were young and foolish?

Exactly. Came for the party. And that was in '71, so I came every year until '77, and I was living in Seattle at the time, and came back for the festival, and met my wife Lenora, within fifty feet of where we're sitting. That's when I moved here to be with her.

And quite the stunning young lady she was ...

Smitten right away, we both were. After I moved here, we both got involved with the local community chorus, "The Highland Camarata". And we met some other hippies who had moved to the mountains, the Mangums, and Leon Frost, that Len knew when she first moved here, and Edwin Ward, and we folks formed "The Courthouse Rambers" to play at a summer talent show that the Camarata had in between their spring and winter chorus sessions.

So that just kind of grew on itself. There was this little spot back here at the Galax tennis courts, where for years, the Ramblers would get together and do funny tunes and cut up.

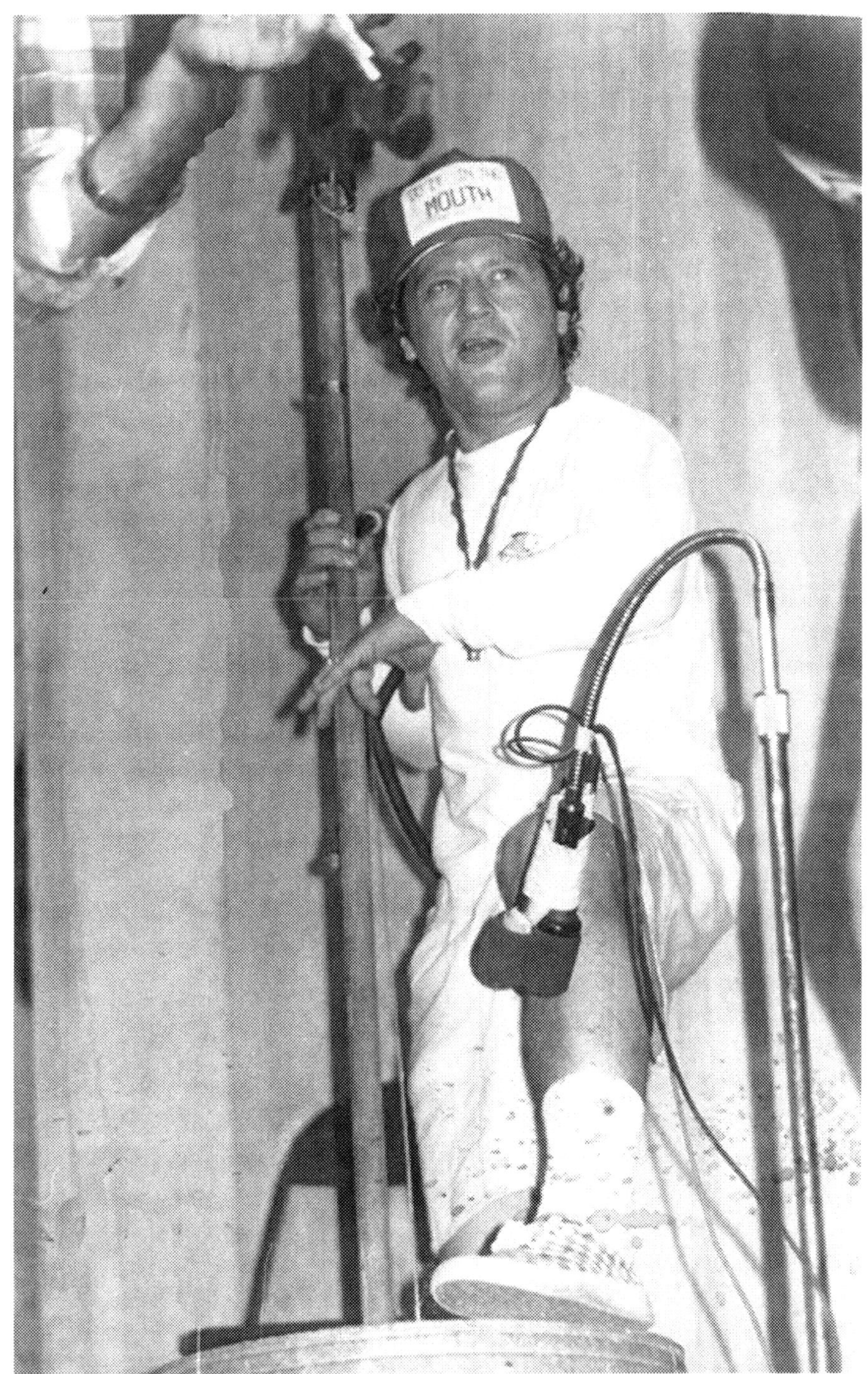

Edwin got married first, to Becky and she came into the group, and then one of Leon's girlfriends played guitar in the group for a while, and then Lisa, his current wife, played mandolin for a while. So it has been as many as four married couples in the Ramblers at its peak.

I had an old Kay bass that I put all kinds of skateboard stickers on ... Sex Wax. I had one on the bottom that said "I don't care about you ... Fuck You."

You were well known for accidentally leaving that bass on stage lying down so people could see that ...

Exactly. We played a few benefits, not many. Mostly private parties and at Galax. We were invited to play for Peggy and David Rockefeller's fifty-fifth wedding anniversary in Tarrytown, NY. They sent a private jet to the Rural Retreat Airport—picked us up, flew us up there, put on a big shindig outside under a tent for a hundred and fifty sit-down dinner guests. Pretty high-falluting.

I always thought that we were more enthusiastic than talented.

Rob and Bet Mangum are pretty serious Old Timey players. And Leon is a genuine hillbilly.

Leon Frost from Piper's Gap. He's a jukebox on the guitar. It was a collection of good musical talent. But our mainstay was a lot of singing and a lot of comedy. A lot of funny, unusual songs. "Billbill" Leon made famous. (About a boy too poor to have a dog, so he had a pig named Billbill).

Leon gave me the worst moment I ever had onstage at Galax. The one time I went on stage with you. So there I was, and you guys are all playing the vamp that you had played a thousand times, and just as we get to the first word, Leon looks at me with this total lost, blank look, as if I was going to remember the words. This total look of horror.

That was Leon. He would get half way through a song sometimes and just draw a blank on the words. I've done that myself.

When I started with the Ramblers, I played washtub. One of John Sturgill's wooden washtubs. When I met Len in '77, I wanted to make some music; I was a trumpet player as a kid. So I took a hose off of a camper, and cut off the end of it and played it like a trumpet. And then Rob Mangum gave me his hot water hose off of his Kenmore, and I put a trumpet mouthpiece on it and it was a dead-on G. Like a bugle. So I played the hose some. That was part of the novelty schtick.

Len started out playing autoharp and Becky was playing dulcimer, and because it was so hard to keep the autoharp in tune, Len started playing washboard and singing. So it was Len on washboard, me on bass, Becky on dulcimer, Edwin on guitar, Rob on guitar, Leon on Bluegrass banjo, Bet on Old Time banjo. So were we a Bluegrass and Old Time banjo band with no fiddle. The Ramblers kinda dissolved three years ago.

But at their peak, you had hundreds of people here.

We would set up a big, stripedy yellow tent with two big center poles. We built a little plywood stage, had lights in there. On Thursday, Friday, and Saturday nights we would have three-four hundred people crowded around.

Now you're a pretty serious bass player.

I don't know about serious. I play more.

Do you care; Old Timey, Country, whatever?

No. Well, I mostly play Old Time. And I'm playing some kind of a Bluegrass-Old Time mix with Tim and Debby Yates. So I play with them some, and in a Swing quartet for about six years with Helen White.

So, through the power of repetition, which is what any music is about, practice, and learning through the chords ... That's kinda made it more fun. So in that regard, as far as being more serious, I realize there are more notes than the one and the five, you know.

Does Casey Hash play Swing with you?

No, he plays like a mix of Folk and Rock, Casey and I play old Fifties tunes and a mix. He's a great entertainer, Casey and I have done a lot of gigs together. Casey is from Elk Creek. As a matter of fact, my wife—when she would come to Elk Creek in the Fifties, knew his dad and uncle, when they were growing up.

Casey is the only person in recent memory with enough nerve to play an accordion in Old Timey music.

He's got quite the set of balls, that guy.

Your wife has strong roots down here.

She used to come visit the country with her mother when she was a kid and fell in love with the country. She moved from Arlington to Grayson County, in '75.

We have camped in this same spot since 1970, right here next to the tennis courts. Part of coming to Galax is being with your friends, in the same spot every year. We finally made buddies, through Leon; I got to pal up to them enough to where they let us take care of getting people parked back here.

The interesting thing about Old Time is the community that goes with the music, the camaraderie that develops, camping together. Everybody leaves their "mantles" somewhere else, because everybody is the same under the string and the mud. So, the idea that you're with your pals, that you stay up all night with, and you do that for so many years in a row, four-five-six, maybe two or three different festivals, four or five days with the same people. Over a period of time you get to know them pretty good. And it's really neat to be able to experience that sense of community with people through the years.

So then to go to a place like Clifftop, where there is a big Yankee infusion, it's not really unsettling, but they're not as inclusive. I do this too; you go to a festival and you get with people you know when you play music. But I still feel like it's open for other people to come jam if they can play the tune.

Nancy Banjo said that there was a point when Bobville was walled off from everybody. Then a few years later, they just opened up and let it happen, and they find a lot better benefits, and the music is a lot better. Getting accepted.

And I don't know if that was due to the sub-culture that the Old Time folks were involved in, and the local rednecks weren't, that kept up that little barrier. But I think the music kind of spilled over that.

That poem of mine that you used to read every year at Galax, that was about that. That was about going from the stalls to 'Over There", which was on the other side of the tennis courts.

Spiritual Journey

NOW A GAY LAPSE IS WHEN YOU COME HOME DRUNK AND GIVE YOUR BUNKIE A BLOW JOB, BUT GALAX IS ANOTHER KIND OF LAPSE ENTIRELY.

FORTY ACRES OF GEEKS AND FREAKS AND BANJOS, CALCUTTA WITH FIDDLES, WOODSTOCK FOR REDNECKS, WITH A YEE-HAW FACTOR OF FORTY. AND YOU'RE LIT UP LIKE TIM LEARY'S CHRISTMAS TREE, AND YOU JUST CAN'T TOLERATE ONE MORE PURPLE HAIRED VIRTUOSO FROM LENINGRAD HERE TO LEARN THE HILLBILLIES HOW TO PLAY "OLD JOE CLARK" AND DRESS BAD.

SO YOU DRIFT PAST THE "DEAD INDIAN NON-BAR AND GRILL", THE COP-SHOP, THE "WE DO IT IN THE MOUTH GANG" AND "THE FIFTY LONG HAIRED FRIENDS OF JESUS". AND DRIVEN BY SOME EMOTION THAT MIGHT HAVE BEEN ENNUI 5OO MIKES AGO, YOU BOLDLY BOOGIE WHERE NO FOOL HAS FREAKED BEFORE.

"AND YEA THOUGH I WALK THROUGH THE VALLEY OF THE THOUSAND FOOT WINNEBAGOS I SHALL FEAR NO EVIL, FOR I AM ALL FUCKED UP."

AND AS YOU TIPTOE PAST THESE WHITED SEPULCHRES, EACH WORTH MORE THAN YOUR ENTIRE FAMILY, YOU REALIZE, WITHOUT EMOTION, THAT THIS IS WHAT AMERICA WILL BE AFTER IT DIES. WHITE AND CHROMED, WITH FLAGS FLYING, THE ONLY SOUND A MUTED HUM FROM THE GENERATORS THAT MAINTAIN THE CRYOGENICS. AND AS YOU LEAVE, THE SECURITY CAMERAS FOLLOW YOU.

AND YOU PIERCE, POINK, LIKE A NEEDLE THROUGH THE EYE OF A CAMEL INTO A STRANGE LAND.... A LAND WHERE THE SEXES DRESS TO ATTRACT EACH OTHER, AND HETEROSEXUALITY RAISES RAMPANT, AND THE SMELLS OF TESTOSTERONE, TOBACCO, AND CHEAP PERFUME MINGLE IN A HEADY INCENSE.

THE YEE-HAW FACTOR BECOMES TRANSFINITE, AND YOU COME UPON A CHROME-PLATED, BY GOD, CANDY APPLE, NO SHIT, PIN-STRIPED, OH YEAH, CUT DOWN, SWEAR TO JESUS, DUMP, FUCKING, TRUCK.

AROUND THIS APPARITION ARE A DOZEN GOOD OLD GRIZZLIES, OLD BOYS WHO COULD EAT WAYLON FUCKING JENNINGS AND BURP UP DAVID FUCKING ALAN COE.

AND GOOD OLD AMERICAN NAMES LIKE DALTON, AND JAMES, AND MANSON, AND QUANTRILL COME TO MIND, AND EACH GRIZ HAS A YELLOW PLASTIC CUP IN IT'S PAW, EACH WITH A CLEAR INCH OF LIQUID, NO ICE, NO FIZZY SHIT.

AND YOU ARE AS TRANSFIXED AS IF YOU HAD COME UPON A PRIDE OF LIONS PLAYING CANASTA, FOR THESE MONSTERS ARE SINGING, SINGING AS SWEET, AND AS PURE, AND AS SILKEN AS THE PEACH SHINE IN THEIR CUPS.

AND THEY ARE SINGING SPIRITUALS.

AND THEY ARE SINGING "NINETY NINE YEARS AND ONE HARD NIGHT," AND THE TATTOOS AND THE SCARS ON THEIR KNUCKLES AND ONE JAILHOUSE, SIDEWAYS GLINT FROM ONE HOODED EYE, TELLS YOU THAT THEY KNOW, THAT YOU KNOW, THAT THEY KNOW, AND IF YOU JUST STAY SHUT UP, HIPPIE, EVERYTHING WILL BE FINE, BOY.

AND SOMETIMES ANGELS ARE OLD LAGS WITH .38'S IN THEIR BOOTS AND BELT BUCKLES THAT COST MORE THAN THEIR DENTURES.

AND JESUS SAID," HE WHO HAS EARS, LET HIM HEAR,"

AND YOU CAN HEAR THE SCRAPE, SCRAPE, SCRAPE OF A BALLPOINT PEN REFILL ON THE CELL FLOOR, UNTIL IT IS SHARP ENOUGH TO OPEN A VEIN TO WHATEVER SHIT THE GUARD WILL SELL YOU FOR THE LAST OF YOUR SELF RESPECT.

AND YOU CAN HEAR THE SUBCUTANEOUS PRICK OF A DIRTY NEEDLE TATTOOING TITS ON SOME PUNK'S SHOULDER-BLADES AND PUBIES JUST ABOVE THE CRACK IN HIS LILY-WHITE ASS.

AND YOU CAN HEAR THE THREE A.M. SILENCE OF SOME LIFER TRYING TO REMEMBER THE ACT THAT GOT HIM HERE, JUST AS DESPERATELY AS IF REMEMBERING COULD CHANGE ANYTHING.

AND YOU CAN HEAR THE SWEATY SINCERITY OF THE ONLY REAL PRAYER;

"FUCK IT, LORD, I GIVE UP"

AND THERE IS NO APPLAUSE AS THE SONG ENDS, FOR YOU DON'T APPLAUD IN CHURCH, BUT IN THE BACK OF THE CROWD AN OLD, OLD MAN SPITS BACCER JUICE WITH THE ELOQUENCE OF A PROPHET.

AND ANOTHER SONG LIFTS TO THE SMOKY SKY.

"AND THERE WILL BE PEACE IN THE VALLEY, FOR ME OH LORD, I PRAY, THERE WILL BE PEACE IN THE VALLEY FOR ME OH LORD, SOME DAY."

AND YOU KNOW, THAT RIGHT HERE, RIGHT NOW, THERE IS.

The Death of the Stalls

I can put in a story here. At the time of the tearing down of the stalls, I was more or less homeless, and had several health problems. I hate people who use the word "issue" when they mean problem, don't you? An issue can be resolved by debate or compromise. A problem requires actual work. Or drugs.

Anyway, I was living in a '76 Toyota Corolla, and had an abscessed tooth that hurt like a bastard, and something called pustular eczema that was eating the skin off my hands. My father was dying, 400 miles away and I was broke ... All I had to sell were a dozen hand carved walking sticks and some fabric paints and blank tee shirts. Somebody had decided that Bobville proper was the inner circle's compound, and had set up a jam tent where the "other ranks" were to camp. One of the rank others was Mike "Lightnin'" Wells, one of the very best white Blues guys in America. We soon figured out that we were second class citizens, not an unusual role for blues guys, and set up a blues ghetto.

I remember telling all and sundry that vegetarians could never play real Old Time, unless they indulged in "Substance B", Bar-b-que. This insight was met with the blankest of stares from the granolas.

Unknown to the hippies, the Bluegrassers were in full dope mode, this was in '91 or so, and there was reefer everywhere. I remember a young band of hot Bluegrassers, dressed all in the very loudest tie-dyes, and awash in moonshine and hashish and LSD. Every so often the mando player would assume a Mercury pose on one foot, and exclaim to the uncaring world, "FTD.... Fucking Tore Down!" Nobody noticed.

I was pretty razzled, and had just given up pot and beer and was not in the best of moods. So I would try to pass out before the Bobville Jam Tent would fire up. One particular Bobvillian, "Clogbob", had brought her own private stage, the "Steppatune". This was an eighteen-inch square piece of plywood so that one could clog even in the deepest mud. Although Clogbob was a petite female, she had a laugh like a drunken Master Sergeant and brogan shoes. All night long it was stompedy-clog-stomp, har-har-har, well into the dawn. I was in some state that resembled sleep. At the very crack of dawn, I crawled out and painted my last tee-shirt, "Who is Old Time Music, and why won't he let me sleep at night?" This was a paraphrase of the bumper sticker, "Who are the Grateful Dead, and why do they keep following me around the country?"

I hung the shirt up on a tent pole to dry, and it was the first thing Lightnin' Wells saw when he woke up to go to work in Hatton's record tent, at six in the morning. He eventually sent me a "Grumpy Smurf" drinking glass, with the legend, "I hate Music!" One of my proudest possessions.

I eventually got enough money up to get to Tennessee, and as a side benefit, Doctor Jack Cahn, MD, fiddler and saint, came up with some free pills that not only knocked the abscess down, but cured the eczema for a few months.

And the next year, Bobville, whether due to my grumping or not, was a lot more open to the common ruck. I had made it a point to introduce any of my redneck friends who had superior pot to the Bobvillians, and that might have had an influence. At least some of the locals bought Nancy Banjo's batik tee shirts. But Mark Rose was cross-culturing all that time.

Mark Rose Interview, Continued

Has the great hippie invasion helped the economy down here?

It's been good for the economy around here, I think. A lot of the hippies that moved here to Grayson County came at the end of Appalachian Power Company buying all the land to build a dam. They didn't build the dam, and so there was all this cheap property available. A lot of hippies started businesses, raised kids ... It's amazing how well the kids that were born here, or brought here, how well they did when they went out into the world. Almost to a fault. I can list thirty or forty instances.

So a lot of those hippies started out trying to be house builders, trained a whole cadre of people who are still in business.

The whole mountain persona, the whole attitude that mountain people have—and it's the same wherever you go with mountain people—is that they are here because they want to be here, not because it's an easy place to be. And the music that goes with that is real important to their lives and their mental health.

And so they have been playing this music, and all their ancestors have played, and the variations on the tunes that evolve as different people play them, it's been going on all along, and these people are pretty humble as a rule. And they get together and play for their own enjoyment, not to please a crowd. And so the hippies came here—some for the music—or came here to get away from cities, the "Back to the Landers" I call them.

By the term, "hippy" I think a lot of people think of longhaired, not necessarily schooled, obnoxious and "taking" type people. But the Back-to-the-Landers were on the falling edge of the hippy movement. I think the mid-Sixties through '74-75, was the peak of that. After that, it was people who wanted to get married, raise their kids, were smart enough to study the demographics to know where they could buy cheap land, have fairly good roads, good water, safe from floating clouds of pollution …

So as these people came here, and discovered the type of people that were here, and then they discovered the kind of music that they played, those people were more vocal about, less humble about the music. And I think that is when the shift kind of started. Cause it is a simple music based on the humble part of the mountain people. And I think the people who came in and saw the value of the music, as far as what it could do for your peace of mind, were a more vocal type of people.

When these back-to-the-landers came to the mountains, a few of them discovered the music when they got here. Not that they tainted it, but I don't think they respected it.

It's pretty simple, if you try and add too many notes, if you try to do too much, then it looses some of the … the simpleness of that repetition and gets cumbersome. It doesn't flow gently, and to me that's part of what appeals to a lot of the Back-to-the-Landers. It was the trance-like elements that went with other types of thinking, you know, of people that meditate. They call it meditation rather than prayer. That meditative quality comes through repetition. I remember the first time I heard "The Red Hots", over at the stalls, I was entranced. And when they got through, man, I was exuberant. I clapped and they turned around and looked at me like "What the …" I spoiled the groove.

And for years, I thought, "What a stuck-up bunch of people". But then I realized years later that I had broken the trance. That still lingers. So even though the tune ends, you don't just abruptly stop. You're still "rolling".

You were really good at evoking applause with the Ramblers.

I enjoy working a crowd … That's what's neat about Old Time Music, there is a hiding place in there.

After I first moved here, Claudine Langille came back from Ireland and she brought three musicians, and Albert Hash's band, came and played at our house. And my neighbor, who never went more than fifty miles from Mouth of Wilson in his whole life, he heard them playing a tune and when they were through, he turned to me and said, "That reminds me of the old fox hunting days." The tune was "Fox Hunter's Reel". And maybe he knew that tune by that name. People like that, whose fathers and grandfathers played Old Time music … my great grandfather played fiddle—a guy named John Rector, a fiddle player from Sparta. I think I kind of have it in my blood.

I've heard stories of Tommy Jarrell turning the corner and seeing some revivalists, and seeing their car up at his own house and turning and going away for a while, hoping that they would leave. I mean, a lot of these people who felt, because the mountain people were so gracious, they would never say to their face, "You're wearing us out."

"Y'all come on in! Stay!" Of course they would stay for five or six hours. And then every day … The other side of that coin was just because people were so gracious, so humble, that they wouldn't say no to people that kind of forced themselves on them.

There's a respect for the music that comes with that old school, that somehow gets lost in the new shuffle. Not that they don't play it right, or not that they are not sincere, or not trying to be traditional, there is just a certain lack of respect there.

Dennis Hall plays with the Bogtrotters and they win Galax every year, with Eddy Bond, and Greg Hooven for years. His dad is Oscar Hall, the head Moose guy. I'll never forget the time I got called by Dennis Hall to play at Oscar's house. I mean, they put a rule in the rulebook one year, no rubber instruments on stage, because of the fucking garden hose I played. They hated to see us coming in, and when we got on stage, the crowd went crazy, for that schticky stuff we did.

But the point was, Dennis called me to play bass with Bobby Taylor, the guy started Clifftop. He was coming to play fiddle, and the bass player couldn't make it, and Leon was going to play mandolin, and I could play bass with them. To me that was the ultimate bridge across from hippydom to Old Time. Right, then I would be accepted ... musically, beyond just who I was, who they still may or may not agree with my politics or my recreations. What happens then is that the local people realize, when you have a respect for the music. .

Sure, some other people have used that exact word. Respect. And there is this thing that happens, where the music will be played, and the rhythm will hit this little step like when a speed-boat, the hull is all wetted, and it hits one quantum, and the hull comes up out of the water, and the boat is sitting on the bottom third of the propeller, it's going like goose shit through a tin funnel, Zooom. And when you get the Old Timey music right at that point, it goes "ping" and it's gone. And you can dance for eight hours.

It freezes time too ...

It stays right there, and becomes effortless ... Hyper-space.

And I can recall moments in my playing in the past ten or fifteen years—I can recall certain moments when that happened—what the ensemble was, who the players were, and it was just like it was ... I close my eyes and I'm right there. It's amazing how that marks your memory banks.

This is such a subtle art from. This is why I want to know why the Japanese like this stuff.

It's that Zen thing. It's that respect thing that the Japanese have for tradition and for simplicity of form, you know. All those elements they bring to meditation and philosophy and living and I think that's in the music.

I never see Japanese guys trying to play the Blues.

No ... That's a good comparison there. There is a certain amount of Soul involved in any kind of music. And I think some is more accessible than others.

Mountain people say very little, and they mean what they say. They are very accepting. That was part of it. Like Tommy Jarrell taking in the Yankees and those guys; they were so accepting, they'd almost let them almost walk all over them.

Being from Kentucky, did you ever listen to John Jacob Niles?

Funny you mention that. In '72, I had a friend whose mother ran this International Music thing at University of Kentucky. And he and I moved the stuff on and off the musical stage. And John Jacob Niles was there two years in a row. And he was a crusty, hateful old fart to work with. I didn't know anything about his music, but now, looking back on it, he was you know ...

What did you think about his music back then?

It was too simple for my taste at the time. Way too simple.

You bring up an interesting point there, about the sound of Old Time Music. When tuners came into favor ...

What happed was you could move from jam to jam and still be in tune because back in the old days, it was all relative. When Tommy Jarrell would play, they'd tune to this tuning fork or whatever and everybody tuned to him. Which was fine as long as everybody was in tune to each other. That was one thing that turned me off to it for years was how out of tune it was—especially in a jam that was more than just a band warming up, or one of each instrument, or five or six or less, when everybody could hear whether they were in tune or not.

Jim Lloyd taught me more about Old Time music than any one person. And he is an incredible Old Time guitar player. His rhythms and the stuff he did were just amazing.

Serious school I took from him. I'd ask him a question how to do something and he wouldn't answer; he would just play it. And later, playing with Nick MacMillian and Chester ... Chester had a way of putting it, that I will never forget. He says. "You have to play the tune." And that's an interesting way to play Old Time Music. Most people say you're playing the song, or your playing in "A", or your playing "Old Joe Clarke". No. You're playing "The Tune".

Chester, he drives the bass line and then picks the melody, kind of, at the same time. And now they play as a trio, and won at Fiddler's Grove last year. As a three piece group. They don't need a bass. And you don't.

Bass was very rare in Old Timey in the old days, because they were too expensive.

Too big and bulky, and nobody had one.

Doesn't seem to have been too much washtub in Old Time, until the hippies showed up.

There is Janice from the "Hilltoppers" that plays the washtub bass. And she's the one first inspired me to play washtub bass. So she is the real inspiration for my bass playing. And I still thank her today, you know. I came down here and I saw her and said, "There is something. I can make that and I could do that".

Of course Johnny Sturgill had that wooden one.

I still have one of those.

I still have the picture of him winning First Prize at Union Grove. We went up and played "Johnny B. Goode" and won. Johnny said, "I have to get my money back." And I asked, "What do you want to play?" And he said, "I don't care." So, "Go Johnny Go" and he went nuts, and he won. And the crowd went wild.

That's the neat thing about it. Then that's as much about entertainment as it is about purity of the music.

And you know, there are some real subtle musicians here. Over there is Will Keys' bus, with the big fan in the back door that looks like a jet engine. I used to come over here and play Swing with Bill Necessary and Will Keys for hours.

I was over in the stalls one time, and somebody tells me about this fiddler who wanted to play "Rubber Ducky". And then he wanted to play "Ragtime Annie". And then he wanted to play "Whiskey for Breakfast." And finally Tom Riccio goes, "Why are you playing all that '70's crap? Who the fuck do you think you are, Henry the Fucking Fiddler?"

And it *was* Henry the Fiddler. And so I had been beating on a mandolin and somebody was rude to me. So I'm walking up the road and I see Bill Necessary … And here comes Henry the Fiddler, steaming. "Hey Bill! Let's play some music. And we sat on the hood of this car and we played "Bill Bailey" … We played all this stuff with ninety-two chords. You know Bill's style; "Every Bar Shall Have Four Chords and Every Chord Shall Have Six Notes."

He's the one that inspired Helen White to play Swing music. I played with Helen and Bill a few times before he passed away.

God, those guys are good! And Wayne Henderson is the best of the bunch. You watch his hands and they don't move.

It's like a runner. These great runners, their heads never bounce. Good dancers the same way. Everything's going but the top of their heads are not moving.

Art Wooten was the best fiddler ever. You would watch his fingers and they would lift just enough to clear the strings by a millimeter. Just exactly enough.

One thing I wanted to mention, was that Old Time Music was started for the dancers. And something about.. so it wasn't up front, you know. The dancers were the front line. The musicians were the record player. The juke-box. That was something else that Chester talked about, the music, "Is it a danceable tune?"

You played these country dances?

The songs are very long; you could play ten or twelve minutes on the same tune.

And the thing that struck me was that every man gets to touch every woman. Every woman gets to embrace every man. Even though they might hate each other. Even though their daughter got pregnant by "that no good son of a bitch, your son …" They still have to have to touch. They have to smell each other's perfume …

There is something humbling about that …

Or leveling.

Leveling … right. That's a much better word.

This defines our community. We are the people who get together Saturday night, and we touch each other.

And it's that community about the Old Time Music that has been real appealing. That's what draws me to these festivals, not just the music, but to get to make music with these people. Or to get to listen to these different combinations of musicians that I like. That only get to play together a few times a year. And the energy they generate … that's a big part of it.

That's the way all music starts out. It seems like the music and the dance, the closer those things can be, the more fulfilling it is.

But the singing and the music is important. It helps the rhythm. And I'm surprised that more Old Time bands don't at least sing a chorus or half a verse, or something.

This guy Pat, nobody can remember his name, used to come by Dave Sturgill's and Dave gave him the best banjo he ever made. Just gave it to him. Because he was the guy that Dave wanted to be. Dave wanted to be George Peagram, and this guy Pat was nuts. Drunk and crazy and shriveled up and mad as shit. He got this beautiful Sturgill Bluegrass banjo, gold-plated, every piece of beauty that Johnny could put on the thing.

Dave gave it to him, and said; "Pay me when you get the money." Like a thousand dollars. And the first thing Pat did was to catch a Monarch butterfly and glue it to the back of the resonator. To make it prettier!

And then he comes back a few months later, and.… "I was out in Las Vegas and had a string of bad luck and had to pawn the banjo, Dave. Would you forgive me?

"I knew you would, Pat." I was there, I seen it. Dave wasn't pissed at all. I asked him later, "You knew that was going to happen, didn't you?"

He said, "I knew that was going to happen. I'm not an idiot. I know how he is." And he wouldn't say anything more about it. A mountain guy, he wouldn't explain himself, but that was like a sacrifice to the god of banjo crazies.

Dave was so smart he couldn't really let his ass show. He did good sometimes. We went up to the "Martha Washington Inn" in Abingdon, Virginia. Somehow they hired him to play on the porch, he had his band, the old farts' band, and he went up there and was talking shit to the tourist people … He knew he had them.

He did this thing where he would do Earl Scruggs' "Foggy Mountain Breakdown" as a frailing banjo song, and called it "Foggy Headed Breakdown" or the "Breaky Mountain Fogdown" or something. He did that and danced around a little bit, and probably did "C-H-I-C-K-E-N". He had a good show.

It takes something to make somebody want to get out there and want to do it full time.

He loved it. He just loved it. That's what he wanted to do. Like Jeremiah Skarie, how does that happen?

He has been winning dulcimer everywhere. He's a shoe-in every where he goes. After years of playing. And he is the most humble person … outside of being totally nuts.

I was sitting right beside him at Elk Creek, and he was drunk out of his gourd when they were calling the finalists in the dulcimer … Five, four, three, two … Number One, Jeremiah Skarie! And I was sitting right there and I said, "Jerry, that's you!"

"Well it is, isn't it! … It's me!" He stumbled on stage with his "Willy, willy good, white Wussian". He's a piece of work. man.

Tom Neuhauser

I'm from Charlestown, Indiana. I make Galax style dulcimers and I've been coming to Galax since 1977. Every year since. Come down here to learn to play the clawhammer banjo, been playing the dulcimer for about ten years, been making them for about ten years.

The very first time they had a festival in Louisville, Kentucky. Right on the river, and they had a group called "The Highwoods String Band". Was probably the mid '70's. And I found out about Galax from Pickin' Magazine. So I came down here, several members of "Highwoods" was here that year, Doug Dourshug, and Walt Koken. Then

I got interested in Clawhammer banjo. I couldn't find anybody in my area that played it, so I kept coming down here and making tape recordings, buying records and tapes, take them home. Found a few books.

I never played anything but the radio and the record player. But dulcimer—about the time I retired, in '94, I joined the Dulcimer Society, started playing clawhammer banjo with them. I got to looking at some of the dulcimers some of the people had and decided a could make a regular dulcimer—Appalachian dulcimer, as well as some of them had. After ten or twenty tries, they started turning out pretty good. I started selling a few of them.

In 1998, I come down here, and we was camped close to the Burrises—we'd been camping with them probably five or six years at that time, and Jen Burris played a Roscoe Russell Galax style dulcimer that belonged to her grandmother. And it was pretty rough—all beat up—so she let me borrow it so I could get a pattern. I took a bunch of pictures of it, measured all the dimensions and everything, and made pretty much a reproduction of the one she had.

But I used better materials than Roscoe did. I used quarter-sawn spruce for the top, I used nice curly walnut for the sides and back, piece of rosewood, for the fretboard, made a real nice instrument, and brought it down here in '99, and give it to Jen, because I got my pattern for the Galax, and she got first place that year. And she's got first place several years on that same dulcimer.

These are a lot bigger than regular dulcimers?

This particular one I kinda got carried away, most of your Galaxes aren't real loud, because they are because the sides are two inches thick, and they are about nine to ten inches wide. So I made this three inches thick, so that doubled my volume right there. And then I made it about two inches wider and about three inches longer. So I got a lot more volume out of it. It has a spruce top and a spruce false bottom and a spruce soundboard ... under the fingerboard. It's got rosewood laminate on the top of a piece of hollowed out spruce. So it barks pretty good.

Was the mountain tradition of making your own instruments important to you?

Yeah. After I made a few reproductions of Russell style dulcimers, I kind of designed my own ... Shaped them a little bit different, kind of a pumpkin seed shape. Found that a couple of Russell's that I saw ... I looked at them and traced them on a piece of paper, drew a center line down and folded it, and the sides aren't the same. They are not symmetrical. So I tried to make mine more symmetrical.

How many dulcimers have you made?

Right at two hundred. The most I ever made in one year was twenty-five.

Michael Jones
Letter

I was strongly influenced by the folk music of the 50's. My dad had "Kingston Trio" recordings which I enjoyed. I remember watching the "Hootenanny" TV Show. I longed for a guitar. When my dad bought one for himself, I began trying to play and my parents soon bought me one. I struggled with learning to play it, but I found I could not put it down. I drifted into listening and playing rock in the '60's but I always loved the acoustic sound and folk music.

I bought a cheap banjo from a friend and learned a few Earl Scruggs tunes until the 5th string fell out and wouldn't stay in. Then one day I saw a poster for the Strawberry Bluegrass Festival that was 100 miles from where I lived. My wife (at the time) and I headed up to Yosemite for one day of the 3-day festival. On the way, I was listening to the Saturday Bluegrass Show. They began playing some really hard core bluegrass to which my wife exclaimed, "What is that shit?" She always said what was on her mind. I thought this is going to be a long day. But as it turned out, she loved the festival. We attended for twenty years.

I was aware of old time music, having heard some of it on radio. The Strawberry Bluegrass Festival had been renamed the Strawberry Music Festival allowing them to include a wider variety of music. I arrived one particular year on a Friday night and had missed most of the music on stage.

On the way out from the stage area there was an old-time group, the "Freighthoppers", playing by the food area. They had played earlier in the day, but I had missed them. As I walked out of the stage area, I was blown away by the drive and sound of the group. I stood there and knew this music moved me more than any other. I had been playing bluegrass music with friends but had grown tired of it. I had also bought an open-backed banjo a year or so earlier as I knew old-time music was what I wanted to learn, but I had little opportunity in California to hear old-time music. I had not experienced music like this. A couple of years later, they played at the "Father's Day Bluegrass and Old-time Music Festival" (which is 90 percent bluegrass and 10 percent old-time music). But it did let me see actual clawhammer banjo players.

I divorced and met my current wife online at a simple living website. We found we were both interested in a more simple way of living. She had been exposed to old-time music in Portsmouth, Ohio at a small festival. My wife wanted to live closer to her family; her mother was in Florida, her grandmother in Alabama, and her children in Ohio. Tennessee was centrally located. I was excited about being close to old-time festivals. So, I retired early and we moved to Tennessee.

We met a man who did not play but was an avid flatfoot dancer. He told us about the best festivals for old-time music. We moved to Eastern Tennessee in June of 2002. The following year we went to a number of music festivals with Mount Airy and Clifftop being our favorites. I became aware of the differences between old-time and bluegrass musicians. It seemed the old-time musicians were more counter culture. They seemed to be more liberal (from the bumper stickers at bluegrass festivals). From my time in California, I had come to the feeling that most bluegrass people were somewhat conservative and rigid in their beliefs. Most bluegrass players had very short hair. I wear my hair long and began to feel that I did not fit in the bluegrass world, but I could see that old-time musicians were different. So, not only did I love the music, but I felt like I fit in with old-time musicians.

One of my wife's daughters moved here from Ohio. We took her to Clifftop. I don't think she was that excited to go, but she had a good time. Then one day she said out of the blue, "I have heard so much of this type of music, I am starting to really like it."

A genuine transmission from the day job computer of: Mark Rubin

Both my parents were musicians. They actually met while both were members of the University of Arizona marching band. My dad always had music on in the house. I remember Copland's American Suite, Joplin's Red Back Book and his beloved German "oom-pah" music on the big Magnavox hi-fi. We even had a rebuilt Wurlitzer 78, the kind with the bubbles going up the sides like in "Happy Days", loaded with an odd mix of Elvis, "The Coasters" and Danny Kaye. Some of my happiest childhood memories are sitting on the floor, with my back pressed up against these huge machines, my eyes closed tight, soaking up every nuance of the sound with my whole body.

Much to my chagrin, the decent middle class American Jewish parents that they were, my folks decided I was going to a violinist and signed me up for one of the first every Susuki Method courses in Oklahoma when I was only six. At an important teachers' demonstration conference on the Suzuki Method, I was asked by the professor in front of the assembled string players, why I had chosen the violin. I replied confidentally that I had no intention of every playing the violin at all; I actually wanted to play trombone but my arms were too short. Humiliated publicly, my parents dropped the violin classes.

Okie dokie. 'Hope this is of some use to you. Quite by accident, around 1989, I fell in with some old hippy Bluegrass pickers in Ft. Worth, who peppered their jam sessions with fiddle tunes and such. When I asked about it, they would say, "Oh, that's Old Time music. It's kind of like Bluegrass, just played poorly". I had been working primarily in the punk rock scene in Dallas, Texas at the time.

Well, this music was in some ways very familiar. My parents were really into square dancing when I was growing up in Oklahoma, so the fiddles and the beat were similar. I was also initially attracted to its heady mix of anarchy and populism; there was no "right" way to do it and anybody could. You got you a banjo and started playing tunes however you heard them or felt them. It was in practice more punk rock than punk rock. It was years before I realized that I alone shared this opinion.

The first artist that interested me, on record, was Clarence Ashley. I went rooting around 78's of his and found the East Texas Serenaders, Charlie Poole and Dock Boggs as well.

I picked up string bass, but eventually claw hammer banjo. I was already living in Austin TX, but that was to make a living playing music period. There were folks down here playing OT, but they were cliquish and none too welcoming to outsiders or young people. It seems to me that OT music to them is an excuse to throw parties, get stoned and fool around with each other's girlfriend. A fairly pathetic sight as they limp into their golden years if you ask me.

Texas is the greatest musical melting pot on Earth. There are so many traditions and cultures running head long into each other for such a long period of time, stewing and recombining together, that it creates a truly vibrant place to explore music. I formed a band with a banjo player and a fiddler I had met at a few jam sessions. We were way too weird to be accepted in the local "OT party" circle, so we naturally gravitated towards each other. We also committed the cardinal sin of playing old time in nightclubs, for money even. We named the band "Bad Livers" and set off on a tour, opening for the "Butthole Surfers".

We were always tagged with the "bluegrass" description, but our approach was always more grounded in OT music. Our best-selling CD "Hogs on the Highway" on Sugar Hill had only claw hammer banjo, for instance. We toured non-traditional venues for 12 years before hanging up our spurs.

(My interest was) Initially the Dock Boggs and Clarence Ashley school of lonely banjo playing. But as I became more aware of my local environment, I was drawn to the styles that are practiced right around here; Bohemian polka, Polish fiddle bands, Tex-Mex accordionists, Zydeco and Cajun music, cowboy yodeling and western swing. Why look up to the east or to old 78's when so many great music is happening all around you? Seems pretty sad to wish you were somebody else who lived someplace else at another time in history. Pathetically self-loathing in fact.

Were drugs or alcohol a factor?

"Certainly. What have you got?"

I like indoor plumbing and penicillin. I'm for civil rights and gay marriage. I am not a re-enactor. (I published) quite a bit. I wrote many reviews for the Old Time Herald and other publications and I've recorded more CD's than I can properly keep track of.

What is your musical career now?

"Busy like hell."

What is your non-musical career now?

"I work at a fiddle shop, which ties in nicely with the rest."

How did OT change your life?

"Sadly, it's reinforced my disgust with hippies."

Do you think OT will survive?

"Hopefully folks will continue to be proud of their own cultural legacies, and work to cherish them rather than have a bunch of self loathing Yankee Jews show up and act as their proxies."

Do you think non-Appalachian people can play OT?

"It's certainly possible, but why would want to? What do they find so distasteful about their own heritage that they would want to adopt someone else's? That's the real question. If all they know of that culture is what they hear off of a record, then the depth of their understanding is only as deep as the needle in the record's groove."

Do you think the emphasis on competition helps or hurts the music?

"This is America and we compete. Always have and should always. Screw music, let the best man win."

Chapter Eleven: Real Southerners

A Letter From Lenora (Fox) Rose

In 1972 I drove down from Northern Virginia with three musician friends and my two grade school-aged children to Elk Creek. We (not my kids) were going to enter the band contest at Independence. 'Back to that story later, but first:

I'd met Muriel about a year before at a festival in West Virginia. We were the only two playing autoharps and we hit it off right away. Then Joel, who played guitar, showed up. He also lived in Northern Virginia and Muriel was from Seattle, staying with an aunt who lived near me, and researching her genealogy. We got together a few times to see if we could pull off being a band. Muriel and Joel moved into my house as renters. The three of us did some traditional tunes like "Banks of the Ohio", "East Virginia", "Maid of Constant Sorrow", but we also did "body music" which was just free-form, improvisational stuff and Joel wrote several pieces. We played and sang at open mics in Washington DC, but mostly just at parties of various friends. We were joined from time to time by other musicians We had no band name.

Sometime in the spring of 1972, I'd brought Muriel, Joel and his girlfriend to Elk Creek for the first time. I carried a tape recorder everywhere I went then; it was rolling one morning as Muriel and I sat at breakfast in my uncle's kitchen. Another neighbor was visiting and he kept calling Muriel "Merle". I think she must have said something about becoming a vegetarian and the neighbor said, "Y'eat swine?" Muriel gave him a puzzled look. "Swine", he repeated. More puzzled looks from "Merle". "Swine ... you know ... swine ... PORK!" I would have to listen to that tape to see what followed but from that little scene came the inspiration for our band name; we were "Merle Swinette and the Mountain Oysters".

In June, at the Independence Fiddlers, it was very wet. How long and how much it had been raining is another piece of information lost in the haze ... of time. Along with Muriel on autoharp or clarinet(!), Joel on guitar or mandolin, myself on autoharp and "voice", was Bob who'd recently begun to sit in on our practices. Bob was a drummer and he'd brought a big congo drum to play. We had no earthly idea that this was a festival dedicated to old time and bluegrass music, or even, exactly what "that" was. We felt *like we were pretty traditional. No one stopped us, so there we were—onstage at Independence. Earlier I'd met Joe Arminger who told me about the threat against the New River: some people wanted to build a hydro-electric dam on it and flood thousands of acres in Grayson County. It was just getting dark as we started to play. The rain stopped, a little breeze came up and I announced that we were "dedicating this to the New River". Then we cut loose with an energetic version of "The Backwater Blues". When we finished, a big roar of applause and cheers came up from the audience. I remember looking out at a bunch of smiling, approving hippy faces. I'm sure we also got some disapproving looks but they didn't register or lurk in my memory banks.*

Our tents were at the base of the hill in the high school ballfield, in the corner where the road turns down into the school property. Earlier that day a pretty good, bearded guitar player dropped by and introduced himself as Rob Mangum. (Later he and wife Bet were members of "The Courthouse Ramblers.") Rob stayed around and jammed with all of us, which included at some point, Wish and probably Joe Arminger. I don't remember Claudine Langille singing with Muriel and me that time (as Wish does) but I do remember getting some unexpected but appreciated applause in the wee hours from a little group of black folks who were standing up on top of the hill by the road.

Claudine Langille and her friend Larry Poole rented a house just over the ridge from my cabin—both our places were up toward the ends of hollows. Claudine had a wonderful, rich, powerful voice. (She's on an album with Henry the Fiddler; someone's on hammer dulcimer and she's singing "Going Over the Waterfall". Nice!) I can hear her now and see her big light-up-the-world smile. She's been back up North for some years. When she lived here—northeast of me, my nearest neighbor at that time was a fine old bachelor farmer who lived to the south of me. A couple of times I'd pass him on the road and he'd shake his head and smile, and tell me he'd just heard Claudine singing up at her house again and how the sound carried right down the hollow to his ears. He loved the old music.

One of my earliest memories was of sitting on my grandparents' front porch in Elk Creek, VA and seeing my great-uncle Olin and great-aunt Elma playing—one on banjo and one on fiddle—and my mother playing the mouth harp. I don't remember the sound of the music but the novelty, the excitement of the moment has stayed with me ever since. It was never discussed, and that was the only time I ever saw or heard of my mother playing the mouth harp (harmonica), but I think it was probably something she turned her back on as being "too country", not sophisticated. She'd grown up poor on the farm, and though she was very intelligent, secretarial school was her highest formal education. She was always quite a jokester, and a talented piano player—by ear, by "the chord method" she'd learned in Roanoke. She also made sure my brother and I got good big doses of country life in Elk Creek from the time we were born, but she often seemed to want to "overcome" the circumstance of her birth. I, on the other hand, longed to live here in the mountains. (When I moved to Grayson County in 1975 with my children, found this old log house and moved into it in 1976, for awhile she thought I'd lost my mind. But I felt like I was finally home.)

In June 1976 I went to the Independence Fiddlers Convention by myself, planning to meet Leon Frost who was going to back me up on guitar when I entered the folk singing contest. He never showed up so I hung out awhile with Wish and Baltimore Joe and some of the Sturgills. (In trade for painting a mural on the wall of the old Piggly Wiggly in Independence that had recently become their instrument shop, John Sturgill built me a "concert dulcimer". Their business closed down before I finished the mural! John had heard me complain that my dulcimer couldn't be heard over the other instruments, especially onstage.) I think we put together a stage band that year, but that's just a guess. It's that haze thing again.

I do remember that Wish, and maybe Joe Arminger too, wanted me to sing the "Grayson County Line" with them. Wish had the sheet music and was optimistic that I could learn the song and perform it later that day. That didn't happen because I was shy about performing a song that I didn't know, especially one where I'd have to read the lyrics from sheet music onstage.

It was at the 1976 Independence Fiddlers Convention I met Evelyn Farmer. She was walking around, cradling her autoharp, and I had mine. She walked up to me with a big smile, introduced herself and invited me to do a tune with her. I don't remember what we sang but I do recall that I was quickly aware I was way out-classed. She could play the autoharp. More than Evelyn's talents as an autoharpist and singer, it's the friendly, welcoming way in which she approached all of the "newcomers" that I admire. It was as if she unconsciously appointed herself to be the "ambassador of good will" between the native-born, local musicians and the "hippies-come-lately". She holds a dear place in my heart.

When the Courthouse Ramblers got together in the early '80's, we learned the "Grayson County Line" and over the years performed it in a few places including at Galax once. (Another sidebar: In 1976, when I did some illustrations for the Grayson County History book, then in production, I met Gene Hughes, co-editor of the book; he'd been commissioned by the Grayson County Historical Society to write that song). Some years later, the CH Ramblers recorded the song on a 45 rpm, "Sounds of Grayson", produced by the Historical Society. I wrote the copy and did the layout and art for the cover. The other performers on the record were Wayne and Carol Henderson on guitars, Wanda Kirk playing old-timey piano and the Highland Camerata community chorus doing a spiritual. "The Courthouse Ramblers": I always said, "what we lacked in talent we made up for in enthusiasm".

Considered a "hippy from up North" by some people around here, at the same time I had a toe in the door by virtue of my ancestry. I had aunts, uncles and cousins living here and there were lots of people in Elk Creek who remembered me from years gone by. I saw both sides of the "them vs. us" thing. I didn't think all "hippies" were naturally wonderful people and I sure didn't think all the native mountain people were a bunch of rednecks. I never felt I had to take sides. People were people. I still feel that way.

The only time I ever won anything at Galax was in 1976. By that time, I was on the verge of giving up the autoharp; it was not an easy instrument to walk around the park and get into jams with; it forever needed tuning. That's a lot of strings to deal with; by the time I'd get it in tune, everyone had gone to bed. So Leon Frost was going to back me on guitar for the Folk Song competition. There I was, in line on a hot Saturday morning, looking around every few minutes to see if I could see Leon, but once again he never showed. So I made a quick decision to sing a capella. When I got to the mic, because there was no one to give me a note, I started singing and realized I was just a shade higher than I'd normally start. I did more than a dozen verses of "Barbara Allen" with a slight "edge" to my voice. That's why I think I got Fifth Place Folk Song that year. That might sound really impressive, but back then there were only five places. I'm still proud to have won that ribbon though.

I was painting the mural in the Sturgill's shop in Independence and John or somebody gave me comp tickets to Stompin' '76. I had no idea what it would be, but I heard it was going to be where the New River Jam had been right after the 1975 Galax Fiddlers. I had gone to that for a day and it was in one of the most beautiful, bucolic settings I'd ever seen. So with that picture in mind, I gave my 4-person tent to friends who came from West Virginia to take with them to Stompin' '76. I can't recall why, maybe my kids were in school, but the plan was my WV pals would set up my tent and have it ready for us when we arrived the following weekend. On Saturday morning, after having to park my car and we three had walked a mile or so, we hitched a ride that took us nearer to the festival site. I could not believe the vendors—the booths with signs advertising all kinds of drugs for sale. Along with that, but mostly because of the huge crowd that kept growing, I began to wonder if I hadn't made a mistake bringing my children We were deposited on a hilltop and when I looked down into the sea of tents and bodies, I wondered why I'd come myself. There was no way I'd ever find my tent and friends. It wasn't a pretty sight and there were some rough-looking thugs nearby.

I felt we were saved when I realized the huge tent we were standing by had an"ALERT" sign on it. (ALERT was the volunteer rescue crew than preceeded the Galax Rescue Squad). And standing in the doorway of the tent was our friend and neighbor in Galax, Tommy Barr, now of Barr's Fiddle Shop in Galax. Tommy was an ALERT volunteer on duty at Stompin' '76. From him we learned that there were no police anywhere around. Crowd control was being handled by some big-name bad rep motorcycle gang. If a vehicle was blocking the road, they pushed it off and down over the bank. There was no food for the masses and only a few porto-potties. There were helicopters flying in and out and announcements over the PA warning people not to "do the whatever-color-it-was" pills. My two kids and I were offered cots in the big tent where we spent the night. I didn't sleep much, between hearing the radio calls come in, the PA announcements and the sound of cars being pushed over banks and people being beaten up. I never heard any music. The next day, Tommy drove the kids and me out to my car.

The Galax Fiddlers the following week (or was it two weeks?) was a far cry from previous ones. Law enforcement, that didn't have the numbers to create a presence at Stompin' '76 were marching around Felts Park three-

and four-abreast and they did create a presence there. Maybe it's the haze but I think I even saw several cops walking side by side with their arms linked—quite surreal.

In 1984, "The Courthouse Ramblers" were just really organizing and learning more than 4 or 5 tunes but we hadn't started going onstage as a band yet. 1984 was the year the Moose decided not to refund money to folk singers, so I spent most of the festival going around Felts Park, wearing my "protest T-shirt" and getting people to sign petitions we later gave to the Moose who disregarded them. We'd gotten wind that the officials at Galax were going to change the rule about refunding the singers, so several of us, including Dale Morris and myself, met with some of the Moose men at Felts Park a few days before the festival. We hoped to convince them to change their minds and give folk singers their money back. I guess because there were hundreds of entrants, the Moose just didn't want to fool with it anymore. Whatever. They wouldn't change their minds. It had gotten my dander up, so in just a couple of days, we had a couple hundred bright orange (for the Scots) T-shirts printed in Kelly green (for the Irish) with the slogan (thanks to my creative daughter!): "PRESERVE TRADITION—DON'T TAX MUSICIANS! Galax 1984". We sold them all. I have one Small left and wish I'd kept one more—in a larger size!

Kirk Sutphin is at least a third generation Old Time musician. Although he is in his thirties, he consciously tries to live in the pre-W.W.II style, and owns a collection of old instruments, two Model A Fords and an antique "Red Belly" Ford tractor. He lives in his grandfather's house, and is sometimes called "Pappy". He is master of the banjo, in several different styles, and is one of the best fiddlers of his generation. To demonstrate his modesty: it was necessary once for me to describe him in print. He wouldn't allow the adjective" famous" or any similar superlative. We finally settled on "Noted", because he does play notes, He lives just down the road from Riley Baugus, they went to school together, and Kirk loves to tell stories with dry wit and accent.

One of his favorites concerns the day when he and Riley were driving through Winston-Salem, and saw some hairy freak. The guy was pretty road-beat, and although he was "festooned" with instruments, they decided to pass him by. Eventually, after a few errands, they drove over to Rich Harkness' house for a few tunes. Rich had a houseguest, a mando-plunker coming in from Tennessee. It was the same raggedy-ass hitchhiker they had bypassed on the highway. Me.

Kirk Sutphin Interview

Now you have to say a word.

A word.

Kirk, known as Pappy. So you been playing music all your life, right?

Pretty much. Since I was eight years old.

And your dad?

My dad played guitar, and my grandpa played fiddle. My dad's Wayne Sutphin and grandpaw was Sid Sutphin.

Who was Paul Sutphin to you?

Paul Sutphin was my grandpa's first cousin. So that would make me and Paul fourth cousins or something.

You're really an expert in all the Old Timey guys.

Pretty much, from around this area ... like a ninety or hundred mile radius around here. But they're just about all gone. I guess in the ... generation, you got people James Burris, from up there in Galax, that plays sort of the festival style of playing. Eddie Bond, he's wide open and Hooven ...

Greg Hooven's not with us any more.

He was real talented. It was a real waste. It's interesting the direction the music's going to be taking, now that a lot of the old guys have gone. I guess I've been labeled a purist in the past so ... I guess there needs to be some purists out there. But I guess I'm not an extreme purist, like it has to be this way or ...

Well, I've had a few visitors ... I guess the furthest visitor was Kiri Mikasa? He's about sixty years old. He taught himself clawhammer from listening to records. From West Tokyo or someplace. He came over a few years ago. And he barely spoke any English ... real poor. He wanted to meet somebody from Round Peak, and I said, "Well, Dick Freeman's dead, and Kyle's dead, Tommy's dead, and Fred's dead ..."

You ain't dead!

But ... I've studied a lot of it. He wanted to meet somebody that was from the tradition and all that, and I told him, "Well put it like this Mikasa, if I didn't know better, and I had my eyes closed, I'd swear he was from Round Peak." And he was so pleased. So gracious. It really tickled him.

But you and Riley are pretty much in the tradition, although I think you said that Riley's family didn't play music.

Not that I know of, but like most families here, somebody played harmonica or a little dab on the guitar or banjo or something. Everybody had somebody musical in the family. Before electricity and all that, that was the entertainment.

You don't make enough money making music ...

No, that's why I paint houses. Probably half and half, I'm not getting rich on either one of them.

But you've got ... How many records out?

I need to take a count of that.

I've got four, I think. "Masters of the Banjo", "Old Roots, New Branches", Sutphin and Friends".

That's "Grandpa's Favorites". That's my latest one. I've been on several other CD's. "Old Holler String Band." That was about the time me and Riley were going up to Tommy Jarrell's house. That's where we met Terry MacMurry. She'd moved down from Wisconsin, learned banjo and liked the people so well she decided to move down.

She wasn't with Paul Brown then?

No ... But that's when I met Paul Brown, at Tommy's house. Pretty much just a gathering place for the Northern people. Came down to learn the music. Tommy was probably the most generous person you would ever meet. He just welcomed everybody into his home, made them feel welcome.

Seemed to have a pretty sharp tongue to him.

Yeah, he wouldn't take a whole lot of junk. He was pretty tolerant of different people. I remember one time, he got up ... there were some visitors there ... got up to get a glass of water from the kitchen. He looked out the window and some guy was sitting cross-legged ... meditating ... And he walked out there ... thought he froze to death or something ... He walked out there and walked around looking at him ... He just shook his head and laughed about it. Never seen anything like that.

I guess one thing I've discovered when I first went to Tommy Jarrell's house, I didn't have any idea of how big of a music scene or whatever you might call it there was out there. Tommy said, "You ever been out to the Mount Airy Fiddle Festival?" And I had no clue of the size of it. And I think, 1983, I went to my first Mt. Airy. I was just amazed at the size of the hodgepodge of people. From New York, and Philadelphia, and West Virginia, and Florida, and how friendly everybody was.

I remember Riley came up after work, on that Friday night, from that seafood place, still had flour on his clothes. Smelling like deep-fried seafood. He was just amazed at all the people that were there, close to our age. We were fairly young then, he being a couple of years older than me. I think we probably stayed up until three o'clock playing music at night with everybody. We wanted to learn all the tunes we could from everybody and meet everybody and we were just taken away by everything. So that's how we, that was out first exposure to the Northerners. Then we had to go to Galax to the Fiddler's Convention the same year. It was the same way. I think we stayed up to four o'clock that night playing music.

You like that Charlie Poole two-finger ... Real clean and percussive ...

They call that the Piedmont Style.

But he would play anything.

It was just the way he played the banjo. A lot of the old guys from that area played like that. One thing I've noticed in teaching banjo at music camps, is that Round Peak banjo playing is a little different ... It's not a rhythm thing. It's predominately melody.

That's one thing I like about Old Timey, there is so much variety. It's not like Bluegrass where it's like this ... In Old Timey, there's no wrong or right way to any of it. Then there's Missouri fiddling, all sorts of other ... Kentucky fiddling.

Tom Mylet said he thought that the most important thing is having respect for the old timers and their music.

And you can tell. Tom Mylet, he really does have respect. He played on my CD with Paul Sutphin and Verlin as the "New Camp Creek Band" That's on "Grandpa's Favorites". We did about three or four cuts on there and it's neat to get that same sound they got back in the Sixties. The key element was Paul Sutphin and his "Clawhammer guitar". And Verlin, with his unique mandolin style. His timing was pretty unique. I'm not exactly sure how he does it. I know a lot of people have tried to figure it out.

I've always had respect for the old guys, tried to meet as many of them as I could. I think that's important. I try to capture a little bit from each one of the old guys. Or as much as you could. You can't listen to the record and capture it. At least I couldn't. That's what I picked up hanging out with Tommy. Little subtleties of bowing and fingering with the left hand.

Well, it's the type thing; music around here, this type of music is a dinosaur. The way Tommy played, was just from his time period ...

Tom Mylet told me that Tommy Jarrell was real old fashioned. He was playing almost a Civil War style. Run that down for me, would you?

Tommy played pretty much like pre-nineteen hundred music.

Who did he learn from?

His dad, Ben, his uncle, Charlie. And neighbors from all around. And he learned some from my grandpa's great uncle. Zach Paine. He was a Civil War vet.

Tell me more about Fred Cockerham.

I didn't get to meet Fred, but I did go to his viewing, right before his funeral. And I saw his wife, Eva, and Tommy was there, and that's really the first time I got to talk to Tommy. That's 1980. And Tommy said, "Come on up and I'll show you what I can on the fiddle. Because at that point, my grandpa had inspired me and my two older brothers to learn to play the fiddle. And Grandpa passed away about a year after we all got us fiddles and started learning a few tunes from Grandpa.

But like I was telling you, I had no idea that there was that many people from New York and Ohio and Florida, Pennsylvania into this kind of music. I thought it was just a handful of people played it. Come to find out it was all over. But, like we were talking about Tommy, Tommy learned from his dad, from an older generation, and he didn't really learn any, a whole lot of new tunes. Maybe a handful. And then Fred Cockerham was more influenced by Fiddlin' Arthur Smith, and some Bluegrass …

So Fred had a more modern influence. My Grandpa didn't play nothing he didn't play when he was a kid. So he wasn't really influenced by later music. And my dad, he was familiar with 1940's music, radio and so was my uncle, Rupert. So I guess there is a time period right in there when people didn't play this music. The younger people, like my dad's generation. So for me to want to play what I do is unique, in a way, for around here.

If you think about it, when radio came about, like Fiddlin' Arthur Smith, that really standardized a lot of the different fiddling. Everybody was like, "Well I'm not going to play like Grandpa, I'm going to play like this". So they kind of altered their styles to fit.

To make some money.

That, and they're just copycats. Do what was popular. I think a lot of people of that generation were maybe ashamed to play mountain music … after they moved down to Winston or wherever, they kind of … they might play a little bit. A lot of people wanted to be up-to-date. I can't see a whole lot of resentment towards the Northerners from people around here, because I'm not sure how many people from the Mt. Airy area play Old Time, that would even have a comment about any Northerners.

Bill Lowe
Deposition

I started playing in 1941 when I was 11 years old. I heard my first OT music from my Uncle Grover Runyons in the mountains of Southeast KY. He played the fiddle and banjo and the moment I heard it, I knew it would be a part of me for the rest of my life. I went to his house as much as I could and listened to him play until he moved away. Then I purchased a guitar from a pawnshop in Williamson, West VA. There after I began a journey into the world of music seeking all the information, styles, types, etc. of music I could find. I began with OT, changed to country in the 50's, returned to OT and OT bluegrass and that's where I've remained until this day.

This was in Pike County Kentucky—up Big Creek. I felt the music the first time I heard my Uncle Grover . I knew it was part of my soul. The feeling in old time music is what it is all about. I took up the guitar first, then learned the old claw hammer style banjo playing. I still play both of them today.

I lived where it originated. At age 18 I left KY for a brief stay in Cleveland, Ohio, joined the Marines and stayed in California for twenty some years, and now retired in Salem, SC. There is less music here than any place I've ever lived.

I started my first band at age 15 named "The Lonely Mountain Boys". I played many a radio show and local show with Ralph and Carter Stanley, Molly O'Day and many more locals who made their mark in the music world. I have always been the leader of my own band. Bill Monroe offered me a job many years ago, but I had 4 children and did not want to be on the road as much as he was.

First and foremost was the Carter Family. I heard them on the radio and tried to duplicate their music. I developed my style of picking from their style. I thought there was only one guitar making all that music I heard on the radio and I tried to get all of that out of one guitar. Of course, I later learned that was not true. That is why my style is so unique, sort of lead and rhythm at the same time ... simple stated. .

There were no festivals when I was young. We had things like fiddle and singing conventions at churches and family gatherings. Being from the mountains the music was a way of life. Today, this is not true. Being from the mountains is so different today ... my personal opinion. There wasn't much else to do when I was growing up and musicians were welcomed by all except some of the church goers who thought it wrong and my dad was one of them. He made me go to a separate building away from the house to play my music and it was not allowed in his house.

Middle part of my life was Doc Watson. He spent a lot of time in California when I lived there and he was not the big shot he is now. He stayed with me weeks at a time ... so did his son Merle. I learned many songs from him and some great picking secrets. We are still good friends today. Kentucky Colonels, Clarence and Roland White were also good friends of mine while living in California. I picked a lot with the great Scott Stoneman.

Did you try to live back to nature?

Musically, yes, lifestyle, no. I grew up that way and wanted a different way of life. Old Timey fulfilled my life dreams of playing, performing and recording. It also keeps me close to where I came from. The music, lyrics, etc. take me back to Pike County KY and that's a good thing. It seems older musicians are not teaching the young the wonderful art of playing the old style. There will always be a desire to keep the past alive.

The best thing about Old Time is the feeling ... the freedom of expression. Worst is people playing it who don't know the history and background of it. New people need to spend time studying the art of Old Time. Visit, talk and pick with those who are from the true vine.

I don't think Outsiders and learn the music. I'll be glad to debate this at length. Others can learn the notes, but not the feeling because they didn't live it. Modern Old Time is not valid; it is not real; it is hybrid music with little feeling and expression. Everyone sounds the same. That is not the way it is supposed to be.

In many ways I also think competition hurts. Those who do not really know Old Time music can get the wrong impression. My opinions are very strong and in some cases may not be printable because I feel today that a lot of younger artists are not spending enough time researching. The get on the train too far down the track. It would be wise for them to listen to old musicians, talk, and maybe play some with them. They could gain a world of knowledge that is so important. The soul they will never get due to the changing environment and lifestyles of today.

William G. "Jerry" Jordan "Jellywhitebread"

Jerry Jordan bought a few of my musical instruments, including a jazz guitar made out of an old Chestnut log from the family farm.

Where to start? For me the idea of the "old time revival" started before I knew it was an idea. Bluegrass was just the music that was heard around the house when I was a baby, my folks were from Jumping Branch W. V., and bluegrass was just what happened when friends or family got together. I considered it all bluegrass, but really there were all kinds of songs that just told a tale. Songs about groundhog pie or possum stew, just something to make you laugh or smile. I heard banjo, guitar, fiddle and a little mandolin. Piano and upright bass once in a while ... the old arts and crafts festival always had the booths with lap dulcimers and hammer dulcimers, but I never heard a lot of them in the local music. For me the music was just something handed down from the old to the young. My grandfather had twelve kids, and between them and their spouses and kids there was a fair amount that carried on the tradition.

It wasn't till I got older that I realized the variety of music that was really out there. I didn't think of it as a revival, 'cause it was always there. In the end I don't think enough of the old music has survived once it was removed from the mountains where I heard it. The world just gets too busy. But when I go back to Monroe and

Summers counties I still hear the old songs, and they are still getting together to play it, though its a lot different than "dueling banjos".

But as far as being part of the revival, I'd have to say I was never part of it. When I was asked to play along with a gathering I was a guitar player, and most of the time it was the G, C, or D chord in one order or another. The one time I got set up with the upright bass, it was 2 feet taller than me, and still only the G, C, or D note was required. Out of the Appalachians, the main revival I saw was with surf music of the early '60's.

When I inquired of my grandfather many years ago where he learned to play the 8 or 9 instruments he played, he said he learned it all as part of church gospel music (he was born in 1915) in Appalachia.

Bill and Janice Birchfield

We're from Roane Mt. Tennessee. We are carrying on the tunes that our families played for generations. My dad Played Old Time Music, and Bill's father was a great Old Time fiddler, Joe Birchfield.

And you make all your own instruments?

Bill: I make my fiddles. I built nine so far. Sold all but three. Some of them's local wood, and the spruce I get from Germany. It's $35.00 a piece for the tops.

You play left handed on right-handed instruments.

I don't string them up backwards, same with the banjo and guitar. I learned the fiddle the wrong way.

Do you play a particular style?

The old time style back in 1910, 1920. I learned from my father and my father's uncle. We played square dances … with my father, we played a lot of them. Started in 1976. Quite a while back. Father's dead, my uncle, grandmas, grandpaws, aunts … All of them in the Birchfield family played some kind of instrument.

Janice: I started playing tambourine, things with rhythm, then started on washtub bass. He actually played about two years before I started playing with the band very often—"The Roane Mountain Hilltoppers."

Bill: We played just in the band when we started. Sugar Grove, Virginia, was the first fiddler's conv ention we went to. We didn't know nothing about fiddler's conventions. I thought it was where you traded fiddles. That's what it sounded like. The first one we ever played at, we took first place.

And we went back for the championship in two weeks, with my uncle and my father and me, and took first place band. I was playing guitar, my Uncle Johnny was playing banjo, and my father Joe was playing fiddle. That's when we named ourselves the "Hilltoppers".

Do you think us people coming down know how to play your music?

I hope you're learning it if you don't.

Janice: People from the Southern Appalachians play OId Time different from people in the Northern Appalachian area.

Bill: They sure do.

Janice: Most of the fiddlers here are long bow fiddlers, and your Northern fiddlers are more short bow fiddlers. They play more like the West Virginia style, some of them.

Bill: The Old Timers pulled the long box, double drones and all that. And they played with a drive hwere the others didn't have that drive.

Janice: We use a lot of cross-tunings.

You think the drive is for dancing?

Bill: Oh yeah. That's the point, right there.

Matt Kenman

I live in the state of Tennessee. Nashville. I used to do Civil War reenactments, quite a bit. Now I do trading and swapping instruments every chance I get. I don't miss no meals.

What kind of music do you play?

I mostly just play what the "Hilltoppers" do. I play with this group and I play with Richard Bowman's "Slate Mountain Rambers". I worked for "The Old Crow Medicine Show" for a while, and I worked for Leroy Troy for years. I even got to work for Marty Stewart one time.

Did you grow up in this music?

I've been around it all my life. I was raised in South Carolina, and then when I was about sixteen I took off for Tennessee. And then I moved around North Carolina and Virginia for a long time. I got with "Old Crow Medicine Show" and started going back and forth to Nashville.

They got pretty famous, and you left them?

We had a parting of the ways backstage of the Grand Ol' Opry.

What would you call their music?

Modernized music. I wouldn't call them Old Time. They are pretty rough musicians, in my opinion. That's pretty much what their crowd is, young folks, the hippy crowd. You don't see a whole lot of the older people there. I played the mandolin and the fiddle and the bones and the banjo. Whatever they couldn't play. I had to fill in and play for them. They were from New York and moved to Boone.

So, what do you think about people moving down to play Old Time and making money?

I think it's highway robbery, when it's making it off the backs of people that's been around Old Time all their lives. They are getting noted for other people's music. But they ain't giving notoriety where it's due. Most time they say, "I learned this from such and such". They didn't, they learned it off their tapes, they didn't learn it from people. Because when you learn it from … Like, I know Bill Birchfield, I've been to his house, we went to the lake fishing, whatever. I know him as a person. And that gets carried into your music. When you hear something off a record, you don't know anything about the people, nothing about them. And it doesn't carry over into your music. You just don't know anything about their lives. You got a piece of history there if you don't have a piece of their life. It carries over into your music; it's got a different feeling. It's a good thing.

And the majority of my tunes, I have to say, I have learned from people, not from records or tapes. There has been a few, like Jimmy Rogers, that I have learned off of tapes. But that's the only way I can learn them, these days.

I play banjo, mandolin, fiddle, bass, accordion, tenor, bones, whatever they want me to play. Every one of my great uncles was a fiddler. In Texas. They played all the dances. They never were formed as a band. They did play together. And they played whatever. Every place they could go get a drink, get a little pay, that's what they would do.

That is so hard for the academics to understand. They talk about the purity of Old Time. They just can't get it though their heads that, you want a gig, and somebody wants you to play "Old Black Joe" … "Hum a few bars and I'll fake it"

It was during the depression and they played music. Somebody offered them twenty bucks and some eating and drinking, they took it. That was a good job. Five dollars, they took it. They done what they had to, to get by. Ninety-five percent of my living is music. But you always got to keep your eyes open for a trade.

What do you think about the hippies that actually care for the music and the people?

I think it's a great thing. If it hadn't been for the Northerners and the hippies, this music would probably have died. It would be dead.

You feel no need to play Bluegrass?

I tried it. And I thought I was really doing something, and I was playing one day, practicing all these fancy licks … this man comes up and says, "Why play all that junk? You can't even recognize the tune. Why not play so you can recognize it walking up, make you want to dance, and when you leave, you feel it and you're still singing the tune."

It made so much sense to me I've not played Bluegrass since. I'm just playing music I come up with. And they didn't call it Old Time Music, they didn't call it Bluegrass, they didn't call it Country. They just called it "making music". They said, "You want to make music?"

And there's been many a time when I'd sit there and play guitar with my dad and all these different ones, and they'd say. "A'ight, if you can't play with us, then we ain't gonna play with you". They'd just put their instruments away. But they wanted you to play the music. And if I didn't play the music, by God, they would put up their instruments for two or three days, just bother you to death and wouldn't play with you. You weren't playing in time with them. You would try to put more in it than it needed. And they broke me of that.

I do collect old records, but I don't study it. Some of the old fiddle tunes and the words … most of these tunes have words to them, but nobody sings them. I'm trying to collect all I can of the words to the fiddle tunes. I'm just proud to play music and keep it as traditional as I can, but you can't be like the records. You can't sing and play exactly like them, because you ain't them. And what made it an appealing band then, was them and they played the way they played. Like, there will never be another Roane Mountain Hilltoppers, they have their sound and that's it.

You will never learn to play the fiddle until you become your own fiddler. As long as you're trying to imitate somebody, you will never become a fiddler. Until you come and put your feeling in it. Then you will become your fiddler.

And you have to know who you are. You have to put your own feet on the ground, inside your own shoes, and say …

Right. You're not a copy.

Gail Gillespie Deposition

Gail is the Editor of "The Old Time Herald" magazine.

I spent much of my youth in the Florida Panhandle, though my dad was in the Air Force & we'd moved around quite a bit before I was in high school. He was from Petersburg, Tennessee where he'd grown up on land that had been in his family since right after the Revolutionary War. He hated old-time music and never really approved of my efforts. He thought the banjo was a horrible, primitive instrument. So, of course it was my favorite from my first memories of hearing it.

Though I didn't call it old-time music until 1966, I was discovering it in the early 60s when I was 15-16 years old. This was the very height of the folk music revival. Joan Baez had recorded a couple of "Carter Family" tunes on her second record and those were my favorites. By 1963 I'd gotten some Woody Guthrie and Cisco Houston, "Carter Family", "Country Gentlemen" and "New Lost City Ramblers" records.

"Jim & Jesse & the Virginia Boys" were on television every afternoon at 3:30 & I rushed home from school to catch them. Before that, I remember hearing & loving country harmony on the radio at my MeeMaw Gillespie's house in Fayetteville, Tennessee in the 1950s When we were at the beach around 1956 we would sit around the kitchen table picking crab meat in the evening, listening to the "Stanley Brothers", who came to us from a radio station in Live Oak, Fla. I was only 10 but I definitely recall loving the instrumental breaks.

I had taken flute lessons in the 4th grade; however, I never read music very well and was turned off lessons for life by a punitive teacher who whacked our knuckles with a drumstick if we played a wrong note.

I started playing old-time music in a band in the early 70s in Gainesville; I liked the do-it yourself aspect of it. You learned it yourself—no lessons, no cruel teachers, and played for the sheer joy of being in the middle of that wonderful sound, sharing it with your friends.

The first instrument I played was the guitar. I received a cheap plywood B&J Serenader parlor guitar for Christmas in 1961; got a small crummy Gibson in 62 and a Martin (I still have this one) in 1963. Borrowed a banjo in 1963 and got my own in 1965, a turn of the century Slingerland. Tried to learn from the Pete Seeger book but wound up defaulting to my own 2-finger picking style based on recordings of the "New Lost City Ramblers", which came in handy when I decided to try and learn Charlie Poole style later on in life.

After Dwight and I met in 74, the usual pattern was fiddle/banjo duets with my husband at home and with the addition of guitars to form a band.

Though I had been a half-hearted hippy in the late 60s, by the time I started playing Old Time, I had little to do with either drugs (marijauna mainly) or of alcohol, so no … but the hippy alternative life style definitely laid the groundwork for old-time music. The escape from meaningless pop music, its replacement with music you could share with friends, meeting "honorary grandparents" like Kyle Creed and Taylor and Stella Kimble, all fit with the alternative subculture.

In the early 70s I lived in a sort of commune, "Big Otter," just outside Gainesville, FL. I say "sort of" commune because most of us had day jobs at the University of Florida or were graduate students there. We lived in homemade houses without electricity or running water—used kerosene lamps, wood stoves & got water from a sinkhole.

Currently I'm mostly a "local musician," and sideman in several old-time bands, and am editor of a magazine about old-time music. I know that there are lots of great players coming up who are deep into it and have a great deal of respect for early sources. They want to "get it right" and they have access to so much more in the way of recordings than we ever did. Though some of the young folks in our area of central NC have found some old guys to visit, I think we baby boomers certainly had more access to real live old-timers.

I have two daughters and both appreciate Old Time, but one daughter is very involved: plays guitar, banjo and banjo-uke and makes banjos. She also made a replica of a Middle Tennessee Music Box dulcimer.

The best thing about Old Time is the support of the greater community. The worst is the insular nature of the community ... things can get cliquish.

I feel some strain between the Yankees and the Southerners. I've felt it before. Though I'm not one of them in terms of class, I get frustrated when it's assumed I'm a Northerner. I want to say,"I know I'm still an outsider, but, hey, I'm a fellow southerner: I called my grandmothers "MeeMaw", grew up eating grits, crowder peas and chess pie and slept under a churn dash quilt! All my relatives say "y'all", know how to catch mullet with cast nets, and put two cups of sugar per quart when they make their "aaahce tea". (I seem to have lost my accent from moving around the world/country between the ages of 6-12 as an Air Force brat).

I think competition changes the music, but whether it helps or hurts it's hard to say. It's definitely limited the kinds of fiddle and banjo styles that you hear now. But it's brought out old-timers to conventions where we might not have otherwise met them and this has allowed the developing of friendships and connections that wouldn't have happened without those very conventions/contests.

Mitchell Badgett
Letter

Well I began learning to play the five-string banjo at the age of 6, about 1961. The song "Old Joe Clark" was the first thing anyone ever showed me. I had little interest in music until one day when I was very young, our family journeyed to my grandmother's brother's family for a get-together. This included a homemade oyster stew for food and their family Bluegrass band, "The Jottumtown Ramblers" as entertainment. My cousin Aubrey Hall was playing banjo in the three-finger style of Scruggs, Reno & Stanley. I knew from that moment on, what instrument I wanted to play and the kind of music I wanted play.

I never traveled to reach this music. It seemed all the best bluegrass and old time was all around me. When I became an adult, I began playing electric guitar and traveled out west in several Top 40 country road/club bands for about 5 years. I just wanted to make some money doing what I loved; playing music. It seemed bluegrass and old time bands could never make any money. Everyone expected you to play for free around home.

The band I've played with the longest and still perform with, are my friends the "Red Wigglers" based in Mt. Airy, NC. We've been together over 30 years now and have played just about every style of music we could think of including some old time. I'd rather play than listen, but all bands intrigue me to watch for a short time. Old time bores me after listening to most bands play the same tune for such a long time, like they were playing for a square dance. There are just too many great melodies out there to only play a few each night.

And I never tried to live "back to nature". While the simple lifestyle and dreams of living on several acres of my own land appeal to me, life was just too fast and cash flow was in too big a demand to kick back and live like my great grandparents did. Music in general opened doors for me that I could have never ventured through otherwise. It also caused some problems, but the good out weighted the bad 10 to 1 in my mind.

OT will survive during my lifetime and maybe my grandchildren's. I'm not so sure after that. I'm sure some of the famous recordings will survive as long as there are music teachers and scholars who are interested in history, but to find an old time band still performing in another 150 years—I doubt it. The melodies and the lively beat are my favorite things. The monotonousness and lack of solos are what I hate the most.

I don't see tension between the Yankees and the Locals. Just the usual adjustment of personalities between strangers and the typical envy or dislike people experience when you hear someone play different from yourself is what I see. Non-Appalachian people can play OT, certainly they can. Will it sound the same? I doubt it. They may be able to get close; close enough that only another musician can tell the difference. You can only copy someone else so far and your own interpretation of the music has to show through. Is that good or bad? It doesn't matter. You have to accept it because that is just the way the art of music is performed. It is alive and in a constant state of flux. Only recordings are locked in time, never to change.

Lynn Worth
An essay for your project.

My name is Lynn Worth and I am from a musical family native to the Blue Ridge Mountains of North Carolina. I was not part of the revival nor do I hate it. I am part of another group—the "next generation" of native Appalachian string musicians who learned from old timers and others. We are usually overlooked by music authorities and historians who focus on revivalists and old timers.

I have two main thoughts on the issue at hand.

- *There is a place for tradition and there is a place for innovation.*
- *Music belongs to everybody.*

I was born (1959) and raised in Ashe County in Northwest North Carolina. I now live in the county next door, Alleghany, a short distance from the Virginia State line. Like everybody my age, I grew up on rock and roll. But I also heard old time and bluegrass music. The albums of Albert Hash and the "Whitetop Mountain Band" were popular, and I enjoyed going to the Ashe County Fiddler's Convention and hearing the music there.

I was in band in school from 4th grade through college, mostly playing by ear. I started playing guitar at age 17 during a particularly snowy winter when a cousin left his Conn six-string at our house. I first played from a Beatles songbook until my fingers were so sore I couldn't stand it, then I taped them up and played some more. I started playing old time fiddle at age 26 when I enrolled in a class through Wilkes Community College, taught by Whitetop fiddler Thornton Spencer. Besides the actual playing, Thornton taught us a lot about fiddles and bows and had great tales to share. The class was informal. Many non-students came, which was a big bonus for hearing more styles and tunes, having other instruments to play along with, and making new friends.

Like a lot of people, I was offered an instrument as an incentive to learn to play. A fiddle hung on the wall the entire time I was growing up. It belonged to my father and his father before him. Neither of them played, but my father loved music of all kinds and passed that love along to me and my brothers. I have many memories of sing-alongs around my mother's piano and records playing all the time. My father told me if I learned to play that fiddle I could have it. My grandfather played mandolin and taught shape note singing. He taught my mother and some of her siblings to play piano by ear.

A highlight of my summer is our family reunion on my mother's side, when my generation and now some of the younger ones get together and jam.

I think the variety in style from musician to musician is the most unique and interesting aspect of old time music. You don't hear it as much in bluegrass, and very little in formal, written music. But an old time tune is as unique as the individual who is playing it. I think this is more true of non-revivalists. Revivalists studied the old timers faithfully and diligently. They play well, they know their stuff, and they sound remarkably like their mentors. Thus, they sound remarkably like each other.

I respect and admire the faithfulness to tradition and the esteem for old timers the revivalists have carried on. I also respect and admire the soul that shows through a person who plays their own unique style. I don't try to live "back to nature" because I never left it to start with. I am a freelance editor and writer for The Gazette newspaper in Galax, VA. I play in two old time bands and a church band.

Old Time has enriched my life beyond description. Period. I think old time will continue to thrive. Hopefully someday it will be appreciated by the general public outside our region, perhaps when the "Beverly Hillbillies" and "Deliverance" are forgotten by future generations and we lose the stereotypic reputation that mountain people are backward, uncultured and uneducated. (That being said, I realize a lot of great old time doesn't even come from the mountains.)

The best thing about old time music is the friendships that it forges. I can't think of anything bad about it. I don't feel any tension between old timers and newcomers. All the old timers I know are happy to share and teach.

I think for most people competition is secondary to the other aspects of fiddlers' conventions. These events provide wonderful social opportunities and terrific entertainment. They inspire musicians to keep practicing and learning. They introduce new people to the hobby and everybody to new friends, styles and tunes.

A rare few take winning so seriously they miss out on the fun, but if that's their thing, I'm certainly no one to judge them for it.

T. J. Worthington Interview

And you moved up from Charleston?

In 1976. To Allegheny County. I wanted to get into some hard labor and live in a place where there were some trees left. Where I live there are five waterfalls within easy walking distance of the house.

It's very different from Charleston. As different as night and day. One thing, Charleston people value education, value money, value appearance. Mountain people don't value any of that. Mountain people value who you are. And Charleston people—that's not even a consideration; it's what you appear to be. I came here to get away from the "what you appear to be" to" what you are". That's the thing I appreciate most in mountain people. Everybody is OK as who they are, no matter if you're totally nuts ... if you've been in an insane asylum, you're still OK. You're just who you are. At square dances you see people that they take care of who will be up in their thirties, forties, fifties, very retarded, but they keep them at home, they take them out in public, take them to square dances.

The Yankee bands don't have the mountain soul. That's the only thing they are missing. I've heard people who've learned from mountain fiddlers, Benton Flippen, Tommy Jarrell and they can play just beautiful, but they're missing mountain soul. At Merlefest I spent all my time in the Old Time Tent. Several bands were really good. The "Wilders", "The Hushpuppies", some others. They were good, and they even had people flatfooting. But something was missing, I could not find what it was. And then the "Clint Howard Band" from Mountain City, got up and played with Doc Watson, and there was the mountain soul. And to me, it just blew everything else away.

But most people would tell you that Doc Watson is not an Old Timey musician, he's been corrupted.

He's not corruptible. If he was, he'd have been long ago. He's still just an old mountain boy from Deep Gap. Otherwise the music wouldn't connect. The sound would be there, but the soul would be missing.

So you were working on a farm, and you bought a piece of land?"

I bought a little old house, and got eight acres around it. I came to a new place inside, I wanted to go off and do semi-solitude and kind of get in tune. But I spent seven years working on the farm, and then painted houses for ten, and then painted pictures for three. And then worked for a lawyer for six and then started this store about two years ago. Just getting along, living among local people. I think I've studied mountain culture the whole time I've lived here.

But too many people coming in just think they are the Beverly Hillbillies. And I wanted to say, "that's not it". Like when I went out to Kansas, I could not convince anybody that life here was not like the Beverly Hillbillies. They wouldn't hear it.

In my first months ... year here ... I was afraid to go out walking, afraid I'd come up on a still, and get shot. Because I believed all that old crap, about what mountain people are like. And right away, I found them extraordinary. In their own personal human way.

Not that there's not stills here.

Oh, yeah, sure. But I was thinking that there were stills everywhere.

And not that you couldn't get shot if you really set your mind to it.

Friend: I was born and raised here ... My daddy was a bootlegger. Phillips, yes, Fred Phillip's daughter. He was a carpenter and he'd build a frame and put a roof on it and put a still in it and run him off some, get it sold, finish the house and sell it, go build him another one. He never got caught, did no time, or nothing. I was raised in a holler, and after he died we had a place called "Brandy Branch." The four of us children were not allowed up Brandy Branch. We'd be out playing, and you'd hear "Kabboom!" And mother would say, "Just be quiet, children, they found another one. You know, I was raised with that, you know, blowing up stills. I never saw one in operation, in my life; only saw them after they blew them up—we'd go look.

TJ: In my years of living here, I have fallen in love with the mountain people, and mountain culture, and I mean falling in love to the point that when I play Ralph Stanley, I cry.

Old Timey, it's not a listening music, it's a social music.

Very much. But I've fallen in love with it. When I first came here, my first year, I went to a Fiddler's Convention. It was Kyle Creed, Albert Hash, Fred Cockerham, Earnest East, those people, and I had no idea who they were. In fact I had never heard the music before. And at the first Fiddler's Convention I fell in love with Old Time Music, and I've been in love with it ever since. And it just gets stronger and stronger. And we have a radio show in Sparta now. WCOK. They didn't play any local music, not any. So I just went to the manager here one day, and I said, "I'd like to do a one hour show, once a week, Saturday morning radio show of regional music." And he said, "Great idea." And I'm thinking "Duh".

Danny Casstevens Interview

Danny Casstevens is a mild-mannered sandy-haired fellow who plays the most weathered Martin in captivity. He is accompanied by Rita Baldwin from Mocksville, NC.

The title of this book is "How the Hippies Ruin't Hillbilly Music."

Well, I don't think the hippies have ruined the music; I actually think they have helped it. Because without young people coming in to it, breathing new life into it ... that's what keeps sustaining it. Through the years. And it's going to change, and evolve, and that's just the natural process. So I really think they have helped it. If anything.

You play both Bluegrass and Old Time. Is the same thing happening in Bluegrass, or is that still more Southern?

Well, to a certain extent, the same thing happens in Bluegrass. You get a lot of people coming down from the cities, coming back to the country, to their roots, they seek out the old fiddlers, Old Time players, and they try to absorb, and learn as much from them as they can.

Rita: And they add their own accent.

Danny: My first musical instrument was a bugle. When I was five years old. I got out and sold greeting cards door to door in the neighborhood. I got up enough points to send off for this bugle. I played trumpet in the elementary school band. And then got into guitar a little bit later.

Rita: I've been playing four years. He's my teacher. Bluegrass and Bluegrass flavored.

Tell me a little about your dad. I always heard that he was the first … second man in North Carolina to play Scruggs style.

Danny: That may be stretching it a little bit. But actually he started playing guitar, and then he switched to the banjo, because that was the new thing. Earl Scruggs had just come on the scene and it was novel. It was new. So he laid down the guitar and picked up the banjo. So there wasn't many banjo players around. He got a lot of playing out of it. This was early '50's. He played all over. He played with a lot of different bands, different people. And my brother, Mike, played the mandolin. And one time, Mom played the bass, we all played. For a very short span of time. And then … Well, you grow up and go your separate ways.

He did a lot of different things. Especially toward the latter part of his life, music was all he did.

I met him in middle seventies, and he had more joy of playing, that was unique. Bluegrass guys appear to be cold and reserved, because they are thinking so hard. And your dad would just play and play and play.

He did enjoy it. And long about that time, was pretty much the peak. They had a good band together and were playing a lot. They did Union Grove, in '76, if I'm not mistaken, when they won the World's Championship Band.

Were you off playing something else?

Yeah, I was actually off doing the Folkie thing, in coffeehouses, you know. It was burgeoning. Sally Spring[55] *she was getting out and hitting the coffeehouses, and we used to play together. We still play together.*

So how did you come back into Old Time?

The Folk Music sort of died out, and of course Rock took that over and became Folk-Rock and if you didn't go electric, you pretty much were sidetracked. And Bluegrass and Old Time were hit really hard during that time and then they started to come back, so there was a lot to do, and a lot of places to go play, and you either played Country or Rock or Bluegrass. So me coming from Bluegrass roots, it was just natural for me to veer back into that direction. I was already familiar with the material, it was a ready-made market, and I really enjoyed it.

Since I started teaching … because not everybody wants to learn Bluegrass guitar; some people want to play Rock and so … I had to adapt my skills to that so I can play a little bit on an electric and a little on acoustic and little on the banjo, mandolin, fiddle so I can teach these.

To me, the cleanliness and harmony and parts playing in the Allman Brothers is pretty much the same thing as Bluegrass.

It's intricate, it's a lot of the weaving of the parts, of harmony playing, and it takes a lot of practice to play that kind of music. It's not easy.

No, it's not. Old Timey is easy.

Well, even that can be raised to a higher level of complexity, with the intricacies of the tunes and the timings that you use.

Do you make your living with music?

Yessir, I do. I make a living teaching music and of course I play on the side and you can't hardly make a living at Fiddler's Conventions … Well I guess you could if you … If you were Wayne Henderson, yeah. But I do make a living with music. It's my livelihood.

That's very rare.

Yeah, and I know that, and I do appreciate that and I feel fortunate to be able to do something that I like to do to make a living. I do Civil War Re-enactments, and painting and so I try to weave them all in together when I can. I use the old Martin, but we play period tunes and try to play them in a period style. I'd like to have a period Civil War Martin but they are rather expensive. One of these days … But I can get by with just the old 18, you know. It's the sound you really want to project. I've got the accoutrements, the uniform … if you just look at it, it looks pretty good.

I'm just sort of free-lance. I do period music for re-enactments, and for period weddings and various memorial services, for Confederates. I double on the bugle, I can play "Taps". I do the ballads, I try to cover a lot of bases. I drag out the old rusty bugle and I can play "Taps" for memorial services.

Chapter Twelve: Fur'ners and Worse

"The Welshman" Robert Gabb

I started playing music when I was six. My mother's a pianist and a conductress. I played cornet, and I went to play guitar when I was twelve, and I played in a punk rock band, and then I ended up in college, playing in a club/cabaret band, and had a blue fucking Mohegan, with these gray stupid Beatle suits on. And we were doing one show and we had to quit for the bingo break, and the guy who was the lead guitar player, I told him, "Chris, let's play some punk rock." He said, "We can't do this, Pat won't give us gigs any more."

So I got up and played "God Save the Queen"—"The Sex Pistols" And Pat says to me, "You will never, ever play with this band again." "That's right, I will never play music again." And I quit playing, and a friend of mine played at the local pub, called me up and he said, "Arnold Finch has moved back from the states, come on down to the pub and see him play." He walked in with a tenor banjo, a five-string banjo, a Dobro, illean pipes, guitar, and that was it. That was hot. So, I start to play music again. But now when I play, I'll play what I want to play. I don't care if I get paid at all. I just play for the pure enjoyment of it.

I was born in 1966. I saw the "Sex Pistols" in 1978, I was about twelve. My brother took me down to see them play. I played with a band called "Exclusive Oar". Played guitar. I started playing banjo, I guess about fifteen years ago, I played tenor, and I started playing mandolin. Then I started playing five-string, I guess, about ten years ago.

What kind of music were you playing tenor with?

Celtic. Pub drinking songs. And when I switched to playing five, then I introduced the punk rock drive to it. Just Old Time tunes played aggressively. Just plunk it. You'll find that root note eventually.

Did music make you move to America?

Yeah. 'Cause when I first started playing, I couldn't get no books, no music, nothing. So I'd go to bluegrass festivals, and watch the bluegrass guys play, and then I'd hum the tune all the way home. That's how I learned to play the tunes. And then I didn't even know what the tunes were called. So I just carried on playing. I just never knew what the tunes were.

I came into Mt. Airy and stayed there, with some people I got to meet, stayed with them. And I got to meet Riley Baugus, and Kirk Sutphin, I played with them a little while. Next year I came back and played a little more.

Is Wales a lot like this area?

Very much the same. West Virginia is even closer … mountain, river, coal mine.

Riley Baugus said. "Anyplace they have coal mines is Appalachia."

And this here with the rolling hills is very much the same. When I first came across, I was playing mostly Irish tunes. I got to figure out that these tunes they're playing here are basically Irish tunes, they've just bastardfied them, and took the minors out of them. They're basically the same tunes.

The only thing I find different is when an American fiddle player gets playing Irish tunes, they just haven't got that down right. And if you hear them playing, it's more basically old time Irish.

About the time you were born, Irish music was a bunch of guys singing standing on tables.

That's what I do! Since the "Pogues" come out, and the "Pogues" reinvented it. Basically, it was Irish-Folk-Cross-Punk Rock. That's when it started to take off real big. That's when the younger crowd started coming into it.

The new Old Timey kids, there is a bunch of real young kids, and I've seen a bunch of skull and cross-bones banjo straps …

They will all jump in on that hippy Old Time scene.

The guy from the "Bad Livers", he hates hippies. "They're no good, they just go to Contra dances and steal everybody's Old Lady".

It's true! I need to start going to Contra dances!

What's your band?

"Doctor Swamp and the Stompers" … Sometimes its "Billy and the Crystal Methodists".

That's almost as good as "The Free Will Backsliders".

Or "The Mt. Aryan Nation". We done that recording and it turned out good … We done sixteen old time tracks and some stuff that I wrote and Jungle Book, "I Want to be Like You", "Friend of the Devil" mixed up with "Rapper's Delight". And "Walking the Dog" and "Mighty Man". I was just sitting out at the house, back about a year ago. I was sitting down playing it. And I was singing it, "Hip, hop, hippity hip hop". It works. So now I'll sing two verses of "Friend of the Devil" and then do some "Rapper's Delight" and then go back.

Oh, I love jug band music. I used to play with the "Thermal Jug Band", and we had Wally the Jug, from the Mungo Jerry Band, play with us. That was a hell of a band. I used to have music at my pub Friday night, Saturday night, Sunday night, but we didn't have no karaoke or nothing. I used to book all the bands and they was always friends. Lots of people used to say, "Every Saturday, you've got all these rinky-tinky bands playing all this hillbilly music". "If you don't like it, there's a bar down the road that's got a rock band."

I don't care for commercial music. I quit … all that commercial deal going on there. As soon as that money starts to come, all the fun's gone out. Galax—I may go for the one night and just drive up. But I won't compete. I got disqualified there once. I did "Y-M-C-A" up on stage, and they disqualified me. Yeah. But they were all up in the bleachers and the stalls and the audience participation was going on.

Yeah. I been thrown off better stages than that one, myself.

I done "Beethoven's Ninth" at Fries and they disqualified me. "Son, this is an old time fiddler's convention", he says, and I said, "Well, if Beethoven was alive, he'd be pretty old now, wouldn't he?"

Chapter Thirteen: The Beat Goes On.

Richard Turner Interview

A restless night, I turn the TV on, like two o'clock in the morning. I go through a few channels, and I see a thing about this Galax Fiddler's Convention. And I say, "God, that looks like fun." They had an 800 number there at the bottom of the screen that you could call for information. So I called and they sent me a bunch of stuff, and the following year, I brought my daughter here. I came because its me—I have a natural love for this music, I was born in Rhode Island. I'm a Damn Yankee, and I would go out in my dad's car, because it had the only radio you could pick up WWVA, Wheeling West Virginia on, and pick up a little bit of this stuff. I would go out there in the middle of the winter, when it was 20 below zero, and just freeze in his car, just to listen to this. And nobody put it on me. It was just a natural, once I heard it, I loved it. Ain't that funny?

So I bring my daughter. She's been playing seven years. She got third place last year here. Fiddler. She's Shara Parker. And we've been traveling around. We flew into Boston, went through there, and went up to Springfield, Mass. because I went to school there. I got a sister in Vermont I haven't seen for a long time. We went up there. We stopped at a little Bluegrass Festival in Vermont that we didn't even know about, until we got there. And she wins First Place at the darn thing. She wins a hundred bucks! And so … see, everything I'm doing is slowly paying off. Hopefully. I'm doing all I can to promote this music.

I'm telling the same story. I won a crystal set, from being a Cub Scout. In Windsor, Connecticut. I ran a hundred-foot antenna, a wire …

To a tree or something?

Exactly. With one earphone, and late, late, late at night, you could get WWVA, and they would sell you baby chicks, and play Bluegrass music and stuff. And there you were.

Nobody put anything in my hand, nobody ever promoted it, and really in New England, all it was, was Rock and Roll when I was a kid. You were almost considered an outcast if they knew you liked this stuff. I hope this stuff is making a comeback. Actually my daughter has got a teacher right there in California, that comes to these things and he is strictly Old Time. He makes more money teaching Old Time fiddle than he did being a regular schoolteacher. He knows a lot of the people down here. He stayed with them. The guy that was in the "Bogtrotters"—Greg Hooven? The last time Dave was here, before Greg died, Dave stayed with him, and jammed with him.

Wouldn't it be nice if we could revive this out on the West Coast? They have some halfway decent festivals out there. But still and all the music is not like it is here. It's just not as good, 'cause it's not as genuine.

Chapter Fourteen: Hippie Kids

Matthew Ball Interview

Matt Ball is at least a third generation musician. His grandfather plays Irish, and his dad, Dave Ball, is one of those multi-polymath-geniuses that seem to be pretty common in Old Timey. Dave collects and builds banjoes, radios, resonator ukes, theremins, and collects Fred Van Eps banjoes. He is a real good pearl engraver. He is an expert on Van Eps, "the" Classical Banjo virtuoso of the 1920's. Matt is tall, quiet, plays many instruments, has just graduated from ETU and has an encyclopedic knowledge of all sorts of hippy music.

So you are Matthew Ball.

I am.

And a third generation musician.

We have been able to trace it back at least to four generations, and we are not sure before that. We figure that there were some at some point. My grand-dad plays Irish accordion, and his father played accordion, saxophone, clarinet, organ ... He was playing in string bands back in the '30's and '40's back in Western Kentucky ... Houston Ball. He played in a group called the "Waikiki Ramblers" ... Where they played such Hawaiian hits as "Paddy on the Turnpike" and "Sally Ann". That was during the Hawaiian craze.

Did your grandfather play professionally?

He has a Doctorate in Music. So he taught at the university level in music. Educational programs. When he was in college he played piano in Jazz bands. And also played with great grand-dad in the Tent Revival circuit in Western Kentucky in the '40's.

My great grand-dad was known as "The Man Whose Accordion Was Saved." He also funded a weekly radio show where he played organ for I don't know how many years. Houston Ball was a cabinetmaker among other things. Heavyweight boxer at one point ...

I was brought to my first Galax when I was eight months old. So, I had to learn to play out of self-defense. I started playing rhythm guitar when I was in Seventh or Eighth grade, like that, and picked up banjo towards the end of High School. I don't have any idea how to do any of that three-finger.

I heard you play some singer-songwriter stuff.

I still play a little of that when I play guitar. We have a weekly jam out in Kentucky, where I live now, that rotates between people's houses. During the summer months we can play out on front yards or in a kitchen, wherever we decide to play.

So why do you like this kind of music? Are you in adolescent rebellion?

Not really, I never went through much rebellion. I've been around it long enough that it's part of me. It's part of my society. Most of the people I associate myself with are musicians, a large percentage of those are Old Time musicians. I really go through phases. I play what I've been listening to. I'll play differently depending on who's fiddling. I prefer to play banjo behind a fiddler.

I sing a little bit, mainly murder ballads, I figured out a while back that most every song I know, somebody dies. Real happy music. I find myself playing in living rooms and front porches rather than playing at music venues. I might play a couple, three paid gigs in a year. Most of the time I don't play for money. I play for the joy of it.

I have been surprised the last few years at the number of people picking up Old Time. There have been a bunch of them that have come to it from Punk Rock. In a way, that attitude is the same, the rocking Punk, or the rocking Old Time scene. They will take that same energy, just playing banjoes and fiddles instead of electric instruments.

Folkies used to call that "Three Chords and a Cloud of Dust".

Same idea. Lots of times more energy than talent. People at all playing levels can get together and play music. And when I was first playing banjo, what helped me more than anything, was getting into big jams where nobody could hear me. That was helping me so I could pick up some tunes and people weren't getting on to me playing the wrong notes.

When I started learning, I learned a couple or three tunes out of a book, and in not too awful long, I figured out that the way the tunes were written down in those books are not the way they are really played. And I see with Bluegrass, I see a lot more of them learning out of books. It's almost orchestrated.

They practice a lot. I remember at the Dave Macon Days Festival in Murfreesboro, they had Dave Macon's grandson there showing us how to read Bluegrass tablature. And outside the window of the Courthouse, John Hartford was whipping up the crowd with frailing banjo. The contrast was poignant.

And to me, practice is not fun. And there is a difference between playing and practicing.

Did you learn from your dad?

We play fairly similarly. I picked up a few things from him when I was first starting out. He showed me the mechanics of clawhammer, and then sent me along with some CD's. So I have been learning mainly by ear. But we play similarly because both of us have learned more tunes from fiddlers than from banjo players.

Your dad is pretty understated, but he is one of the most incredible banjo players; didn't he win at Galax?

He's placed here, several times. He's never won. He's won Mt. Airy a couple of times. And won Dave Macon Days once.

To Be Continued . . .

So there is no mystery. There never is. In a wide screen, digitally enhanced, multi-track world where everybody has fifteen minutes of fame—anybody with a hit record is a demigod, the slut de jour is a diva—there is something so attractive about real people, who play real music after real work. It's not some Cinemascope alternative universe, sound by Dolby. It's right there, on back porches all over the world. Warts and all. Some people still can turn off the television, and pick up cheap guitars and make music. Not perfect music, but music. Music for themselves, music for their community. Sometimes it's Blues, or Old Time, or Bluegrass, or Grunge or Garage Rock, or Alt/Punk/Jazz/Ska/Rap stuff. But it's real.

It's real, and it's America. It's your music, and you can't let them rob you of it. Carry on.

Portfolio

33 54TH Annual OLD FIDDL

Appendix: Some Old Time Band Names

Gleaned From Galax Programs

1976	
Deadheads and Suckers	James Leva
Lettuce Rock String Band	Sheila Rice
1979	
Average Pink Band	Yul Luvitt
Newly Lost Pigmy Polecats	Steve Feldman
1980	
Unquenchable String Band	Mark Palinos
Geezer Hollar Cretones	Eddy Haskell
1981	
Hot Shots	Fidel Castro
Molten Aquarius String Band	Jim Wexler
Bubba Bond and the Round Peak Leather Boys	Frenchie Fried
Nuke Waste Creek Boys	I.M. Glowing, 3 Mile Island
Swami Tommy and the Round Creek Zen Boys	Hugh Backwitters
Stella Doro and the Lady Fingers	Janey Lewis
1982	
Chicken Chokers	Fox Watson
Nee Ningy	Ted Ponter
Woodchucks in Babylon	Keith Griel
The Cahn Men	Jack Cahn
The Flying Buttress Brothers	

Newly Evicted Expo City Ramblers	Ken Bronson
Cacaphones	L. Dorsey Worthy
Ladies Waist Band	Ann Kinnamon
1983	
Belligerent Brothers and Somebody's Wallet	Pete Beale
Low Riders of the Vertical Smile	Brian Stewart
Toot the Root and the Walkertown Studs	Fuzzy Turl
Pearl and the Oystertones	Barbara Swell
The Vomitones	Butch Lust
Buckwheat and the Dupremes	Buckwheat O'Course
Dick Buttkiss and the Tightends	Alex Karrass
Chester Drawers and His Bureaucrats	
The Ramps	Tom Riccio
Poly Vinyl and the Chlorides	Ben T. Zenning
1984	
Gina and the Tonics	Gina Banjolini
Razor Lickers	Bunk Naess
Cousin Curtis and the Cash Rebates	Curtis Buckhannon
Fiddlin' Retreads and the High Speed Blowouts	David Winston
Poodle Humpers	Pierre
Fountain City Frogstranglers	Mary Edna Thompson
Wee Weeny	Richard Small
Mumbilly Dreamland	Darrell Acuff
Nuclear Sledgehammer	Kenzo Bronson
Screaming Seam Squirrels	Pop Fart
1985	
Rhythm Gorilla	Koske Bosco Takaki
Los Knotheads	
Dr. Boo Boo and the Not-so-Hot-Shots	
Groan Mt. Be Boppers	
Place Named Rambler Boys	
Richard Cheese and the Smegma River Ramblers	
Rat Loyalty	
Felonious Mum and the Tasteless Troubadours	

Mumbilly Jihad	
Hardly Breathing String Band	
Jawbone and the Babylonians	
Loin of Man	
Swine, Women and Song	Hoagie Seibert
Bio Satellite Relay Explorers	
Alabama Jew Boy League	
Burning Jello	
1986	
Tumors of Ignorance	Billy Pleasure
Dead Sea Squirrels	Joe Anthrax
The Sudafed Sisters	N. Spainhour
Fat Mumbillies From Space	Moloy
Red Bud Roundabouts	Phil DeBong
Morphic Resonance	Pauline Morphy
Pick-a-bob String Band	Steve Mason
1987	
Rebop Ramblers	Elaine Gibson
Floating Pineapple String Band	Allen P. Reed III
Otter Chaos	Pete Peterson
OK Bayou Dance Band	Jamal
Ragtime Annie and the Panty Raiders	
Roadkill Ramblers	Geoff Seitz
Pliocene Potentates	
Foolish Pride String Band	Ben Williams
Toad Stompers	
The Eskabillies	Wolf
Tongue in Groove String Band	Larry Marks
Rugby Gully Jumpers	Wayne C. Henderson
Tammy Fay-Do-Do	I. Shoppe
1988	
Babs and Her Bionic Boobs	Winda Wilson
Psyco Delta Phonic Hicka Billies	Greg Krolicle
Goober and His Tuber	Spud Daede

Alias R. and His Nobodies	Seth Hedu
Polly Plywood and Her Pretty Pumkins	Denmark
No Flies Ennui	Adam Rose
Grunwald's 42 String Impossibility	Ken Bloom
Sharpton Ridge Boys and Tawana	Rev. Al
Alaric and the Smokey Mt. Visigoths	Lee Lorinzoni
Shrunken Mumbilly Edsels	William Mum
Collard Aristocracy	Buz Lloyd
O Zone	Haile Unlikelie
Characteristics of Mortar	Dirk Powell
Zombie Lust	Harry Bolick
I Cure Fits String Band	Don Mussell
Hillbilly Hokumites	Billy Ransom
The New Old Mtn. Topper Valley Hill Rambler Ningie Boys	
Bottom of the Barrel Bunch	Scottie Holbrook
Fred Zeflyn and the Secret Society of Mum	
Alabama Goober Grabbers	Wahoo Lou Lou
1989	
Dr. Hyde Glue	Chuck Webster
Rare Vertical Mumbillies	U. P. Wright
Don Mussell And the Mountain Oysters	Rachel Goodman
Pickled Possums	Bette Drake
1989	
Enyheenywanawrekaweeny	Winda Wilson
Smokey Fog Boys	Pete Peterson
1990	
Cool As Grits	Koske Takaki
New Crusty Nostrils	Alan Firth
Russell Up-some-grub	Russ Childress
Buddha Belly and his Bosom Buddies	Karen Falkowski
Fifty Longhaired Friends of Jesus	
A Fool And His Money	Steve Wish

Index To Photographs

Front Cover	Cover Band L-R Ed Bell, Unknown, Dea?, Rick Friend, Wish (stw)
Back Cover	Union Grove 1975 L-R Rob Mangum, Tom Jensen, Chris Sekerak (Pruney), Wish (stw)
Page xii)	Will Keys and Wish circa 1987 (Sluys)
Page 6)	Views of Union Grove and Kyle Creed Band 1977 (Mylet)
Page 27)	Wish and Tom Jensen Folkies, circa 1965 (Gilberto)
Page 29)	Jam at Union Grove with Earl White circa 1974 (Sekerak)
Page 32)	Dave Sturgill circa 2000 (stw)
Page 33)	Pruney and Norma circa 1974 (Sekerak)
Page 34)	Doug Baker and Earl White Galax 1985 (Sluys)
Page 37)	One wall of the Sturgill Front Room circa 1975 (Sekerak)
Page 40)	Pruney's Cabin circa 1975 (Sekerak)
Page 44)	Jeremiah Skarie circa 2004 (stw)
Page 55)	"The All-nighters" Galax 1991 Jacki Spector is center with ribbon on banjo. (Sluys)
Page 58)	John Sturgill World's Champion Bass Player Union Grove 1977 (stw)
Page 60)	The Skyland Strings; Sue Cahill with Sturgill mandolin. L-R Carol Seace, Sue, Ken Powers, Dave Sturgill. Circa 1975 (Sekerak)
Page 61)	Johnny's Workbench circa 1975 (Sekerak)
Page 63)	Nancy Sluys circa 2003 (stw)
Page 66)	Horsehair and Catgut Stringband 1979 Ft. Lauderdale Fl. L-R L.J. Slavin, Chuck Anton, Nancy Sluys, John Minier, Bill Sluys
Page 69)	Back of the Stalls Galax 1985 (Sluys) L-R Matt Levine, Tony Marcus, Bob Willoughby, Dave Grant, Unknown. Joe Thrift in background.
Page 71)	Fiddlin' Nancy Banjo circa 1984 (Sluys)
Page 73)	Canaan Valley Connecticut Music Festival circa 1965 (Gilberto)
Page 74)	Bob Naess, Rich Harkness, Joe Thrift, circa 1984 (Sluys)

Page 77)	Joe Thrift circa 2004 (stw)
Page 79)	Nancy Cory circa 2004 (stw)
Page 81)	Ken Bloom circa 2006 (Bloom)
Page 86)	"Hilo Hattie and the Papayan Hawaiians" Galax 1989 Harry Bolick, Ken Bloom, John Hatton, Matt Levine
Page 94)	Tom Mylet circa 1975 (Mylet)
Page 95)	Marianne and Tom Mylet's Wedding Picture 1975 (Mylet)
Page 97)	Top) First Brandywine Friends of OT Music Picnic circa 1973
	Bottom) Tom, Marianne and children with Percy Creed circa 1994
Page 109)	Dick Tarrier at Mt. Airy Festival 1985
Page 112)	Wish with homemade bass Galax Stalls 1987 (Sluys)
Page 116)	Galax Mud circa 2004 (stw)
Page 118)	Hoagie Siebert and Ron Cole Galax 1984 (Sluys)
Page 123)	Trina Royer, Meridith McIntosh, Sally Freund Galax 1988 (Sluys)
Page 125)	Mark Rose Circa 1984 (Rose)
Page 127)	Leon Frost circa 2004 (stw)
Page 130)	Blues Jam at Banjo's after Mt. Airy Festival 1989. Lightning Wells, Bill Sluys, Ransom, Michelle Belanger, Wish. (Sluys)
Page 131)	Mark Rose circa 2000 (Sluys)
Page 142)	Kirk Sutphin circa 200. Riley Baugus in background (stw)
Page 148)	Bill Birchfield circa 2004 (stw)
Page 149)	Matt Kenman circa 2004 (stw)
Page 161)	Dave Ball wins a ribbon, Galax 1987 (Sluys)
Page 165)	Bosco at Galax (Sluys)
Page 166)	Wish with Dragon Mandolin Galax 1984
Page 167)	Judy "Jake" McGee "Mother of Bobs" Galax 1983 (Sluys)
Page 168)	Rich Hartness Galax 1984 (Sluys)
Page 169)	Top) Debbie Gitlin and Riley Baugus Mt. Airy 1986 (Sluys)
	Bottom) Ken Bronson and Tom Riccio 1987 (Sluys)
Page 170)	Group at stalls with mud Galax Circa 1982 (Sluys)
Page 171)	The Red Hots on Stage Galax 1989 (Sluys)
Page 172)	Tina Liza Jones and daughter Liza 1986 (Sluys)

Endnotes

1. http://www.contemplator.com/history/childbio.html
2. http://www.electricscotland.com/history/other/minstrelsy_intro.htm
3. http://carl-sandburg.com/biography.htm
4. Mark Twain, "Life on the Mississippi" Chapter 38
5. Wikopedia "Country Music?
6. http://libweb.uoregon.edu/speccoll/photo/ulmann/niles.html
7. http://en.wikipedia.org/wiki/Aaron_Copeland
8. http://www.press.uillinois.edu/f99/yung.html
9. Extracted from "The White Top Folk Festival: What We (Have Not) Learned," David E. Whisnant, University of North Carolina at Chapel Hill. August 6, 1998. Copyright 1998 by David E. Whisnant
10. Union Grove, The First Fifty Years, Pat J. Ahrens, Union Grove Old Time Fiddlers' Convention Inc. 1975
11. Williams, Herman K. "The First Forty Years of the Old Fiddlers Convention" Self Published Book.
12. http://www.swarthmore.edu/bulletin/archive/97/mar97/folkfestivals.html
13. http://www.ieee-virtual-museum.org/collection/people.php?taid=&id=1234680&lid=1
14. http://www.harrysmitharchives.com/1_bio/index.html
15. http://mikeseeger.info/html/oldtime.html
16. Most of this chapter is based on "THE JEWGRASS BOYS" BLUEGRASS MUSIC'S EMERGENCE IN NEW YORK CITY'S WASHINGTON SQUARE PARK, 1946-1961 By Timothy Josiah Morris Pertz
17. http://www.singout.org/
18. http://www.folkways.si.edu/projects_initiatives/broadside/home.html
19. "Mayor Of MacDougal Street" Elijah Wald Da Capo, 2005
20. http://julianwinston.com/music/me_and_music.php
21. Guy Carawan has the credit for "We Shall Overcome"
22. Now at Davis Library, UNC at Chapel Hill, NC

23. Captain Alfred M. Hubbard, CIA., "Acid Dreams" Lee, Martin A. and Shlain, Bruce Evergreen, 1985
24. "The American Square Dance"; by Margot Mayo (1948)
25. http://www.roryblock.com/Pages/LifeStory.htm
26. Actually made by Fiddler Doug Reid, brother of W.B. Reid
27. http://www.greengrasscloggers.com
28. Named after Clogarina Beverly Cotton
29. "Foxfire 3", Edited Eliot Wigginton, Anchor Press/Doubleday, Garden City, NY, 1975, pp. 168-185
30. http://www.concert-promotions.com/StompinSite/users.rcn.com/hal2002/index.html
31. Love Valley is a dude ranch sort of place not too far from Union Grove. http://www.lovevalley.com/
32. Don Palifka's broken toe.
33. "Walking Tall"
34. Jan. 18th, 1978 http://www.eng.uab.edu/cee/faculty/ndelatte/case_studies_project/Hartford%20Civic%20Center/hartford.htm
35. The cute one.
36. Record Jacket Copy, "The Even Dozen Jug Band" Collector's Choice ASIN: B0000631PE, 1964
37. http://www.htfiddler.net/ent/bio.htm
38. http://www.tepel.org/articles/sapoznik.html
39. Newscaster for NPR
40. "Clapton's Guitar; Watching Wayne Henderson Make the Perfect Guitar" Allen St. John, Free Press, 2005
41. NB. Do not wear polyester pants to fight grass fires. You have been warned.
42. "Will The Circle Be Unbroken" Nitty Gritty Dirt Band, 1972
43. This is the understatement of the book
44. "The band that made bluegrass obsolete" Future Kaleidoscopes David Lindley & Chris Darrow. Vocals & guitar Steve Cahill banjo & dobro Pete Madlem, Richard Greene on fiddle.
45. "Hey, Y'all! Watch This!
46. Gastonia, NC is still known as "Little Chicago"
47. http://www.chriswig.com/music.aspx
48. http://www.fretlesszithers.com/index.html
49. The Birth of NORML The National Organization for the Reform of Marijuana Laws. I was there, smoking pot with a million Narks. They had great pot.
50. "String Bands in the North Carolina Piedmont", Bob Carlin, McFarland, 2004
51. From the story telling of Sidney Sturgill
52. He hated this joke.
53. Mandolin Player on the Cover of this very book

54. Louisa County, Northwest of Richmond
55. Sally Spring is a legendary singer-songwriter in the Carolinas. Her recent CD "Mockingbird" is available nationally.

978-0-595-42305-7
0-595-42305-1

Printed in the United States
79382LV00008B/151-180

9 780595 423057